*The United Nations
and the Control of
International Violence*

The United Nations and the Control of International Violence

A LEGAL AND POLITICAL ANALYSIS

John F. Murphy

ROWMAN & ALLANHELD
Totowa, New Jersey

ROWMAN & ALLANHELD PUBLISHERS

Published in the United States of America in 1982
by Allanheld, Osmun & Co. Publishers, Inc.
(A Division of Littlefield, Adams & Company)
81 Adams Drive, Totowa, New Jersey 07512

Library of Congress Cataloging in Publication Data

Murphy, John Francis, 1937–
    The United Nations and the control of international
violence.

    Includes bibliographical references and index.
    1. United Nations. 2. Pacific settlement of interna-
tional disputes. I. Title.

JX1977.M827   1982   341.23   81-69989
ISBN 0-86598-079-9

82   83   84/10 9 8 7 6 5 4 3 2

Printed in the United States of America

Contents

Foreword

The first thing I notice in looking at the state of mankind is a palpable contradiction which makes all stability impossible. As individuals, we live in the civil state, under the control of the Law; as nations, each is in the state of nature. (Jean-Jacques Rousseau, *A Lasting Peace and the State of War**)

Jean-Jacques Rousseau, the eighteenth century sage, was neither the first nor the last to note that domestic politics and international politics appear to be governed on different foundations and according to different principles. If the domestic order is ideally the abode of justice perfected by "the union of force and Law," the international realm is a state of nature in which claims of right either are unsupported by adequate sanctions or are advanced as veils for self-interest and brute force. In every deed, the international state of nature is one of perpetual strife in which treaties and covenants are often but devices in the "continuation of the war." For Rousseau, as for Thomas Hobbes, the international system is in a state of war.

What was particularly characteristic of Rousseau was the supreme pessimism of his conclusions, for he not only rejected the possibility of moderating the ill-effects of international anarchy, but held that even justice in the domestic realm was ruled out by the exigences of international intercourse.

For, living as we do at once in the civil order and in the state of nature, we find ourselves exposed to the evils of both conditions, without winning the security we need in either. The perfection of the social order lies, doubtless, in the union of force and Law.

*C. E. Vaughan, translator and editor (New Haven: Whitlocks, Inc., no date), pp. 126–27.

But such a union is only possible when force is controlled by Law; whereas, so long as the prince is regarded as absolutely uncontrolled, it is force alone which speaks to the subject under the name of Law and to the foreigner under the name of reason of state: so taking from the latter the power, and from the former the very will to offer resistance. The result is that, in both cases, brute force reigns under the empty name of justice.†

For Rousseau the only escape from this dilemma was either an alliance among states that would deter aggression or a condition and policy that would isolate the domestic community from the intrusions of external commerce and strife. But alliances, he held, were themselves instruments in the international strategy of conflict, and relative isolation, even in Rousseau's day, was simply impossible for a state in the heart of Europe, as would shortly be the case for all societies. The universal result, as he remarks, is that "brute force reigns under the empty name of justice."

If the strife of international anarchy and the distortions that it introduced into the domestic realm were apparent in Rousseau's day, it can hardly be said that the problem has abated since then. Indeed, if it would come as no surprise to Rousseau, it is nonetheless disconcerting to many latter-day pundits that the transformation of traditional empires into a multitude of independent states and the increasing interdependence of those states have made violence even more central to the problem of international affairs. Alas, superimposed on the traditional conflicts among states is transnational and subnational acts of revolutionary turbulence, terrorism, and assassination. At the very time that the United Nations succeeded in defining "aggression" (GA Res. 3314 [XXX], December 1974), the whole exercise appeared strangely futile, for not only do ancient practices of interstate force continue, but the General Assembly seemed to sanctify acts of violence arising from putative claims of self-determination, freedom, independence of foreign domination, anticolonialism, and antiracism. Surely sufficient room through which to drive not only tanks, but molotov cocktails, bombs, and high-powered rifles. The result is too often a decrease of order and the dominion of brute force under the "empty name of justice."

The problem to which Professor John Murphy turns—the incidence of international violence and its control—is not only inherently interesting, but it remains the essential issue of international law and organization. Many would seek to ignore this issue by concentrating on more apparently manageable issues or by dismissing the universal organization that has been entrusted with concern for

†Rousseau, *A Lasting Peace,* p. 127.

international peace and security as either itself part of the problem or an absurd irrelevance. One can hardly deny that the resolution of various functional disputes among states may reduce the incidence of violence or that the United Nations has often dissolved into demagogic rhetoric and inflammatory posturing. Yet the general problem of a violence that seems structural and endemic in character remains, and the United Nations continues to be the only institution sufficiently universal in membership and legitimate in its Charter-based mandate to exert any broad authority, however fragile, in this area.

The great virtue of Professor Murphy's study is that he understands both the dimensions of the problem and the limitations of the instruments available to cope with it. Moreover, he is concerned not only with traditional issues of interstate force, but with those kinds of nontraditional violences that threaten to upset even the ancient foundations of diplomatic comity. As he demonstrates, in such circumstances the international legal canon can hardly be conceived as a static code of public order but reflective of and part of a dynamic process of change. So defined, the perspective of the international lawyer is skillfully related to the analysis of violence and international organization undertaken by political scientists and moral philosophers.

Professor Murphy's study is thus not only a comprehensive and sophisticated text on the role of the United Nations in the control of the whole range of international violence, but also an important contribution to bridging the gap that often separates the legal analyst from the social scientist. One of the untoward results of the increases of methodological sophistication in recent years has been greater confusion in the dialogue among the various disciplinary specialists. Armed with particular forms of questions, precise definitions, and special jargons, the commentators on violence, law, and political organization more and more speak past, rather than to, each other. On the basis of his wide-ranging experience and extensive scholarship in fields that cut across the disciplines, John Murphy is able to break the communication barrier. The result is not only a superb monograph on violence and international organization, but a splendid contribution to the methodological foundations upon which future works may be constructed.

ROBERT S. WOOD
Chairman, Department of Strategy
Naval War College

Acknowledgments

In a sense the genesis of this book goes back to 1964, when I began work in the office of the Assistant Legal Adviser for United Nations Affairs, Department of State. It was there that I first became interested in the United Nation's role in the control of international violence—an interest that has continued to this day. During my period in that office I had the good fortune to have as supervisors of my work three outstanding international lawyers, John Lawrence Hargrove, Herbert Reis, and Stephen M. Schwebel, whose substantial knowledge of the United Nations and high standards of legal craftsmanship were invaluable guideposts to me. I am grateful to all three of these gentlemen, although it should be understood that none is responsible for any errors or infelicitous language there may be in this book. Sole responsibility for these lies with me.

I am also grateful to Martin Dickinson, then Dean of the University of Kansas Law School, for permitting me to take a year's leave of absence, and to Admiral Edward F. Welch, Jr., President of the Naval War College, for selecting me to serve as the Charles H. Stockton Professor of International Law at the college for 1980/81. This gave me the time to do the research necessary for the writing of the book as well as access to the superb library and stimulating intellectual atmosphere at the college.

I especially appreciate the time spent by Professors Frederick H. Hartmann and Robert S. Wood of the Naval War College in reading and commenting on drafts of the manuscript for this book. Their comments have been most helpful. Again, responsibility for errors or infelicitous language is solely my own.

Ruth L. Meierowitz, my secretary at the Naval War College, typed many drafts of the manuscript with unfailing good humor and high competence. The same may be said of Janice Riley and Mary Williams of the secretarial staff at the University of Kansas Law School, who continued this work upon my return to the university.

A special note of gratitude goes to my wife, Anita K. Head, Professor of Law and Law Librarian at the George Washington University Law School. Her constant support, fine judgment, and belief in my ability to undertake and complete this project have sustained me throughout these one and a half years.

Introduction

In recent years the United Nations has not been held in great favor. The apogee of this negative image was reached in the wake of the 1975 Zionism resolution, when the United Nations came to be regarded by some as "a dangerous place," dominated by states hostile to basic United States and free world interests. After the emotional reaction to the Zionism resolution had quieted down, the attitude seemed to shift slowly from one of outrage or alarm to indifference or even ridicule. The United Nations came to be viewed as largely irrelevant to the broader issues of international relations, since action on important matters was taking place outside the United Nations in bilateral or regional negotiations. No longer was the organization considered to be a dangerous place, but rather a theater of the absurd or a mere debating society.[1]

Disillusionment with the United Nations has been especially pronounced with respect to the organization's performance in maintaining international peace and security—its primary role under the Charter. Many have felt that the United Nations has failed to keep the peace. Some have even claimed that, far from maintaining international peace and security, the United Nations has promoted violence through its support of wars of national liberation and international terrorism.[2]

Any analysis of the United Nation's performance is greatly complicated by the elusive nature of international violence. The models for the drafters of the UN Charter's provisions prohibiting "the threat or use of force against the territorial integrity or political independence of any state" were Italy's invasion of Ethiopia and the march of Hitler's troops into Poland. That is, international violence was thought to involve aggression by the armed forces of one state against another state for the purpose of conquest or political domination. To be sure, the post-World War II period has had a large number of such acts of aggression—the recent invasion of Afghanistan by the Soviet

Union being a prominent example. But traditional acts of aggression have also been accompanied by a rise in revolutionary warfare that does not fall neatly within the scope of the Charter. This revolutionary violence, moreover, has been supported at a minimum in principle and often in practice by member states of the United Nations. Other forms of international violence have similarly come to the fore, such as international terrorism, wars of assassination, and surrogate warfare.

Terrorism, in particular, has become a prevalent form of international violence during the 1970s. Many of these violent acts have been committed by private individuals in the furtherance of a particular cause. Others have involved private individuals acting under the sponsorship of governments. Still others have taken place in the course of revolutionary war or in the context of traditional armed conflict.

These forms of unconventional violence have posed grave problems for the law and practice of the United Nations and have enormously complicated the political milieu in which the United Nations operates. Current international law and procedures have simply been inadequate to deal with the problem and efforts to remedy the situation have run into many obstacles.

This book will examine the United Nation's record in coping with international violence from several perspectives. First, it will explore the United Nation's record with respect to traditional uses of armed force, i.e., state-to-state conflict. Next, it will consider the United Nations and revolutionary wars. Then it will turn to unconventional violence—including wars of assassination, surrogate warfare, and officially sponsored terrorism. Finally, the book will focus on the United Nation's response to private acts of international terrorism.

In each area the approach will be to examine principles of the United Nations Charter, as well as applicable general principles and procedures of international law, with a view to determining their adequacy in the context of today's political, economic, and social realities. It will then shift to a consideration of illustrative UN actions. In this connection the book will focus on the practice of the Security Council, the General Assembly, the secretary-general, and the International Court of Justice—the primary organs of the United Nations with jurisdiction over international violence. The exploration of case histories will be selective, with no attempt to examine every instance of the United Nation's response to international violence. As to each area, there will be a concluding chapter with recommendations as to possible improvements in UN law and practice.

A primary purpose of this study is to attempt to bridge the gap between the approach of the social scientist to the United Nations and that of the international lawyer—a gap also present in their respective approaches to international law generally. The social scientists attack the "legalistic-idealistic" approach to foreign policy as unrealistic, inelastic, and therefore incapable of dealing with moral questions or questions of national expediency. One view of the social scientist regarding international lawyers is aptly summarized by Michael Walzer, a leading moral philosopher, in a recent work:

> Now, the language with which we argue about war and justice is similar to the language of international law ... Legal treatises do not, however, provide a fully plausible or coherent account of our moral arguments, and the two most common approaches to the law reflected in the treatises are both in need of extra-legal supplement. First of all, legal positivism, which generated major scholarly works in the late nineteenth and early twentieth centuries, has become in the age of the United Nations increasingly uninteresting. The UN Charter was supposed to be the constitution of a new world, but, for reasons that have often been discussed, things have turned out differently. To dwell at length upon the precise meaning of the Charter is today a kind of utopian quibbling. And because the UN sometimes pretends that it already is what it has barely begun to be, its decrees do not command intellectual or moral respect—except among the positivist lawyers whose business it is to interpret them. The lawyers have constructed a paper world, which fails at crucial points to correspond to the world the rest of us still live in.

> The second approach to the law is oriented in terms of policy goals. Its advocates respond to the poverty of the contemporary international regime by imputing purposes to that regime—the achievement of some sort of "world order"—and then reinterpreting the law to fit those purposes. In effect, they substitute utilitarian argument for legal analysis. That substitution is certainly not uninteresting, but it requires a philosophical defense. For the customs and conventions, the treaties and charters that constitute the laws of international society do not invite interpretation in terms of a single purpose or set of purposes. Nor are the judgments they require always explicable from a utilitarian standpoint. Policy-oriented lawyers are in fact moral and political philosophers, and it would be best if they presented themselves that way. Or, alternatively, they are would-be legislators, not jurists or students of the law. They are committed, or most of them are committed, to restructuring international society—a worthwhile task—but they are not committed to expounding its present structure.[3]

For their part, international lawyers would reject this analysis as simplistic. They would point out that one cannot draw such a sharp line between the law as it is and as it ought to be, since international law is a dynamic process constantly undergoing change. The lawyers might also contend that the social scientists and other "realists" have misunderstood the nature of law, morality, and power, as well as their interrelations.[4]

In spite of the current emphasis on interdisciplinary studies, the social scientists and the lawyers have mostly been speaking past each other. The absence of interchange has been detrimental to both disciplines. It is time for a dialogue to begin.

NOTES

1. See especially Daniel P. Moynihan, *A Dangerous Place* (Boston and Toronto: Little, Brown & Co., 1978); William F. Buckley, Jr., *United Nations Journal* (New York: G.P. Putnam's Sons, 1974).

2. See L.C. Green, "The Legalization of Terrorism," Yonah Alexander et al. (eds.), *Terrorism: Theory and Practice* (Boulder: Westview Press, Inc., 1979), pp. 175–97.

3. Michael Walzer, *Just and Unjust Wars* (New York: Basic Books, Inc., 1977), pp. xii–xiii.

4. For an excellent discussion of both the social scientist and the legal perspective and of ways in which they might be reconciled, see John Norton Moore, "The Legal Tradition and the Management of National Security," W. Michael Reisman and Burns H. Weston (eds.), *Toward World Order and Human Dignity* (New York, London: The Free Press, 1976), pp. 321–64.

PART ONE

The United Nations and Traditional International Violence

ONE

A Brief History of Approaches to Peace Through International Organization

PRE-LEAGUE OF NATIONS

In a sense, the history of approaches to peace through international organizations begins with the first gatherings of men into societies for their mutual protection. As Aristotle noted, man is a political animal, and he recognizes the need for the creation of institutional devices and systematic methods for regulating his relations with others. In ancient Greece this institutional arrangement took the form of the city-state. The Greek city-states in turn came up with the conception of the federation for peace as a structure for relations between themselves. These federations were not, to be sure, "leagues of nations" in the modern sense of the term as they were drawn entirely from Greece itself. Nonetheless, they represent an accomplishment in cooperation, especially since they made frequent use of arbitration as a peaceful means of settling disputes and developed the general arbitration treaty. Arbitration did not prove to be a panacea, however, as disputes between the Greek city-states often resulted in outbreaks of violence.[1]

The first institution that maintained peace on a worldwide basis was the Roman Empire. This was a national rather than an international peace, imposed regardless of the wishes of the people and enforced by the might of Roman arms. There was no need for and no use made of arbitration as developed by the Greek city-states.

With the collapse of the Roman Empire, the peace and order that had characterized the empire at the zenith of its power gave way to incessant petty warfare. This pattern was broken for a brief period around A.D. 800 when the Frankish king Charlemagne, who revived the title of "Roman Emperor in the West," imposed orderly rule on most of Europe. But Charlemagne's empire was soon torn apart by civil wars among his grandchildren, and, in the ninth century, western Europe was again invaded by pagan peoples from beyond its borders. The result was that once more it proved impossible to maintain orderly central government over large areas.

In the wake of the chaotic conditions of the ninth and tenth centuries, the institution of feudalism arose. The major cohesive force of feudalism was a relationship of mutual loyalty between individual lords and their vassals rather than a common loyalty of all citizens to the state. Because feudalism developed under conditions of near anarchy, early feudal society was decentralized and torn by frequent war. Historians are divided, however, over the issue of whether feudal institutions necessarily tended to perpetuate this state of affairs. At least in principle, all the warring lords owed allegiance to a chief feudal lord, who, in turn, had a duty to maintain peace and justice. Hence some historians view feudalism as a constructive response to the difficult problems of the age that produced it by providing a working basis of government for the newly emerging European states.[2]

A measure of world peace was provided by the rise of the papacy and the Holy Roman Empire. But neither the universal church nor the empire was as successful in maintaining the peace as the Roman Empire had been. The breakup of the unity of medieval European Christendom and the parallel decline in the empire, caused in part by the rise of the spirit of nationalism, resulted in the birth of the modern state system. This set the stage for the possible development of true international organization, or, as Inis Claude has pointed out, *interstate* organization.[3]

There had been a number of peace plans proposed by scholars and statesmen from the fourteenth century on.[4] Such thinkers as Dante, Dubois, Emeric Crucé, the Duc de Sully, William Penn, the Abbé de Saint-Pierre, Rousseau, Bentham, and Kant had presented plans, on a global or European scale, that stressed the need for comprehensive organization and a high degree of integration between states. Although at least one plan envisaged the achievement of peace through the creation of a unified world-state under the secular rule of one supreme prince,[5] most of the proposals called for the coming together of the several states in a league equipped with common supranational organs.

It was not until the nineteenth century, however, that the world was ready for an international organization.[6] Even then, statesmen did not follow the utopian model. Rather, they emphasized the principle of separate and independent sovereignties while attempting to achieve new arrangements that would allow the sovereign units of the old system to pursue their interests and manage their affairs in an age of technological and commercial interdependence.

The first example of this process in the nineteenth century was the Concert of Europe, which followed the Congress of Vienna in 1815. The Concert of Europe was not a permanent international organization, but periodic meetings among the Great Powers held some thirty times during the century in order to deal with pressing political issues. These included, among others, "the maintenance of existing peaceful conditions, the substitution of pacific for violent methods of manipulating the distribution of power, the agreement upon the ground rules for playing the competitive game of imperialism, and the formulation of general international legislation applicable to the ordinary relations of states."[7] Although the Concert of Europe did not create an independent international organization with supranational authority, it did produce "the prototype of a major organ of modern international organization—the executive council of the great powers."[8]

An important step toward the establishment of a modern form of international organization was taken at the Hague conferences of 1899 and 1907. These two conferences were convoked in a time of peace to consider the major problems associated with the maintenance of international peace and security in general rather than to maintain peace in a particular crisis or to terminate a specific war. Also, the Hague conferences took a more universalist approach than the Concert of Europe. The 1907 conference included the representatives of forty-four states, including most of the Latin American Republics. One author has even suggested that the Hague conferences "ushered in the heyday of the small states."[9]

There were other accomplishments at the Hague conferences. The idea of a regular assembly of nations, first introduced as a basic plank in the platform of the Concert of Europe but only carried out from 1815 to 1822, was revitalized. The conferences also constituted a precedent for the proposition that collective diplomacy should codify and develop international law, establish standing procedures for the peaceful settlement of disputes, and promote the principle that pacific solutions should be sought by disputants and facilitated by disinterested states. This precedent served as the basis for much of the work leading to the creation of the League of Nations.

Another precedent for the League of Nations was the development in the nineteenth century of public international unions—such as the International Telegraphic Union and the Universal Postal Union—concerned with problems in various essentially nonpolitical fields. These unions produced the first genuinely permanent international machinery with a permanent staff to give continuity to the organization; carry out functions of research, correspondence, and publication; and make arrangements for the next conference of states. In particular, they promoted the concept that there is an area where states have an interest in cooperation rather than in conflict.[10]

THE LEAGUE OF NATIONS

As Inis Claude has noted,[11] the nineteenth century may be viewed as the era of *preparation for* international organization and the years since 1914 as the era of *establishment of* international organization. There was, indeed, a substantial measure of continuity between the principles, organs, and practices of the nineteenth and early twentieth centuries and those adopted by the League of Nations. The Concert of Europe was the forerunner of the League Council, in which the Great Powers assumed major responsibility for keeping the peace. The Hague conferences had anticipated the League Assembly, where the small states could participate on a permanent basis with established membership and responsibilities. The recognition of arbitration as a form of third-party decision making well suited for the settlement of certain kinds of international disputes, which dated back as far as the Greek city-states and was emphasized at the Hague conferences, foreshadowed the Permanent Court of International Justice.

The precipitating factor for the creation of the League of Nations, of course, was the carnage of World War I. Cooperation among the Allied powers during the war produced the appropriate psychological conditions for an alliance for peace and resulted as well in some novel features of the League system. The most important of the novel features were the principle of the guarantee by member states of the political independence and territorial integrity of each member against external aggression, and the use of collective measures— economic, financial, and, perhaps, military—to defeat aggression. Also fundamental to the League's approach to maintaining peace was the concept that war could be avoided if procedures were provided for allowing peoples and governments cooling-off periods during which they could face facts and turn to peaceful means for settling their disputes.

During its first decade the League enjoyed a substantial measure of success in spite of the failure of the United States to become a member.[12] The years 1924 to 1929 were a period of apparent general prosperity, relative peace, and promising cooperative efforts in the economic and social fields. But this veneer of prosperity contributed to the failure of governments to take steps necessary to deal with the basic problems of economic maladjustment and imbalance resulting from the war. The bubble burst in 1929, and the years 1930 to 1936 saw a worldwide depression of unprecedented breadth and depth. The depression helped to bring to power expansionistic, authoritative regimes in Germany, Italy, and Japan. These regimes challenged the peace-keeping capabilities of the League, and the League proved unequal to the challenge.

More properly put, the Great Powers, on whose support the peace-keeping capabilities of the League depended, declined to meet the threat. The United States, as a nonmember, gave only limited support; Great Britain and France, for a variety of political, economic, and social reasons, failed to fulfill their responsibilities as League members. As a result, the League was unable to check Japanese aggression in Manchuria in the early thirties or to sanction Italy effectively after its attack on Ethiopia in October 1935. No attempt whatsoever was made to use League machinery and procedures to prevent German remilitarization of the Rhineland in March 1936 in clear violation of the Treaty of Versailles and the Locarno Pact or the outbreak of war when it became imminent as the result of the Czechoslovakian crisis and the threat to Poland. The expulsion of the Soviet Union in 1939 following its attack on Finland was, in a sense, the League's last gesture as an institution designed to prevent and punish aggression.[13]

BACKGROUND TO UNITED NATIONS CHARTER PROVISIONS ON THE CONTROL OF INTERNATIONAL VIOLENCE

Despite the collapse of the League, or perhaps because of it, there was agreement among the Allied powers early in the course of World War II that some form of international organization should be created after the war to maintain international peace and security. In particular, the governments of China, the USSR, the United Kingdom, and the United States so agreed at Moscow in 1943.[14] This led in turn to a meeting of these countries' representatives at Dumbarton Oaks in 1944 where an agreement was reached on proposals that became the basis for further discussion at San Francisco in April–June 1945. The United Nations Charter, signed on June 26, 1945, entered into force on October 24 of that year.

The new United Nations system drew heavily on the League as a guide for its machinery. For example, the Permanent Court of International Justice, while formally superseded by its successor, the International Court of Justice, served as the basic model, with relatively few modifications, for the new World Court. Similarly, the decision was made to renew the League's effort to achieve peace through international organization instead of through world government. The United Nations was to be an international organization, moreover, that would be dominated by the Great Powers, in spite of the declaration in Article 2, paragraph 1, of the Charter that "The Organization is based on the sovereign equality of all of its Members."

Like the League, the United Nations was also created to deal with wide-ranging subject matter. Great Britain and the Soviet Union had favored limiting the role of the new organization to the political and security sphere.[15] But, in accordance with the functional approach to peace, the decision was made that the United Nations could do its job properly only if it was authorized to explore the economic, social, and ideological causes of armed conflict.

Not only were the Great Powers to be in a position to dominate the peace-keeping functions of the United Nations; the organization of these functions was based on the fundamental premise of Great Power unity, especially between the United States and the Soviet Union. To be sure, the drafters of the Charter were aware that it would be difficult to maintain the Great Power cooperation that characterized the war effort. But there was a widespread agreement that there was no hope for a peaceful world unless the Great Powers cooperated in preventing and punishing aggression.[16]

NOTES

1. Sylvester J. Hemleben, *Plans for World Peace Through Six Centuries* (New York and London: Garland Publishing, Inc., 1972), pp. xi–xiv.

2. See e.g., Joseph R. Strayer, "Feudalism in Western Europe," in Ruston Coulborn (ed.), *Feudalism in History* (Princeton: Princeton University Press, 1956), pp. 22–25.

3. Inis L. Claude, Jr., *Swords into Plowshares* (New York: Random House, 4th ed., 1971), p. 21.

4. Sylvester J. Hemleben, *Plans for World Peace,* pp. 1–41.

5. That of Dante. *Ibid.,* p. 11.

6. Inis L. Claude, Jr., *Swords into Plowshares,* pp. 21–40.

7. Ibid., p. 27.

8. Ibid., p. 28.

9. Ibid., p. 30.

10. Ibid., pp. 28–34.

11. Ibid., p. 41.

12. Leland M. Goodrich, *The United Nations in A Changing World* (New York and London: Columbia University Press, 1974), p. 5.

13. Ibid., p. 7.

14. Ibid.

15. Inis L. Claude, Jr., *Swords into Plowshares,* p. 67.

16. Ibid., pp. 72–75.

TWO

The United Nations System
for Maintaining International
Peace and Security

The purpose of this chapter is to examine, in brief outline, the law of the United Nations Charter as it relates to the peaceful settlement of disputes, prohibitions on the use of force by states, exceptions to these prohibitions, and the authority of the United Nations to use force. In each area, where appropriate, comparison will be made with the law of the League Covenant. This chapter will also serve as a backdrop to Chapter 3 where we will turn to a description and assessment of the United Nations in practice.

PEACEFUL SETTLEMENT OF DISPUTES

The Charter requires that "all Members shall settle their international disputes by peaceful means in such manner that international peace and security, and justice, are not endangered."[1] Later the Charter is more specific about the peaceful means that should be employed when it states that "The parties to any dispute, the continuance of which is likely to endanger the maintenance of international peace and security, shall, first of all, seek a solution by negotiation, enquiry, mediation, conciliation, arbitration, judicial settlement, resort to regional agencies or arrangements, or other peaceful means of their own choice."[2] The Charter further obligates parties to such a dispute, if they fail to settle the matter by the means specified, to refer it to the Security Council.[3]

The obligation of member states who are parties to a dispute to submit it to the Security Council is limited in scope. It applies only if the continuance of the disagreement is "likely to endanger the maintenance of international peace and security" and only if efforts to settle it by the peaceful means specified have failed.[4] In its discretion, any member of the United Nations may bring any dispute to the attention of the Security Council or the General Assembly.[5]

For its part, the Security Council is given "primary responsibility" under the Charter for the maintenance of international peace and security.[6] The council is required, "when it deems necessary," to call upon the parties to a dispute likely to endanger the maintenance of international peace and security to settle it by peaceful means.[7] The council is also authorized by the Charter to recommend appropriate procedures for settling such disputes[8]—while bearing in mind that "legal disputes should as a general rule be referred by the parties to the International Court of Justice."[9] The council's authority to recommend terms of settlement is normally limited to situations where it is satisfied that the efforts of the parties to settle peacefully have failed and that the continuance of the dispute is "in fact" likely to endanger the maintenance of international peace and security.[10] If all the parties so request, the council may also make recommendations without regard as to whether the dispute is likely to endanger the maintenance of international peace and security.[11]

It has generally been thought that the Security Council's authority in the area of pacific settlement of disputes is limited to making recommendations.[12] This view, however, is now questionable in light of the language in the Advisory Opinion of the International Court of Justice on Namibia.[13] There, in advising that the Security Council resolutions on Namibia had created obligations for both member states and nonmember states of the United Nations, the court quoted with approval a statement of the secretary-general that "the powers of the Council under Article 24 are not restricted to the specific grants of authority contained in Chapters VI, VII, VIII and XII . . . the Members of the United Nations have conferred upon the Security Council powers commensurate with its responsibility for the maintenance of peace and security. The only limitations are the fundamental principles and purposes found in Chapter I of the Charter."[14]

Under this view of the Charter, it is unclear what the limits of the council's decision-making power are. The limits could be as narrow as the "fundamental principles and purposes found in Chapter I of the Charter." But even if the council must at least be acting in the "maintenance of international peace and security" under the first paragraph of Article 24 of the Charter, it would arguably have the authority to mandate particular terms of settlement for a dispute. As we shall see, the council may have done this in the context of the Arab-Israeli conflict.

By the terms of the Charter, the General Assembly is assigned a relatively subsidiary role in the maintenance of international peace and security. It is to serve as a forum for public discussion and multilateral diplomacy designed to achieve the peaceful adjustment of unsatisfactory situations and the acceptance of the principles of cooperation.[15] Although it can discuss any question relating to the maintenance of international peace and security brought before it by a member state,[16] the assembly is prohibited from making recommendations while the Security Council is dealing with the issue.[17] In cases where "action" is required, the assembly is required to refer the issue to the Security Council.[18] However, as we shall see, the International Court of Justice has given a narrow interpretation to the word "action" and an expansive one to the "measures" that the General Assembly may recommend for the peaceful adjustment of any situation "which it deems likely to impair the general welfare or friendly relations among nations."[19] Hence, in practice the assembly has assumed a greater role in the maintenance of international peace and security than a strict reading of the Charter would indicate.

Under the Charter, the secretary-general is made the chief administrative officer of the United Nations.[20] An issue that has arisen regarding the secretary-general, and one that has created tension in the organization, is the extent to which he can also be regarded as an international executive with some measure of autonomy—both from the member states and from the organization itself. Some measure of support for such a role is found in the terms of the Charter. The secretary-general is specifically directed not to seek or receive instructions from any government. He and his staff are to act as international officials responsible only to the organization.[21] The secretary-general's authority to bring to the Security Council any matter he believes may threaten the maintenance of international peace and security[22] has been interpreted to include the right to conduct independent inquiries and to engage in informal diplomacy regarding potentially dangerous situations.

The International Court of Justice was established as the principal judicial organ of the United Nations in the hope that it would become a primary institution for the peaceful settlement of disputes between states. Like its predecessor, the Permanent Court of International Justice, it has been a great disappointment to its most ardent supporters. During the thirty-three years that the court has been functioning, it has had on the average only one contentious case a year and one advisory opinion every other year. From the very beginning of the court's existence, however, it was obvious that powerful member states of the United Nations viewed the court with distrust. Proposals advanced during debates on the Charter to give the court jurisdiction over any question or dispute relating to the interpretation of the Charter were given short shrift,[23] and the court's jurisdiction was limited to giving advisory, nonbinding opinions on any legal question, and only then if requested by a designated organ of the United Nations or its specialized agencies.[24]

Similarly, a large majority of member states favored giving the court compulsory jursidiction over legal disputes.[25] But both the

United States and the Soviet Union strongly opposed this proposal and declared that they would not become parties to the court's statute if the proposal were adopted.[26] Consequently, the so-called compulsory jurisdiction of the court is limited to situations where the states concerned have expressly consented to such jurisdiction, either on an *ad hoc* basis, or in advance of the dispute through a declaration.[27] As of January 1, 1979, however, there were only forty-five states that had filed declarations recognizing the court's compulsory jurisdiction.[28] This compares unfavorably with the degree of state acceptance of the compulsory jurisdiction of the Permanent Court of Justice.[29] Moreover, many of the declarations filed with the I.C.J. are qualified by crippling reservations. Perhaps the most notorious of these is the so-called Connally Amendment, which reserves to the United States the right to decide whether a dispute involves a matter essentially within its domestic jurisdiction. Considering these substantial limitations on its competence, the court has performed more admirably in the area of peaceful settlement of disputes than it is usually given credit for. We shall explore this proposition further at a later stage in our deliberations.

PROHIBITIONS ON THE USE OF FORCE BY STATES

Grotius, in his distinction between the just and the unjust war, stated that "war ought not to be undertaken except to enforce rights."[30] The Covenant of the League of Nations prohibited members from resorting to war in some circumstances, but not all; in particular, members were permitted to resort to war in cases where specified means of peaceful settlement had failed.[31] The covenant also obligated members of the League "to respect and preserve against external aggression the territorial integrity and existing political independence of all Members."[32] Ambiguities raised by the terms "aggression" and "war" caused problems for the League, however, and the drafters of the United Nations Charter decided on a different approach.

Article 2(4) of the Charter provides:

> All Members shall refrain in their international relations from the threat or use of force against the territorial integrity or political independence of any state, or in any other manner inconsistent with the Purposes of the United Nations.

But this approach was not uniformly followed elsewhere in drafting the Charter, and this has raised questions as to the proper interpretation and application of Article 2(4). For example, Article 1 proclaims the first purpose of the organization to be the maintenance of international peace and security by taking effective collective measures to prevent or remove "threats to the peace" and to suppress "acts of aggression or other breaches of the peace." It does not use the words "force" or "threat of force." The application of the qualifying words "in conformity with the principles of justice and international law" to the organization's first purpose, moreover, has led some to claim that, unless law and justice are served, recourse to force may be justified. Similarly, some have cited the principle of self-determination in Article 1(2) to support the contention that force can be used on behalf of "wars of national liberation." Also, as we shall see later, the Security Council is directed "to determine the existence of any threat to the peace, breach of the peace, or act of aggression" and to make recommendations or decide on measures to restore international peace and security. This means that there is "no necessary identity between what is legally prohibited by Article 2(4) and what the Council seeks to control in the discharge of its responsibilities."[33]

EXCEPTIONS TO PROHIBITIONS ON THE USE OF FORCE BY STATES

Total elimination of the right of states to use armed force would, of course, be hopelessly utopian, and there are exceptions to the prohibitions on the use of force contained in the United Nations Charter. What these are, and their scope, has been a matter of considerable debate. We shall begin with an exception explicitly encompassed within the Charter's system for maintaining international peace and security.

Self-Defense

Grotius included within his category of just wars a war fought for the purpose of self-defense,[34] and self-defense has always been recognized as sufficient justification for the use of armed force. Prior to the adoption of the United Nations Charter, the standard test for judging whether the use of force was justified as an act of self-defense was that of American Secretary of State Daniel Webster in the context of a dispute with Great Britain over an attack launched from Canada against the small steamer *Caroline* while it was docked on the American side of the Niagara River. There, Secretary Webster stated that the use of force in self-defense should be limited to cases in which the "necessity of that self-defence is instant, overwhelming, and leaving no choice of means, and no moment for deliberation."[35] At an earlier time Webster had declared a requirement of proportionality that "the act, justified by the necessity of self-defence, must be limited by that necessity, and kept clearly within it."[36] Thus the use of armed force should be for the purpose of defense and not for punishment.

Article 51 of the U.N. Charter provides:

> Nothing in the present Charter shall impair the inherent right of individual or collective self-defence if an armed attack occurs against a Member of the United Nations, until the Security Council has taken measures necessary to maintain international peace and security. Measures taken by Members in the exercise of this right of self-defence shall be immediately reported to the Security Council and shall not in any way affect the authority and responsibility of the Security Council under the present Charter to take at any time such action as it deems necessary in order to maintain or restore international peace and security.

The words "if an armed attack occurs" have raised the issue whether Article 51 has limited the scope of the self-defense doctrine. Some have argued that the words should be read literally so as to eliminate the possibility of anticipatory self-defense available under the *Caroline* doctrine. In their view, this is necessary because the advent of nuclear weapons means that an error in calculation or intelligence might result in a nuclear holocaust in the name of self-defense. Others counter that in this age of long-range and massive strike capability any absolute prohibition on anticipatory self-defense would mean that states confronted with the necessity for defense would have to assume the posture of "sitting ducks."[37] This dispute has not been definitively resolved by the United Nations itself.

Humanitarian Intervention

The use of force allegedly on the basis of humanitarian concerns has traditionally taken place in three contexts. First and foremost from a historical perspective, force has been used to protect the lives and property of a country's nationals abroad when the host country's government has shown itself unable or unwilling to provide such protection. This use of force has been defended as an exercise of self-defense. Second and much more controversially, force has been used to stop another country's government from engaging in a massive violation of the human rights of its own citizens. Third, the doctrine has been invoked, on one side or the other, in cases of intervention in civil wars or in wars of national liberation.

The second type has most often been the focus of attention in debates over humanitarian intervention. It is unclear from the historical record whether there has ever been a clear case of humanitarian intervention—that is, one not primarily motivated by ulterior motives of gain on the part of the intervening state.[38] From a traditional legal perspective, it is also unclear whether such purity of motive is a requirement for a lawful intervention.[39]

Assuming *arguendo* the validity of humanitarian intervention under traditional law, the primary focus of recent debate has been on its compatibility with the United Nations Charter. Some argue that humanitarian intervention violates the terms of Article 2(4) because it impairs the territorial integrity and political independence of the state where the intervention takes place and because it cannot be justified as an act of self-defense. They also contend the record indicates that humanitarian intervention has been used as a cloak for interference in the internal affairs of small states who cannot oppose the intervening forces of a great power, and that it may encourage counterintervention by other states and risk an escalation of the conflict. At the most, they assert, the humanitarian motives of the intervening state might be considered by way of a political plea in mitigation in domestic and international forums.[40]

Those who support the doctrine of humanitarian intervention dispute the allegation that there has never been such an intervention and dismiss the presence of mixed motives as irrelevant for policy prescriptions. They note the language of Article 2(4) that requires member states to "refrain in their international relations from the threat or use of force against the territorial integrity or political independence of any state, or in any other manner inconsistent with the Purposes of the United Nations" and argue that humanitarian interventions, far from being inconsistent with the purposes of the organization, promote the protection of human rights—a primary purpose of the United Nations. They contend further that an intervention for such limited purposes does not threaten the territorial integrity or political independence of the state against which it is directed. The inability or unwillingness of the United Nations to act to protect human rights is stressed by these commentators. In their view, "article 2(4) suppresses self-help insofar as the organization can assume the role of enforcer. When it cannot, self-help prerogatives revive."[41]

Again, as we shall see, this debate has not been definitively resolved by the practice of states or by the response of the United Nations to such practice during the postcharter period. State and UN practice do, however, lend a substantial measure of support to the anti-humanitarian intervention thesis.

Other Alleged Justifications for the Use of Force

There have been a number of other justifications for the use of armed force advanced by commentators and states. Some may be dismissed summarily; others raise more serious issues.

In the first category, some have claimed that armed intervention may be justified in order to assist in the process of "modernization."

Professor Friedmann has aptly pointed out the absurdity of this contention:

> Even if one were to accept "modernization" as a generally acceptable value of world order—a proposition made doubtful by man's recent preoccupation with environment and his discovery of the devastating effects of much of his "modernization"—the ambiguity of the criterion is only too obvious. Does it mean compulsory democratization, conversion of an agricultural to an industrial economic structure, the redistribution of land, or total socialization?[42]

More serious have been claims of a right to intervene to insure self-determination. The validity of these claims has been particularly difficult to analyze because "self-determination is a concept of quintessential ambiguity whose scope is a matter of considerable debate."[43] In particular, it is unclear whether self-determination applies only to peoples located within a colonial territory or extends as well to ethnic or religious groups seeking to secede from an established country. Some have even claimed that the right to self-determination is synonymous with the democratic principle of free choice of government by the people, although there is, unfortunately, little support in state practice for this contention.

At times self-determination has been cited as justification for extending armed assistance to a government at its request against a local rebellion. More often it has been relied on to justify supplying arms or coming to the direct military assistance of rebel groups or one of several factions competing for authority within a single country.

The communist states have avidly pressed the claim that armed support for wars of national liberation is compatible with Article 2(4) of the Charter, on the ground that such aid allows oppressed people to exercise their right to self-determination. This claim has not enjoyed general support in the United Nations. But, as we shall see, it has been widely supported when applied to particular contexts, such as southern Africa, the West Bank, and the Gaza Strip.

Finally, the United States contended during the Cuban missile crisis that its "quarantine" of shipping in and out of Cuba was a regional peace-keeping exercise taken pursuant to Chapter VIII (Regional Arrangements) of the Charter. Others claimed that the American use of force constituted an enforcement action, which could only be authorized by the Security Council pursuant to Article 53(1) of the Charter.[44] No authoritative determination of this issue was ever made by a UN organ.

UNITED NATIONS AUTHORITY TO USE FORCE

Under the Covenant of the League, primary responsibility for enforcement of prohibitions on the use of force was placed on member states rather than on the League council. Thus, under Article 10 of the Covenant, member states undertook "to respect and preserve as against external aggression the territorial integrity and existing political independence of all members of the League." Similarly, under Article 16 of the Covenant, if it were deemed that a member state had committed an act of war "in disregard of its covenants under Articles 12, 13, or 15", all other members of the League were obligated to impose economic and financial sanctions against a Covenant-breaking state. However, the apparently automatic nature of these sanctions was nullified by a 1921 interpretative resolution of the League Assembly,[45] leaving the decision whether to apply them to each individual state. Also, military sanctions against a Covenant-breaking state were neither automatic nor mandatory, and the 1921 resolution weakened the universalist character of these sanctions by stating that military assistance would normally come from the geographic area concerned.

By contrast, the United Nations Charter gives "primary responsibility" and considerable discretion for maintaining international peace and security to the Security Council.[46] The council is authorized under Chapter VII of the Charter to determine the existence of any threat to the peace, breach of the peace, or act of aggression, and to make recommendations and decisions as to whether economic or even military sanctions should be employed.[47] Any such decision of the council is binding upon member states under Article 25 of the Charter. At the same time the five permanent members of the council—the United States, Great Britain, the U.S.S.R., China, and France—are able through the veto power to prevent any enforcement action of which they disapprove.

The decision-making authority of the council regarding the use of armed force, however, has been largely rendered null because the permanent members failed to agree on the armed forces to be made available to the Security Council in accordance with the terms of special agreements concluded between the council and member states.[48] In the absence of these agreements, the council has been unable to make binding decisions to use force, and any measures taken by the United Nations or under its auspices requiring the use of armed force have been based on voluntary contributions. The breakdown in the wartime collaboration between the five permanent members of the Security Council and the frequent use of the veto by the Soviet Union have also contributed to the collapse of the Charter concept of a Security Council acting in concert and supported by a permanent peace-keeping force.

In place of this concept, and in order to fill the vacuum, the combination of a strong secretary-general and a more active General Assembly has created an entirely different system from the one outlined by Chapter VII. Under this system, the United Nations has operated on an ad hoc basis, and the role of its military forces has been limited to a "watchdog" function and to serving as a buffer, or "plate glass window," between the parties to a dispute with their consent. As we shall see, the new role of the secretary-general and the General Assembly has raised legal and political issues that remain unresolved to this day.

NOTES

1. Article 2(3).
2. Article 33(1).
3. Article 37(1).
4. See the relationship between Articles 33(1) and 37(1).
5. Article 35(1).
6. Article 24.
7. Article 33(2).
8. Article 36(1).
9. Article 36(2).
10. Article 37(2).
11. Article 38.
12. See e.g., Leland M. Goodrich, *The United Nations in a Changing World* (New York and London: Columbia University Press, 1974), p. 111.
13. Advisory Opinion on the Continued Presence of South Africa in Namibia (South West Africa) [1971] I.C.J. Rep. 16.
14. Paragraph 110 of the Court's opinion.
15. See generally Articles 10, 11, 12 and 14.
16. Article 11(2).
17. Article 12.
18. Article 11(2).
19. Advisory Opinion on Certain Expenses of the United Nations [1962] I.C.J. Rep. 151.
20. Article 97.
21. Article 100(1).
22. Article 99.
23. Leland M. Goodrich, *Changing World*, pp. 32–33.
24. Article 96.
25. Leland M. Goodrich, Edvard Hambro and Anne Patricia Simons, *Charter of the United Nations* (New York and London: Columbia University Press, 1969), p. 545.
26. Ibid., p. 547.
27. See Article 36 of the Statute of the Court.
28. Department of State, *Treaties in Force* (1979), p. 292.
29. There are currently 157 parties to the statute of the court—Liechtenstein, San Marino, and Switzerland, in addition to 154 members of the United Nations. Although the number of parties to the court's statute has

grown rapidly, the number of them accepting the compulsory jurisdiction of the court has remained fairly constant. By contrast, in 1938, 38 of the 54 parties to the Statute of the Permanent Court of International Justice had accepted the court's compulsory jurisdiction. Leo Gross, "The International Court of Justice: Consideration of Requirements for Enhancing its Role in the International Legal Order," *The Future of the International Court of Justice* (Dobbs Ferry: Oceana Press, 1976), vol. I, pp. 22, 30.

30. Quoted in Hedley Bull, "The Grotian Conception of International Society," Herbert Butterfield and Martin Wright (eds. and contribs.), *Diplomatic Investigations: Essays in the Theory of International Politics* (Cambridge: Harvard University Press, 1966), pp. 51, 55.

31. For discussion, see Robert S. Wood, "The League of Nations in Retrospect: Legal Doctrines and Political Conceptions," Robert S. Wood (ed. and contrib.), *The Process of International Organization* (New York: Random House, 1971), pp. 59–68.

32. Article 10.

33. Leland M. Goodrich, Edvard Hambro and Anne Patricia Simons, *Charter of the United Nations*, p. 46.

34. Hedley Bull, "Grotian Conception," pp. 54–55.

35. J. B. Moore, *Digest of International Law* (1906), p. 412.

36. Mr. Webster to Mr. Fox (April 24, 1841), 29 *British and Foreign State Papers* (1857), pp. 1129, 1138.

37. For excerpts from articles and books exploring both sides of the issue, see Louis Henkin et al., *International Law: Cases and Materials* (St. Paul: West Publishing Co., 1980), pp. 929–38.

38. Thomas M. Franck and Nigel Rodley, "After Bangladesh: The Law of Humanitarian Intervention by Military Force," *American Journal of International Law* 67 (1973):275–305.

39. For a general discussion of these and other issues, see Richard Lillich (ed.), *Humanitarian Intervention and the United Nations* (Charlottesville: University of Virginia Press, 1973).

40. Ian Brownlie, "Humanitarian Intervention," John Norton Moore (ed.), *Law and Civil War in the Modern World* (Baltimore and London: Johns Hopkins University Press, 1974), pp. 217–28.

41. W. Reisman, *Nullity and Revision* (New Haven and London: Yale University Press, 1971), p. 850. See also Richard B. Lillich, "Humanitarian Intervention: A Reply to Ian Brownlie and A Plea for Constructive Alternatives," John Norton Moore (ed.) *Law and Civil War*, pp. 229–51.

42. Wolfgang G. Friedmann, "Intervention and International Law," quoted in Louis Henkin et al., *International Law*, p. 925.

43. John F. Murphy, "Self-Determination: United States Perspectives," Yonah Alexander and Robert A. Friedlander (eds.), *Self-Determination: National, Regional, and Global Dimensions* (Boulder: Westview Press, 1979), pp. 43–61.

44. See Quincy Wright, "The Cuban Quarantine," *American Journal of International Law* 57 (1963):546–65.

45. See Robert S. Wood, "League of Nations in Retrospect," p. 64.

46. Articles 27, 39.

47. Articles 38, 41, 42.

48. See Articles 43–47.

THREE

The Security Council

In our examination of United Nations practice in this and the following three chapters, we will attempt to be at once descriptive, analytical, and evaluative. To this end, examination of UN practice will be undertaken for several purposes. First and foremost, we will seek to evaluate how well the United Nations has fulfilled its role in maintaining international peace and security. At the same time, as previously noted, some Charter provisions are ambiguous, and, as the International Court of Justice has advised,[1] UN actions may serve as a valuable guide to the interpretation and application of these provisions. Such an examination may also reveal lacunae in the Charter that need to be filled or ambiguities that need to be clarified.

Our focus in this and the following three chapters will be limited to a consideration of UN responses to traditional acts of international violence, i.e., to situations where there has been the threat of or an actual crossing of international boundaries by the armed forces of one state without the consent of the governmental authorities of the state whose boundaries have been violated. Consideration of the difficult legal and political questions associated with more indirect interventions is reserved for later chapters.

As we explore UN responses to international violence, we will be evaluating the organization's efforts toward finding peaceful settlements as well as its effectiveness as an enforcement agency. Although, strictly speaking, only the Security Council would appear authorized by the Charter to serve in an enforcement capacity, we shall see that the General Assembly has also assumed this role and that the secretary-general, and even the International Court of Justice, have performed, at least indirectly, an enforcement function from time to time.

PALESTINE

As already noted, the Soviet Union and the United States were unable to agree on the terms of agreements making available to the

25

Security Council the armed forces necessary for the discharge of its responsibility to enforce the peace as envisaged by Article 43 of the Charter. The disagreement between the Soviet Union and the United States related to such matters as the size and composition of the armed forces to be contributed by the permanent members, the provisions of bases, the location of forces when not in action, and the time of their withdrawl.[2] The implications of this failure became apparent early as the conflict in Palestine between Jews and Arabs became more violent. Secretary-General Trygve Lie attempted to salvage the talks on permanent military forces by suggesting informally to Great Britain and the United States that an armed force be established in Palestine out of the "minimum units which the Big Five were committed to place at the Security Council's disposal," which he believed would be "more than adequate" to keep the peace.[3] Both Great Britain and the United States rejected the proposal because of fear of Russian troops in Palestine, and the secretary-general therefore never introduced it to the Council. Accordingly, it proved impossible for the Security Council to implement the General Assembly's plan for a partition of Palestine into a Jewish and an Arab state. Indeed, the United States reversed its position on partition in the Security Council and called instead for a temporary trusteeship over Palestine.[4] This proposal was not adopted, the mandate was terminated on May 14, 1948,[5] the Jewish community in Palestine immediately proclaimed the State of Israel within the territorial boundaries of the partition plan, and the new state was quickly recognized by a number of states, including the United States and the Soviet Union. Almost simultaneously, however, Egypt, Syria, Transjordan, Lebanon, and other Arab states intervened, as stated in a cablegram of May 16 from the secretary-general of the League of Arab States to the United Nations secretary-general, "to restore law and order and to prevent disturbances prevailing in Palestine from spreading into their territories and to check further bloodshed."[6] Thus began the first of five Arab-Israeli conflicts in the Middle East.[7]

The Security Council was slow to react to the crisis, and when it did on May 22 it limited itself to a call for a cease-fire.[8] This resolution was ignored by the Arab states, and it was not until several days later on May 29 that the council adopted a more strongly worded resolution calling for a four-week cease-fire by June 1, instructing the Mediator on Palestine and the Truce Commission for Palestine to supervise its observance, and referring for the first time to Chapter VII of the Charter by way of warning.[9]

The Arab states refused to abide by the June 1 deadline, and it was only after lengthy negotiations through UN mediators that they finally agreed to a truce on June 11. However, after four weeks and the expiration of the truce, the Arab states refused to agree to its extension, and hostilities were resumed. In response, on July 15 the council adopted its most rigorous resolution in which it took account of Arab rejection of appeals for the continuation of the truce and determined that the situation constituted a threat to the peace within the meaning of Chapter VII. It declared that failure to comply with the resolution would demonstrate the existence of a breach of the peace requiring action under that chapter and ordered a cease-fire "until a peaceful adjustment of the future situation of Palestine is reached."[10] This resolution was more effective, and a second cease-fire went into effect on July 18.

The second cease-fire was frequently violated despite efforts by UN mediators to maintain it. In an effort to find a solution to the crisis, Count Bernadotte, the Chief UN Mediator, recommended a number of changes in the General Assembly's plan; e.g., that the Israeli Negev "should be defined as Arab territory."[11] The next day Bernadotte was assassinated in the Israeli sector of Jerusalem. The murderers were never apprehended, and after the International Court of Justice advised that the organization had the standing to bring an international claim,[12] Israel paid reparations to the United Nations. Ralph Bunche was appointed Bernadotte's successor.

In October, the cease-fire broke down completely, and heavy fighting took place between Israel and Egypt. By resolution of October 19,[13] the Security Council called for restoration of the cease-fire and suggested withdrawal of troops as well as negotiations between the parties, either directly or through the United Nations. After a series of similar calls by the council, negotiations between Israel and Egypt, under the chairmanship of Ralph Bunche, began at Rhodes in January 1949. Largely through Bunche's efforts, for which he was awarded a Nobel Peace Prize, these negotiations resulted in the signing of an armistice agreement on February 24. This was followed by similar agreements between Israel and Lebanon, Jordan, and Syria. These armistice agreements specified that they were concluded without prejudice to territorial rights and that the armistice demarcation lines were not to be construed as political boundaries. The agreements also established demilitarized zones and set up Mixed Armistice Commissions (MACs) to supervise the implementation of the truce. The chairman of each MAC was the chief of staff of the U.N. Truce Supervision Organization (UNTSO).[14]

Conclusion of these armistice agreements was an outstanding accomplishment of the United Nations. The same may not be said, however, of the other UN actions regarding the situation in Palestine. Particularly, the Security Council failed to take the steps necessary to implement the General Assembly's partition plan, although it was crystal clear that the Arab States were going to resort to force against the projected Jewish state. But it must be remembered that the United Nations can be only as effective in preventing the outbreak of international violence as its member states—especially the permanent members of the Security Council—wish it to be. In the case of Palestine, neither Great Britain nor the United States was willing to provide the Security Council with the forces necessary to prevent the outbreak of violence in Palestine and the invasion of the territory by Arab states.

The reasons for this unwillingness are worth a brief examination—although one has to speculate somewhat to do so—because neither Great Britain nor the United States spelled out their positions publicly in great detail. We have already noted the reluctance of Great Britain and the United States to have Soviet troops introduced into the Middle East. Under the plan proposed by Secretary-General Lie, however, the Soviet component would have been only a small part of the overall force and would have been under the command of the United Nations. Moreover, even if the cold war had progressed to the stage where the introduction of any Soviet armed force into Palestine was simply unacceptable, it was incumbent upon the United States and Great Britain to suggest other alternatives. But the British announced categorically and self-righteously that they would have no part in implementing a partition plan that was opposed by the Arab states.[15] For his part, the permanent representative of the United States to the United Nations, Warren Austin, argued that the Security Council had no authority under the Charter to use force to implement the partition plan.[16] Secretary-General Lie's observation on this contention is compelling:

Ambassador Austin's doctrine that the United Nations did not have the power to enforce any type of political settlement is sound as a general proposition . . . The United Nations does not have the power to impose a political settlement, whether it be unification or partition, except in special circumstances. Such circumstances exist when all the parties in control of a territory hand it over to the United Nations to determine its fate. In the case of Korea all the parties did not do that. In the case of Palestine, on the other hand, the United Kingdom was the sole Mandatory power, and it had handed over the whole territory to the United Nations for disposition. Clearly, I felt, the Organization in these circumstances had full constitutional power not only to maintain order inside the territory but, even more, to resist any attempt from outside to overthrow its decision.[17]

One might add to Secretary-General Lie's observation that, in any event, the Security Council had the authority and the primary responsibility under the Charter to maintain peace, through the use of force if necessary. Great Britain's abandonment of the mandate, the Jewish community's proclamation of the State of Israel, and the

Arab states' threats to intervene with force precipitated an imminent threat to peace that, had its permanent members been willing, the council had ample authority to handle.

As a result of the council's failure to deal with the crisis in Palestine, the United Nations has had the Arab-Israeli conflict on its agenda for the length of the organization's existence. We shall return to this unhappy situation on several more occasions.

KOREA

The next major test for the Security Council was one that challenged the very existence of the United Nations. At the Potsdam Conference of July 1945, the United States and the United Kingdom agreed that Korea should "in due course . . . become free and independent." At the end of the war, however, the country was divided, as Japanese forces north of the 38th parallel surrendered to forces of the Soviet Union, and Japanese forces south of that line surrendered to United States units. In December 1945 the United States, the United Kingdom, and the U.S.S.R. agreed in Moscow to the establishment of a provisional government for the whole of Korea and to the creation of a Joint Commission that would supervise its formation.

In 1947 the United States proposed that elections take place in each zone. The Soviet Union rejected this plan and proposed instead that all troops be withdrawn from Korea by January 1, 1948. The United States then brought the question of elections to the General Assembly, which established a United Nations Temporary Commission on Korea to facilitate and expedite the elections.[18] Challenging the assembly's resolution as illegal, the Soviet Union refused to participate in its implementation. As a result, the commission was not permitted to enter North Korea and supervised elections in South Korea only. Following the election, and after the elected representatives had met in Seoul as the Korean National Assembly, the General Assembly declared that a lawful government—that of the Republic of Korea—had been established in Korea and created a new commission to bring about unification of the country.[19]

In the summer of 1949, United States and Soviet troops had been withdrawn from Korea, leaving North and South Korean forces guarding each side of the 38th parallel. There were frequent border incidents. On June 25, 1950, the United States and the commission informed the United Nations that North Korean forces had invaded South Korea.

In response to the invasion, the council first passed a resolution calling for a cessation of North Korea's actions.[20] When this resolution was ignored, it recommended that member states "furnish such assistance to the Republic of Korea as may be necessary to repel the armed attack and to restore international peace and security in the area."[21] Passage of the second resolution allowed the United States to bring its defense of Korea—an action it would have taken in any event—under the auspices of the United Nations.

At the same time the United States resisted efforts on the part of the secretary-general to involve the United Nations more deeply in the defense of Korea. The secretary-general proposed informally to the United States the formation under Security Council auspices of a "Committee on the Coordination of Assistance for Korea" to promote and supervise UN participation in the military action.[22] Although the proposal had the support of the Europeans, the strong resistance of the Pentagon to anything more than a minimal role for the United Nations led the United States to reject it. In view of the United States monopoly over available armed forces, the council had no choice but to accept the American decision. As a result, UN "supervision" over the forces in Korea was limited to the receipt of periodic reports from the United States. Secretary-General Lie later expressed the opinion that American resistance to letting the United Nations play a more substantial role "no doubt contributed to the tendency of Members to let Washington assume most of the responsibility for fighting."[23] Be that as it may, the UN role was not insignificant. Fifteen governments ultimately contributed ground, naval, or air forces, and many others made significant contributions of ancillary support, such as shipping, medical facilities, and supplies.[24]

The Soviet delegate returned to the Security Council on August 1, 1950, and blocked any further action by the council. On October 7, 1950, the General Assembly, noting that the objectives of the Security Council had not been attained, established the United Nations Commission for the Unification and Rehabilitation of Korea.[25]

In the meantime, the Inchon landing of September 15 had radically turned the tide of battle in Korea, and the North Korean army was in full retreat. This sudden change of circumstances raised a crucial question: Should United Nations forces cross the 38th parallel dividing the two Koreas or be content with having driven the North Korean forces out of South Korea? The view of the United States, which was shared by the secretary-general and many other member states, was that UN forces should proceed into North Korea in order to defeat decisively the North Korean forces, preclude any further aggression on their part, set up conditions for free elections throughout Korea, and thereby unify the country.[26] To this end the United States introduced, and the General Assembly adopted, a resolution which recommended that "all necessary steps be taken to ensure conditions of peace throughout the whole of Korea"[27] and that elections be held under UN auspices toward the unification of all Korea. The resolution declared that United Nations forces entering North Korea should not remain any longer than necessary for achieving this objective.

In response to the stalemate in the council and at the initiative of the United States, the assembly also adopted on November 3 the famous "Uniting for Peace" Resolution.[28] The resolution provided that the General Assembly would meet to recommend collective measures in situations where the Security Council was unable to deal with a breach of the peace or act of aggression. Under the resolution, whenever a veto prevented the council from acting, a special emergency assembly session could be convened within twenty-four hours by a procedural vote of any seven members. By way of institutional provisions, the resolution recommended that all member states earmark units of their armed forces to be maintained in readiness for future use under either council or assembly resolutions and authorized the secretary-general to appoint a panel of military experts to advise governments, on their request, about setting up the earmarked national units. It also established a fourteen-member Collective Measures Committee to study further methods to improve the ability of the United Nations to meet future cases of aggression.

It wasn't long before the United Nations had occasion to use its new procedures. The fundamental premise underlying the decision to cross the 38th parallel—that the People's Republic of China would not intervene in the fighting with its own forces—proved false. On November 29, as the UN forces were driving to the Yalu River, North Korea's boundary with Manchuria, Chinese troops intervened in massive numbers. Imminent victory threatened to become a rout as UN forces retreated rapidly. Initially, the secretary-general attempted to work out a cease-fire through negotiations with the communist Chinese. These proved to no avail, and on February 1, 1951, with the Security Council unable to act, the General Assembly, acting under the Uniting for Peace procedures, passed a resolution condemning the Chinese action as aggression, calling upon them to withdraw their forces from Korea, and recommending that all states lend every assistance to the UN action in Korea.[29]

During the winter of 1951 the initiative passed again to the UN forces and the North Korean forces were driven back to the 38th parallel. This time there was no sentiment in favor of crossing the line. Nonetheless, negotiations were long and difficult, and the conflict continued until an armistice agreement was finally concluded at Panmunjom on July 27, 1953. Although there have been several incidents, hostilities have not been renewed. At the same time, a permanent settlement of the conflict has eluded the United Nations.

With the possible exception of its actions regarding southern Africa,[30] Korea has been the Security Council's only exercise in collective security. The council was to engage in this exercise only because of fortuitous circumstances, the most important of which, of course, was the absence of the Soviet delegate from the council at the time of the North Korea invasion of the South. This removed the certainty of a Soviet veto. Also important was the ability of the United Nations Commission in Korea to report immediately from the scene and thus convince the council that North Korean forces had in fact invaded the South.[31] Except for the presence of the commission in Korea, there almost surely would have been substantial debate in the council over which side was the aggressor.

Perhaps the most debatable aspect of UN action in Korea was the decision to cross the 38th parallel with the goal of unifying the country by the force of arms and creating a new, democratic government. This goal went considerably beyond the more limited purpose of denying the North Koreans military sanctuaries. Precedent for the goal of punishing the aggressors might be found in the Nuremburg trials, where high-ranking Nazi leaders were punished for crimes against peace, defined under the Nuremberg charter as wars of aggression or wars in violation of international treaties. The attack by North Korea upon the South was clearly an act of aggression in violation of the United Nations Charter. But the Nuremberg trials and punishment of the Nazi leaders depended upon realization of the war goals of the Allies, namely, the unconditional surrender of Germany, occupation of that country, annihilation of the German government, and its replacement with one acceptable to the Allies. It is highly questionable whether these goals were appropriate for UN forces in Korea.

It is even questionable whether they were compatible with the UN Charter. Article 39 of the Charter authorizes the Security Council to "determine the existence of any threat to the peace, breach of the peace, or act of aggression" and to make recommendations "to maintain or restore international peace and security." This provision would seem to permit the temporary occupation of enemy territory, pending a peace settlement or for some period of time stipulated in the settlement. It would not appear to justify forceful unification, even as a measure against further attack. The goal of *conquest* of North Korea would also seem incompatible with the doctrine of proportionality, which, as we have seen, is an integral component of the right of self-defense.

The principle of proportionality raises some serious moral issues regarding UN goals in crossing the 38th parallel. In the words of Michael Walzer:

> The argument at this point might be put in terms of proportionality, a doctrine often said to fix firm limits to the length of wars and the shape of settlements. In this instance, we would have to balance the costs of continued fighting against the value of punishing the aggressors. Given our present knowledge of the Chinese invasion

and its consequences, we can safely say that the costs were disproportionate (and the aggressors never punished). But even without such knowledge, a strong case might have been made that Acheson's "roundup" did not warrant its likely price.[32]

Walzer goes on to say:

Because of the collective character of states, the domestic conventions of capture and punishment do not readily fit the requirements of international society. They are unlikely to have significant deterrent effects; they are very likely to extend rather than restrict the number of people exposed to coercion and risk; and they require acts of conquest that can only be aimed at entire political communities. Except when directed against Nazi-like states, just wars are conservative in character; it cannot be their purpose, as it is the purpose of domestic police work, to stamp out illegal violence, but only to cope with particular violent acts. Hence the rights and limits fixed by the argument for justice; resistance, restoration, reasonable prevention.[33]

In its police action the United Nations was unable to fulfill even its more limited, and clearly legitimate, goal of ensuring that North Korea would not resume its aggression against the South. On the contrary, with the Chinese intervention and the difficulty of the UN forces in returning to the 38th parallel, the North Koreans were in a position to drive a hard bargain in negotiations over an armistice and prolonged the process for two years. Whether this would have happened had General MacArthur heeded the warnings of the People's Republic of China that it would intervene if UN forces continued their drive to the Yalu River is problematic.

SUEZ

The Security Council played only a modest role in the Suez crisis—one of the most spectacular and dangerous examples of interstate violence arising out of the Arab-Israeli conflict; nonetheless, it is worth a brief examination. For the Suez crisis represents a situation where the Security Council was prevented from fulfilling its primary responsibility for maintaining international peace and security by states normally dedicated to upholding the United Nations in its peace-keeping functions.

By way of background, it will be recalled that the first Arab-Israeli conflict ended in the armistice agreements of 1949. However, the armistice between Israel and Egypt deteriorated rapidly.[34] Fedayeen raids occurred frequently from the Sinai and the Gaza Strip and led to increasingly severe Israeli retaliation. On the ground that it was exercising legitimate belligerent rights, Egypt closed the Suez Canal to Israeli shipping and kept it closed in disregard of a 1951 Security Council resolution[35] that denied the compatibility of the exercise of belligerent rights with the armistice. Egypt also controlled the entrance to the Gulf of Aqaba at Sharm el Sheikh, which overlooked the Strait of Tiran. In justification of this action, Egypt again relied on belligerent rights and on the fact that the navigable passage of the straits fell within its territorial waters. In response Israel contended that the gulf could not legally be closed to blockade one riparian and that the straits constituted an international waterway, which, under customary rules of international law, could not be unilaterally closed to Israeli shipping.[36]

Tensions between Israel and Egypt continued to mount, and in 1956 the Security Council asked the secretary-general to undertake urgently a study of the amount of compliance with the armistice agreements. The report submitted by the secretary-general on May 9 took note of the escalation of violence between Egypt and Israel and observed:

A chain of actions and reactions was created which, unless broken, is bound finally to constitute a threat to peace and security.

13. The development could have taken another turn, if the Government and citizens of one country had felt able to assume that transgressors from the other country—in violation of the provisions of the armistice agreement—had acted without any instigation or approval by the authorities and the authorities had taken active counter-measures, including appropriate punishment for transgressions. No reason would then have existed for acts of reprisal which might be considered, by the country taking action, as acts in self-defence; instead a complaint to the other party would have been the natural outlet for reactions[37]

The secretary-general observed further:

64. There is not in all cases an adequate functioning machinery for resolving disputes concerning the interpretation, or implementation of the obligations assumed by the parties under the agreements. Obviously an assurance to comply with the armistice agreements has little practical bearing on the situation to the extent that any party can reserve for itself the right to give to the obligations its own interpretation, which may be different from the one which in good faith is maintained by the other party.

65. A further weakness is that no procedure has been established

for the handling of conflicts covered by the general clauses in the armistice agreements. For example, the first article of the several agreements established a right to security and freedom from fear of attack. The parties have in many cases complained of actions from the other side as being in conflict with this stipulation. Were diplomatic relations maintained, such complaints would undoubtedly be handled through normal diplomatic channels and might in that way to a large extent be resolved. In cases of this kind which the party may not wish to bring to the Security Council, there is at present no such possibility available within the framework of the armistice regime as applied.

66. . . . The Governments, while taking note of my observations concerning the procedural weaknesses indicated, have not gone further into the matter.[38]

On June 4 the Security Council unanimously adopted a resolution[39] urging the parties to cooperate with the chief of staff and the secretary-general in order to put into effect the proposals of the report. No such cooperation was forthcoming, however, and conditions along the demarcation lines continued to deteriorate. Relations between Egypt, on the one hand, and England, France, and the United States, on the other, also came under increased strain culminating in the United States decision not to finance the construction of the Aswan Dam and Egypt's announcement on July 26 of the nationalization of the Suez Canal and its intention to use funds from the collection of tolls to defray the costs of building the dam. Although the decree of expropriation provided for compensation to the shareholders in the company established to operate the canal on the basis of the market value of their shares as of July 25, and President Nasser indicated that he remained bound by the obligation in the Constantinople Convention of 1888 to keep the canal open at all times, the hostility of the British, French, and United States reaction was pronounced. Attempts at compromise were unsuccessful, and on September 12 the United Kingdom and France placed the issue before the Security Council for the first time.

At this point, United States secretary of state John Foster Dulles, fearing the imminent use of force, proposed a Suez Canal Users' Association (SCUA), which would take the form of an international organization with ships at each end of the canal. Dulles added, however, at a press conference, that the United States would not back up SCUA with the use of force. Egypt and the Soviet Union protested to the Security Council, claiming that the establishment of SCUA was incompatible with Egyptian sovereignty and constituted a threat to the peace.

At the United Nations, Secretary-General Dag Hammarskjöld was lending his good offices to private negotiations between the French, British, and Egyptian foreign ministers. These negotiations resulted in substantial agreement on six points: (1) free and open passage through the canal without discrimination, overt or covert; (2) respect for the sovereignty of Egypt; (3) the insulation of the canal from the politics of any country; (4) the manner of fixing tolls and dues to be settled between Egypt and the users; (5) a fair proportion of the dues to be allotted to development; and (6) in the case of disputes, unresolved affairs between the Suez Canal Company and the Egyptian government to be resolved by arbitration. These points were then incorporated into a draft resolution,[40] which was unanimously adopted by the Security Council on October 13.

On the surface, then, prospects for a peaceful settlement of the dispute were favorable. But appearances were deceiving, for in London, Paris, and Tel Aviv, government officials were deciding in secret to use force in the form of an Anglo-French "police" action, following an Israeli attack upon Egypt. The United States was not informed of these plans.

The Israeli attack upon Egypt came on October 29, whereupon the United States promptly asked the Security Council to determine that a breach of the peace had occurred and to order Israel to withdraw behind the armistice lines. The chief of staff of UNTSO confirmed that Israeli troops had violated the armistice and crossed the international frontier. Israel defended its action as security measures to eliminate Egyptian fedayeen bases in the Sinai peninsula and claimed that this action was self-defense under Article 51 of the UN Charter. On October 30 Britain and France, through their veto power, prevented the Security Council from taking action and sent a joint ultimatum to Egypt and Israel calling upon both sides to stop all warlike action and withdraw ten miles away from the canal. The ultimatum also demanded that Egypt permit the "temporary occupation by Anglo-French forces of key positions at Port Said, Ismailia, and Suez," and threatened force if compliance was not forthcoming.

With the Security Council unable to act, the matter was then transferred to the General Assembly under the Uniting for Peace procedure. We will consider the actions of the General Assembly regarding the Suez Crisis—particularly the establishment of the United Nations Emergency Force—in the next chapter.

As for the performance of the Security Council in the Suez crisis, a review of the record leaves one with two strong impressions. First, the council performed extremely well in attempting to resolve the disputes peacefully. Second, the council also functioned as envisaged by the founders of the United Nations—i.e., the United States and the Soviet Union acted in concert in dealing with the blatant acts of aggression. Only the extraordinary fact of British and French aggression and their consequent vetoes prevented the council from filling its responsibilities.

The observations and recommendations of the secretary-general's report regarding violations of the armistice agreement between Egypt and Israel, which were adopted by the Security Council, highlighted, in diplomatic fashion, Egypt's failure to carry out its obligations under the agreement to prevent fedayeen attacks from its territory against Israel. The recommendations of the secretary-general's report offered Egypt an opportunity to save face with respect to its past violations while contributing to a strengthening of the armistice arrangements. But Egyptian willingness to refrain from supporting guerrilla attacks against Israel was simply not present.

Similarly, the six points agreed upon by the foreign ministers of Britain, France, and Egypt through the good offices of the secretary-general and incorporated into a resolution by the Security Council were a solid basis for a settlement of the dispute between Egypt, Britain, and France concerning expropriation of the Suez Canal and might have contributed to an easing of tensions between Egypt and Israel, especially since the first point called for free and open passage through the canal without discrimination, which presumably would have included Israeli shipping. Britain, France, and Israel, however, were not interested in a peaceful settlement, but rather in the overthrow of President Nasser—an objective totally incompatible with the United Nations Charter and subversive of the responsibilities of the Security Council. The courageous stand of the United States in the council against its closest allies in support of fundamental norms of the Charter was a highpoint in the history of the United Nations. As we shall see in the next chapter, United States support for Charter norms continued throughout the duration of the Suez crisis.

THE SIX DAY WAR

Although we will be considering the General Assembly's actions on the Suez crisis in some detail in the next chapter, it is necessary to touch upon this subject briefly at this juncture in order to give some brief background to the Security Council's consideration of the Six Day War that broke out in June 1967. At its Emergency Special Session, summoned by the Security Council under the Uniting for Peace procedure, the General Assembly adopted a series of resolutions calling for a cease-fire, a return to armistice lines, and the creation of a United Nations Emergency Force in the Middle East (UNEF).

Pressure from the United Nations, the Soviet Union, and the United States induced Britain, France, and Israel to accept a cease-fire, and, upon the arrival of UNEF forces, British and French troops began to withdraw. Israel delayed its withdrawal until it received assurances that the United States viewed the Gulf of Aqaba and the

Strait of Tiran as international waterways, and that it would be prepared "to join with others to secure general recognition of this right."[41] Since Israel refused to permit the stationing of UNEF forces on its territory, they were positioned solely on Egyptian territory.

These arrangements helped to prevent major hostilities in the area for almost ten years. Through the latter part of 1966, however, fedayeen incursions into Israel grew in number and intensity. These attacks sometimes moved through Jordan or Lebanon, but for the most part they were mounted in Syria, where a new and radical government had come to power earlier in the year. Two especially serious incidents in October that resulted in the deaths of several Israelis caused Israel to appeal, as it often had before, to the Security Council. This appeal was unsuccessful. A relatively mild resolution, calling on Syria to take stronger measures to prevent such incidents, was vetoed—as had been others before it—by the Soviet Union.[42] Early in November, moreover, Syria and Egypt concluded a "defense agreement," involving a joint military command and other measures of "coordination and integration" between the two countries.

In response to these developments, Israel retaliated massively, but against moderate Jordan rather than against the more militant Syria. The justification given by Israel for the attack was that there had recently been thirteen acts of sabotage committed on Israeli territory from Jordanian bases. As a result of the attack, UN observers reported, eighteen Jordanian soldiers and civilians were killed and fifty-four wounded.

The Israeli attack was widely regarded as a disproportionate, illegal act of reprisal. Although self-defense—that is, proportionate defense against an illegal use of force—is permissible, retaliation is not. Defined as a subsequent, punitive military response, retaliation was contrary to the United Nations Charter and damaging to the whole structure of the armistice agreements.[43] As a consequence, the Security Council, by a vote of fourteen to zero, with one abstention, censured Israel "for this large-scale military action in violation of the U.N. Charter and of the General Armistice Agreement between Israel and Jordan," and warned Israel "that actions of military reprisal cannot be tolerated and that if they are repeated, the Security Council will have to consider further and more effective steps as envisaged in the Charter against the repetition of such acts."[44]

The double standard applied by the council in these two instances was obvious and contributed to the already substantial Israeli bitterness and distrust toward the United Nations. It also contributed to an atmosphere in which Israel became more inclined to rely on self-help measures rather than recourse to peaceful settlement through the United Nations.

In 1967 the conflict escalated to the point of crisis. At Egyptian request, the UNEF was withdrawn. Egypt reimposed the blockade against Israeli shipping in the Strait of Tiran and massed forces in the Sinai. In sharp contrast to their actions in the Suez Crisis of 1956, neither the Soviet Union nor the United States proved willing to take political initiatives at the United Nations regarding the UNEF, either by calling for a meeting of the Security Council, proposing constructive resolutions in the meetings of the council that did occur, or by bringing effective pressure to bear on the Arabs and Israelis in support of a continuing UN role in the Middle East. Rather, they used the United Nations as a forum for debating the merits of the opposing positions of the Arabs and Israelis. The Soviet Union even went so far as to argue that there was no dangerous crisis in the Middle East and that the situation therefore did not warrant any significant actions on the part of the United Nations.[45]

It is unclear which side fired the first shot.[46] On June 5, 1967, however, the Israeli Air Force mounted a massive attack on Egyptian military airfields. Syrian, Jordanian, and other Arab forces soon joined the battle, but within six days Israel had occupied large areas of territory, including the Gaza Strip, the Sinai, the Golan Heights, East Jerusalem, and the West Bank of Jordan. Again the superpowers failed to take effective action inside or outside the United Nations to deal with the crisis. Because of their disagreement from the outset over whether there should be an unconditional or a conditional cease-fire, the Security Council did not agree on any formal cease-fire resolution until the second day of the fighting. The superpowers also failed throughout the week of fighting to bring effective pressure to bear on the parties to stop the fighting. Consequently, the war came to a halt only when the Israelis had achieved their desired territorial objectives and halted their forward motion of their own accord.

Once the cease-fire went into effect, the Security Council passed several resolutions concerning humanitarian assistance to civilians and prisoners of war and called upon Israel not to take unilateral measures to change the status of Jerusalem.[47] The council had considerable difficulty, however, in taking any action beyond these resolutions.

The Soviet Union and the Arab states argued that the council should declare Israel the aggressor and require it, under Chapter VII of the Charter, if possible, to withdraw to the Armistice Demarcation Lines as they stood on June 5th. In exchange for Israel's withdrawal, the Soviet Union offered only vague assurances that Israeli maritime rights in the Strait of Tiran would be "no problem," and that a document might be filed with the secretary-general, or a Security Council resolution adopted, that would finally end any possibility of claiming that a "state of belligerency" existed between Israel and its neighbors.[48]

Israel's position was substantially different. In its view, the Arab states had repudiated the armistice agreements by going to war. The parties should therefore meet alone and draw up a treaty of peace. Until negotiations for that purpose began, Israel would not weaken its bargaining position by publicly revealing its peace aims, although it did state publicly that it had no territorial claims as such and was occupying the captured territory only for purposes of national security and the protection of its maritime rights as well as its rights in East Jerusalem.

Because of the incompatibility of these views, it took five months of difficult negotiations, inside the United Nations and out, before the Security Council could act. When it did, on November 22, 1967, it adopted the now famous Resolution 242. Because of the importance of this resolution, it is quoted below in its entirety:

The Security Council

Expressing its continuing concern with the grave situation in the Middle East,

Emphasizing the inadmissiblity of the acquisition of territory by war and the need to work for a just and lasting peace in which every State in the area can live in security,

Emphasizing further that all Member States in their acceptance of the Charter of the United Nations have undertaken a commitment to act in accordance with article 2 of the Charter,

1. Affirms that the fulfillment of Charter principles requires the establishment of a just and lasting peace in the Middle East which should include the application of both the following principles:

(i) Withdrawal of Israeli armed forces from territories occupied in the recent conflict;

(ii) Termination of all claims or states of belligerency and respect for and acknowledgement of the sovereignty, territorial integrity and political independence of every State in the area and their right to live in peace within secure and recognized boundaries free from threats or acts of force;

2. Affirms further the necessity

(a) For guaranteeing freedom of navigation through international waterways in the area;

(b) For achieving a just settlement of the refugee problem;

(c) For guaranteeing the territorial inviolability and political independence of every State in the area, through measures including the establishment of demilitarized zones;

3. Requests the Secretary-General to designate a Special Representative to proceed to the Middle East to establish and maintain contacts with the States concerned in order to promote agreement

and assist efforts to achieve a peaceful and accepted settlement in accordance with the provisions and principles of this resolution.

4. Requests the Secretary-General to report to the Security Council on the progress of the efforts of the Special Representative as soon as possible.

Resolution 242, issued under Chapter VI of the Charter, was adopted unanimously after assurances from key countries that they would accept the resolution and work with the secretary-general's special representative towards its implementation. Shortly after promulgation of the resolution, however, controversy arose regarding interpretation of its provisions. In particular, Israel and the Arab states disagreed whether the resolution required an Israeli commitment, in advance of negotiations, to withdraw from the occupied territories. They also disagreed whether the resolution required withdrawal from *all* the occupied territories or only a negotiated withdrawal to "secure and recognized boundaries."[49]

In addition to this debate over the proper interpretation of Resolution 242, not all the parties accepted the resolution as the basis for a peaceful settlement of the conflict. Syria rejected Resolution 242 on the ground that the resolution contained no explicit reference to the Palestinians. It only affirmed the necessity "[f]or achieving a just settlement of the refugee problem." In the Syrian view, the Palestinians could not be viewed just as refugees, but as displaced persons with an inalienable right to return to their homeland.[50]

Pursuant to Paragraph 3 of Resolution 242, Secretary-General U Thant designated Gunnar Jarring, ambassador from Sweden to the Soviet Union, as the Special Representative who would proceed to the Middle East. Neither Ambassador Jarring's efforts, however, nor talks among the Soviet Union, United States, France, and Great Britain produced an agreement acceptable to both Arabs and Israelis. The Arab states continued to stand on the policy adopted by the Arab League and the Palestine Liberation Organization (PLO) in the Khartoum Resolution: "no peace with Israel, no recognition of Israel, no negotiations with it, and insistence on the rights of the Palestinian people in their own country."[51] The PLO adopted a national charter in 1968, in which it declared the establishment of the State of Israel to be "entirely illegal" and proclaimed as its goal the total liberation of Palestine.[52]

The cease-fire between Israel and the Arab states steadily deteriorated. In the spring of 1969, President Nasser, concerned that prolonged Israeli occupation of the territories seized in the Six Day War would strengthen their claims to permanent sovereignty over them, announced that the cease-fire was no longer valid and began a "war of attrition" against Israeli defenses along the Suez Canal.

United States secretary of state William P. Rogers succeeded in negotiating an "at least" 90-day standstill cease-fire agreement between Israel, Egypt, and Jordan, which went into effect on August 7, 1970. In an effort to undermine the Rogers initiative, the Popular Front for the Liberation of Palestine, a splinter group of the PLO, sponsored a series of hijackings and attacks on commercial aircraft. These precipitated major clashes between PLO forces in Jordan and King Hussein's army. Syria intervened on behalf of the Palestinians, but withdrew when the United States threatened a counterintervention.

With the death of President Nasser in 1970, Anwar el-Sadat became president of the United Arab Republic. The standstill cease-fire was extended despite failure to resolve the dispute over the interpretation of Resolution 242. During this period, Egypt indicated for the first time a willingness to enter into a peace agreement with Israel if basic differences could be resolved. However, as we shall see in the next section of this chapter, no such peace agreement was concluded; rather the fifth Arab-Israeli conflict broke out in 1973.

The performance of the Security Council regarding the Six Day War was—with one exception—less than inspiring. Particularly, the council failed to take any positive steps toward preventing the outbreak of the war. This was due mainly to the obstructionist tactics employed by the Soviet Union during the council's deliberations. The Soviet Union vetoed any attempt in the council to call upon Syria or other Arab states to fulfill their obligations under international law to prevent the use of their territories for guerrilla attacks against Israel. When the crisis came to a head with the removal of the UNEF, the Soviet Union ridiculed the council's attempts to deal with the problem.

Not all of the responsibility for the council's ineffectiveness, however, lies with the Soviet Union. As Professor Oran Young has noted:

> . . . the American role during the upswing phase of the crisis was marked by hesitancy, indecisiveness, and weakness. While the activities of the Soviet Union tended to exacerbate the crisis by encouraging one of the protagonists, the indecisive activities of the United States led to a situation which allowed the crisis to run its own course with a striking lack of significant and forceful external efforts to regulate the contest. Throughout this phase, the United States relied almost exclusively on a series of rather hesitant verbal reactions, thereby avoiding more forceful initiatives or conditional threats. In particular, this was the case with regard to the withdrawal of UNEF, the lack of political initiatives within the United Nations, the problems posed by the Egyptian blockade of the Strait of Tiran, and the American efforts to restrain the Israelis.[53]

Professor Young suggests that some primary reasons for United States indecisiveness were:

First, the long-standing American commitment to a balance of power policy in the Middle East operated as a pressure on the United States to avoid activities favouring either of the protagonists in the 1967 crisis. Second, the concurrent American preoccupation with the problem of Vietnam generated strong domestic opposition to more active policies that might lead to extensive involvement of the United States on a second foreign front. Third, a sharp division of public opinion in the United States between pro-Israel sentiments and a strong desire to avoid involvement in a potentially violent situation led to an unwillingness on the part of the executive to act decisively without clear Congressional support. Fourth, the Egyptian initiative in blockading and possibly mining the Gulf of Aqaba both reduced the range of responses open to the United States and raised fears that any effective American action to raise the blockade might bring on the United States the onus for touching off violence and creating a situation of great danger in the Middle East.[54]

Because of the failure of the Soviet Union and the United States to act effectively, either in concert or separately, the council was slow in responding to the actual outbreak of war. Implementation of the council's tardy calls for a cease-fire was also hindered by the superpowers' unwillingness to bring the necessary pressure to bear on the belligerents to stop the fighting.

The one exception to the council's dismal record regarding the Six Day War is its unanimous adoption of Resolution 242. Although this resolution does not refer to some of the key problems in the Arab-Israeli conflict—such as the status of Jerusalem and the rights of the Palestinians—it does provide a framework for negotiations and, as we shall see later, has been the basis for some major breakthroughs in the efforts to bring peace to the area. The adoption of Resolution 242, therefore, was an outstanding diplomatic achievement and was dependent upon substantial willingness to compromise between the superpowers—a willingness absent throughout most of this period.

THE 1973 ARAB-ISRAELI WAR

As shown in the preceding section of this chapter, despite the Security Council's unanimous adoption of Resolution 242, little progress was made toward bringing about a peaceful settlement of the Arab-Israeli conflict within its framework. On the contrary, in 1969 Egypt initiated the so-called war of attrition designed to weaken Israel by constant fedayeen attacks. From 1967 to October 1973, the Security council met on a number of occasions to consider violations of the cease-fire, but was unable to act effectively. Then, on October 6, 1973, Yom Kippur, the Jewish Day of Atonement, Egypt and Syria launched a surprise attack against Israel, which was joined by several other Arab states. Egypt and Syria defended their attack on the ground that they were acting in self-defense to recover their territories illegally occupied by Israel since 1967. The illegality of the Israeli presence in the occupied territories was premised on the Arab interpretation of Resolution 242 that Israel was required to withdraw from all the occupied territories in advance of any peace settlement.[55] This argument and its supporting premise had long been rejected by Israel and the United States, among others. Israel felt entitled to remain on the cease-fire lines of 1967 as the occupying power until the parties themselves reached an agreement in conformity with the principles and provisions of the resolution.[56]

Although the council first met on October 8 at the initiative of the United States, it was not until October 22 that it took action. This was because the Arab states enjoyed substantial success in the early days of the fighting, and the Soviet Union was accordingly unwilling to support a cease-fire resolution in the council. The tide began to turn, however, as counterattacks advanced Israeli forces to within twenty-two miles of Damascus and succeeded in establishing a bridgehead west of the canal behind Egyptian lines, fifty miles from Cairo.

As a result of Israel's success on the battlefield, the Soviet Union invited American negotiators to come to Moscow for urgent consultations. The outcome of these meetings was the council's adoption of Resolution 338,[57] which made mandatory Resolution 242. Resolution 242 was cast in the form of a recommendation to the belligerents to adopt certain principles as the basis for peace in the Middle East. Resolution 338, however, confirmed that the parties should start to implement Resolution 242 immediately after the beginning of a cease-fire and was a *decision* of the Security Council that negotiations to this end should start immediately.[58] Subsequent Security Council resolutions urged that the two sides return to the positions they occupied when the cease-fire became effective. Also, a new United Nations Emergency Force was created, this time by the Security Council rather than by the General Assembly. In response to Resolution 338's call for negotiations, a Geneva Peace Conference on the Middle East was convened. Two public sessions and one closed session were held, but the talks were discontinued after all three proved fruitless.

Shortly after the cease-fire went into effect, President Sadat decided, on the basis of a variety of political, economic, and social factors, to eschew further resort to force and pursue a "political settlement option."[59] Aided by Secretary Kissinger's shuttle diplomacy, negotiations led in January 1974 to a limited agreement on the disengagement of Egyptian and Israeli forces[60] and to the more comprehensive Sinai Interim Agreement in September 1975.[61] In the words of Secretary Kissinger, Egypt and Israel pledged in the interim agreement "not just to disentangle their forces in the aftermath of war, but to commit themselves to the peaceful resolution of the differences that have so long made them mortal enemies."[62] To this end, Egypt and Israel agreed that the United Nations Emergency Force established by the Security Council should continue its peacekeeping functions. Similarly, in the Agreement on Disengagement between Israeli and Syrian Forces of May 31, 1974,[63] the parties agreed to a United Nations Disengagement Observer Force (UNDOF) to supervise maintenance of the cease-fire.

Egypt and Israel eventually progressed beyond their interim agreement to the conclusion of a peace treaty.[64] At this writing no such progress has been made between Syria and Israel or between Jordan and Israel. Israel remains in occupation of the Golan Heights, the Gaza Strip, and the West Bank of the Jordan, and the key problems of Palestinian rights, East Jerusalem, and Israel's territorial security remain as unresolved as ever.

The actions of the Security Council with respect to the 1973 war followed a pattern similar to that of the council's actions regarding the Six Day War. Nothing to speak of was done to prevent the outbreak of the conflict, and the Soviet Union was unwilling even to consider a cease-fire resolution until it became clear that the Arabs had begun to lose their early advantage. When American and Soviet perspectives on the situation converged, the council adopted Resolution 338, which is a major breakthrough in the Arab-Israeli conflict in that it creates an obligation for all the parties to negotiate a resolution of their dispute within the framework of Resolution 242. To be sure, all the Arab States except Egypt have ignored the council's directive, but, at a minimum, it enhances the pressure on these states to come to the negotiating table with Israel as well as strengthening Israel's case in the political bodies of the United Nations.

The position of the United States in the Security Council during the 1973 war is worth a brief notice. Although the facts clearly indicated that the Arab attack was an act of aggression, the United States deliberately maintained a silence in the council concerning the illegality of the attack. This was unfortunate. Apparently this stance was taken in the hope of inducing the Soviet Union to support a constructive resolution in the Security Council rather than merely arguing the Arab case. But this hope proved forlorn. The Soviet Union showed no interest in cooperating with the United States and was a ferocious defender of the Arab aggression. Thus, from a *realpolitik* perspective, the American soft-handed approach in the council was a failure. More important, this reticence may have undermined the fundamental norms of the United Nations Charter against the use of force. At Nuremberg, high-ranking Nazi officers were sentenced to death for crimes against peace, such as the planning and waging of an aggressive war. For over two weeks during the 1973 war, the Arab states were not even asked to agree to a cease-fire. As Professor Eugene Rostow, former under secretary of state, has commented, the United States' silence in the council "measures the ominous recent decline in the influence of international law on international politics."[65]

CYPRUS

The international violence involving Cyprus does not lend itself to easy classification. It could be considered a case of revolutionary violence—and hence treated in a later chapter of this book—because of the Greek Cypriots' rebellion against the established order and their efforts to effect *enosis,* or union with the Greek mainland. Or, depending on the particular perspective, the actions of the Turkish Cypriots to have Turkey intervene militarily on their behalf and effect a partition of the island could be regarded as a revolution against oppression by the Greek Cypriot majority. Overall, however, it appears appropriate to consider Cyprus as a case study of traditional violence. The conflict over Cyprus, and the resultant military inter-ventions by Turkey, raise fundamental issues of the protection of an ethnic minority—issues characteristic of the post-World War I period. The Turkish threat and actual use of force in Cyprus, therefore, appears to follow a traditional pattern of international violence appropriate for coverage in this chapter.

The story of the dispute over Cyprus is long and complicated and will be told only in brief outline here.[66] For centuries Cyprus has been a focal point of conflict, although the island is small and has few natural resources. Its importance lies in its strategic location. Control over the island permits hegemony over the eastern Medi-terranean. As a consequence, Cyprus has been successively occupied from before the Byzantine era by Richard the Lionhearted, the Templars, Franks, Venetians, Turks, and British. Britain, the last colonial power over Cyprus, acquired the island in 1878 from Turkey.

As early as 1830 there was substantial sentiment on the island in favor of *enosis.* This sentiment increased rapidly in intensity during the next century until 1931, when Greek Cypriots burned the British governor's house in large-scale demonstrations for union with Greece. After World War II such riots became commonplace, and, in a plebiscite among Greek Cypriots in 1949, ninety-six percent of the eligible voters favored union with Greece. Most Greek Cypriots thought of themselves as Greeks living on Cyprus, although their ancestors had lived there for centuries, and the same was true of Turkish Cypriots with respect to Turkey.

In 1950 Archbishop Makarios III became the head of the Greek Orthodox Church in Cyprus and soon asserted leadership of the Greek Cypriot people in secular as well as spiritual affairs. He proved to be a tough and effective promotor of Greek Cypriot interests.

Britain at first strenuously resisted giving up its control of Cyprus. In the United Nations General Assembly, it claimed that Cyprus was a matter essentially within its domestic jursidiction, and that therefore Article 2(7) of the Charter precluded discussion by the assembly of the problem. Although the assembly, at the insistence of Greece, discussed "self-determination for Cyprus" several times, it was never able to come up with a resolution that could command a two-thirds vote.

In 1954 the British Minister of State for Colonial Affairs said that "there can be no question of any change of sovereignty in Cyprus."[67] This precipitated a series of riots that were never completely put down, and the guerrilla campaign on the island continued—not only against the British, but also between Greek and Turkish Cypriots.

The violence on Cyprus, which raised the risk of a direct confrontation between Greece and Turkey over the island, greatly concerned Britain's allies in the North Atlantic Treaty Organization (NATO). As a consequence, in 1958 Paul Henri Spaak, the secretary-general of NATO, urged Greece and Turkey, both NATO members, to negotiate with Great Britain regarding Cyprus's future. These and other efforts resulted in a meeting in Zurich in February 1959 between the Greek and Turkish foreign ministers.

At the conference it soon became clear that there could be no agreement on either *enosis* or partition of the island. Instead, on February 11, 1959, the prime ministers of the two countries initialed drafts of a "Basic Structure of the Republic of Cyprus," a "Treaty of Guarantee between the Republic of Cyprus and Greece, the United Kingdom and Turkey," and a "Treaty of Alliance between the Republic of Cyprus, Greece and Turkey." One year from the date of the signing, Cyprus was to become an independent republic with a Greek Cypriot president and a Turkish Cypriot vice president.

The basic structure contained twenty-seven "Points," the last of which was that "All the above Points shall be considered to be basic articles of the Constitution of Cyprus." Under the draft treaty of alliance, a permanent tripartite military headquarters with 950 Greek troops and 650 Turkish troops was to be established. The proposed treaty of guarantee would bind Cyprus, Greece, Turkey, and the United Kingdom to prohibit all activity tending to promote "directly or indirectly either the union (with Greece) ... or partition of the Island."[68] The three guarantor powers would also "recognize and guarantee the independence, territorial integrity, and security of the Republic of Cyprus. . . ."[69] Under Article IV, in the event of any breach of the treaty provisions, the parties would consult together, but "in so far as common or concerted action may prove impossible," each would reserve "the right to take action with the sole aim of reestablishing the state of affairs established by the present Treaty."

At a later conference in London, which included, for the first time, representatives from the Greek and Turkish communities, Britain agreed to the Zurich proposals on several conditions, including British sovereignty over two base areas on the island and the insertion of an additional article in the treaty of guarantee to assure that Greece, Turkey, and Cyprus would "respect the integrity of the areas to be retained under the sovereignty of the United Kingdom." The British conditions and the additional treaty article were accepted by the other parties.

After further negotiations regarding British base rights on Cyprus and long-term economic aid, final agreement was reached between the parties on July 1, 1960. Cyprus became independent a month and a half later when the accords were formally signed at Nicosia. In elections held earlier in December, Archbishop Makarios had been chosen president, and Dr. Fazil Kutchuk, running unopposed, had been elected vice-president.

As commentators have suggested,[70] perhaps the 1960 accords were bound to fail, based as they were on the deep distrust between Greeks and Turks, and constitutional protection of Turkish representation at every level of the government and Turkish veto power over all crucial decisions. Nevertheless, the settlement worked reasonably well for about two and a half years. Then, Archbishop Makarios began to chafe under the restrictions of the constitution that, in his view, conferred rights on the Turkish Cypriots "beyond what is just." On December 5, 1963, the Archbishop proposed to the guarantor powers thirteen major revisions of the constitution. Although a number of the proposed changes raised no major problems, and some even would have provided the Turkish Cypriots with more protection than before, six of the proposed revisions would have repealed basic articles for which the Turks had fought hard at Zurich and London— the vice-president's power to veto, the requirement of separate majorities in the House for passage of important legislation, separate municipalities, separate judicial systems, a limited security force, and assurance of thirty-percent representation in the public service. Not surprisingly, the Turkish government promptly rejected the proposals, the Archbishop refused the rejection, and, within days, set off by what normally would have been a trivial incident, fighting began between the Greek and Turkish communities on the island.

As calls for peace by Archbishop Makarios and Dr. Kutchuk, as well as calls by the British, Greek, and Turkish governments, failed to stop the fighting, the threat of a Turkish invasion grew. The three guarantor powers then informed the government of Cyprus of their readiness to assist, if invited to do so, in restoring peace and order by means of a joint peace-keeping force under British command and composed of British, Greek, and Turkish contingents already present on the island under the treaties of establishment and alliance. The British suggested that the guarantor powers would be acting as a "regional arrangement" established under the treaty of guarantee and authorized by Chapter VIII of the United Nations Charter. Upon acceptance of the proposal by the government of Cyprus, the force was immediately established. Shortly afterward, the British government announced a conference in London of the guarantor powers and representatives of the two communities to attempt to find a solution to the Cyprus problem, and the four governments jointly requested the United Nations secretary-general to appoint a representative to observe the progress of the peace-keeping operation.

At the London conference, the British government developed a plan with the United States for an enlarged peace-keeping force drawn from NATO nations. Despite strenuous efforts to induce him to accept it, Archbishop Makarios rejected the plan. Although he was prepared to accept an international force on the island, he insisted that it be under the Security Council, that it not include Greek or Turkish troops, and that its mandate include protection of the territorial integrity of Cyprus and assistance in restoring normal conditions.

On February 15, 1964, Britain requested "an early meeting of the Security Council ... to take appropriate steps to ensure that the dangerous situation which now prevails can be resolved with a full regard to the rights and responsibilities of both the Cypriot communities, of the Government of Cyprus and of the Governments party to the Treaty of Guarantee."[71] Almost simultaneously, the Cypriot ambassador to the United Nations requested an emergency meeting of the Security Council, stating "the increasing threat from war preparations on the coast of Turkey opposite Cyprus coupled with the declared intentions of the Turkish government to interfere by force in Cyprus has made the dangers of invasion of the Island both obvious and imminent."[72]

In the Security Council, Cyprus raised a key issue:

Since this point has been made relevant to the whole issue, I should like, with permission, to put a simple question to the Members signatories to the Treaty of Guarantee. I do not insist on an answer tonight. Is it the view of the Governments of Greece, Turkey and the United Kingdom that they have the right of military intervention under the Treaty of Guarantee, particularly, in view of the Charter? On this I must insist on having an answer.

It is very relevant to the whole issue, and I think the Council must have an answer to it before it forms a final opinion. I think the question is simple. It requires an answer, and I quite agree with the representative of Turkey—let us have all our cards on the table.[73]

The answers of each of Cyprus' partners in the treaty of guarantee differed markedly. The representative of Turkey avoided the issue, arguing that the situation in Cyprus was "too tragic to use that kind of stratagem."[74] The representative of Greece replied categorically that the treaty gave no such right of unilateral military intervention;[75] the representative of the United Kingdom also in effect avoided the issue, arguing that it was not the task of the Security Council to consider hypothetical situations.[76] For his own part, the representative of Cyprus contended that Turkey was of the view that the treaty of guarantee gave it the right to intervene militarily in Cyprus, and that this interpretation of the treaty was contrary to peremptory norms of international law; namely, the provisions of Article 2(4) of the UN Charter prohibiting the unilateral use of force.[77]

There were eight separate meetings held over a period of two weeks in the Security Council on the Cyprus question. Meanwhile, the heavy fighting on the island continued. Finally, on March 4, 1964, the council adopted a resolution by a vote of eleven to zero.[78]

In its resolution the council did not address the issue raised by Cyprus, thereby declining to act as a legal tribunal. Rather, the resolution noted that "the present situation with regard to Cyprus is likely to threaten international peace and security." It called upon all members "to refrain from any action or threat of action likely to worsen the situation in the sovereign Republic of Cyprus" and upon "the communities in Cyprus and their leaders to act with utmost restraint." The resolution also recommended the creation, "with the consent of the Government of Cyprus," of a United Nations peace-keeping force in Cyprus (UNFICYP).

The consent of the Greek Cypriot government was immediately forthcoming. On March 6, however, fighting again erupted in Cyprus before any such force could be established and spread to various parts of the island. In response to pleas from the Turkish Cypriot community, the Turkish fleet began maneuvers off the southern coast of Turkey near Cyprus, and on March 13, Turkey informed the UN secretary-general that unless peace was restored on the island it would intervene militarily in the conflict. This time, as support for its threatened unilateral action, Turkey specifically cited Article IV of the treaty of guarantee.[79]

The Security Council met at once in response to the threat. In the council's debates, the representative of Cyprus argued again that the provisions of the United Nations Charter prohibiting the unilateral use of force ruled out the Turkish interpretation of Article IV that it had the right to intervene militarily. The Cypriot representative also argued that the Charter had to be interpreted in the first instance by members of the Security Council without reference to the International Court of Justice.[80]

On March 13 the Security Council unanimously passed a resolution[81] that reaffirmed "its call upon all Member States, in conformity with their obligations under the Charter of the United Nations, to refrain from any action or threat of action likely to worsen the situation in the Sovereign Republic of Cyprus, or to endanger international peace" and requested the secretary-general to implement the council's resolution of March 4. Turkey did not invade, and the next day the first contingent of Canadian troops landed on the island as an advance guard of the United Nations force.

By May of 1964 the UN force had reached its planned level of about 7,000 men. Initially, the force enjoyed some success in maintaining peace on the island. However, the situation continued to deteriorate, and the crisis came to a head when, at the beginning of August, a Cypriot government force launched a series of attacks against the Kokeing-Mansoura area on the northwestern coast, one of the last stretches of seashore held by Turkish Cypriots. The Cypriot government claimed that it was a main landing spot for arms and other supplies from Turkey and that it was a center of Turkish Cypriot terrorist activity. The Turkish view was that the Archbishop intended to wipe out the inhabitants of the area. The United Nations force had a unit in the area, and the Greek Cypriot attacks violated an express assurance given by Archbishop Makarios to the United Nations force commander. When the fighting began, the UN force commander tried unsuccessfully to negotiate a cease-fire and evacuate women and children from the area. After these failures, the United Nations unit withdrew, rather than get involved in the fighting itself.

On August 7 and 8, Turkish air force planes bombed the Greek Cypriot forces attacking the Turkish Cypriot enclave. On August 8, both Turkey and Cyprus requested that the Security Council be convened as a matter of urgency. For two days and nights the Security Council debated. All were agreed that the council should call for a cease-fire; the issue was whether it should also condemn Turkey as an aggressor. Before the council, in addition to arguing that it had a right to intervene under the treaty of guarantee, Turkey alleged that its air attacks were limited to military targets and that they constituted a legitimate act of self-defense.[82]

The resolution[83] adopted by the Security Council on August 9 called for an immediate cease-fire by all concerned and reaffirmed an urgent appeal just addressed by the president of the council "to the Government of Turkey to cease instantly the bombardment of and the use of military force of any kind against Cyprus, and to the

Government of Cyprus to order the armed forces under its control to cease firing immediately." The wording of the resolution reflects the strong tendency of the United Nations to avoid the issue of who was at fault and simply call on all sides to stop shooting. At the same time the resolution does imply a measure of disapproval of Turkey's actions by its lack of evenhandedness in its appeals to the governments of Turkey and Cyprus.

The Security Council, at six month intervals, renewed the mandate of UNFICYP, which quite successfully limited the violence on the island to manageable proportions. In the meantime a number of efforts to mediate the dispute proved unavailing.[84] The debate in the council was between those favoring a unitary state of Cyprus (Greece and the Greek Cypriots) and those favoring a federated state (Turkey and the Turkish Cypriots). Greece and the Greek Cypriots indicated that they no longer viewed *enosis* as a viable solution. However, Turkey argued that, under a unitary state, the Greek majority would rule and there would be nothing to prevent that majority from voting in favor of *enosis*.[85]

Then the situation suddenly changed drastically for the worse. On July 15, 1974, a coup engineered by Greek army officials who supported *enosis* overthrew Archbishop Makarios. The Security Council met on July 16 and 19, but failed to take any action on either of those days. On July 20, Turkey intervened militarily in Cyprus.

France claimed that the council's delay in acting on the Greek army officials' coup had convinced Turkey that it had no alternative but to resort to force.[86] Be that as it may, the council responded with alacrity to the Turkish invasion, adopting a resolution that demanded a cease-fire, the end to foreign military intervention, and the withdrawal of all military personnel not sanctioned by international agreement. The resolution also called for Greece, Turkey, and the United Kingdom to enter into negotiations on an urgent basis.

Nevertheless, the fighting continued, and between July 20 and August 30 the council adopted eight resolutions. On August 15, in response to reports of heavy UNFICYP casualties, the council demanded respect for the international character of the force,[87] and on August 16 the council formally disapproved of unilateral military action against Cyprus—a direct slap against Turkey.[88] Also on August 16, Turkey accepted the council's call for a cease-fire, after it had gained control of the northern third of the Island.

At the end of 1974—after a change of government in Greece—Archbishop Makarios returned in triumph to Cyprus to resume the presidency of the island. The Security Council continued to renew the mandate of the UNFICYP, although, under the system of voluntary contributions established to finance the force, the budget deficit for operating expenses continued to grow. But little progress was made toward resolution of the dispute between the Greek and Turkish communities in Cyprus. On the contrary, in February 1975 the Turkish Cypriots declared the area under their control to be the "Turkish Federated State of Cyprus." This was rejected by the Greek Cypriot community, but became, in effect, a *fait accompli*. The United States Congress imposed an arms embargo against Turkey by way of sanction, but lifted it in 1978 in response to assurances from the administration that progress was being made in intercommunal talks toward a resolution of the dispute. With the death of Archbishop Makarios in 1977, Syros Kyprianou succeeded to the presidency and then, in early 1978, was elected to his own five-year term. At this writing, the negotiations over Cyprus continue with no resolution in sight.

Operating in an extraordinarily difficult milieu, the Security Council performed admirably its primary responsibility for maintaining international peace and security. The council's establishment of the UNFICYP helped keep the level of violence on Cyprus to tolerable levels, except in those instances where either the government of Cyprus or the government of Turkey decided to engage in large-scale military assaults. In these instances, the force could not be expected to prevent violence since it was not equipped by its mandate to serve as an enforcer of the peace, but only operated as a peacekeeping force designed to cope with small-scale outbreaks of violence and depended on the continuing consent of the Cypriot government for the fulfillment of its mandate.

The council also acted rapidly and responsibly with regard to the Turkish invasion threat in 1964 and the subsequent bombing. In the first instance the council's May 4 resolution creating the UNFICYP helped to persuade the Turkish Government not to make good on its threat. The May 13 resolution's response to the Turkish bombing implicitly disapproved of it while indicating the obligation of the Cypriot government to cease its use of military force against the Turkish Cypriot community.

The Security Council was unable to head off the Turkish invasion of Cyprus in 1974 and was, as suggested by France, slow in reacting to the highly combustible situation created by the Greek military officers' coup. Nor was the council able to bring the fighting in Cyprus to a halt until Turkey had fully gained its objective of occupying one third of the island and effecting a *de facto* partition.

The council made no attempt to rule on the many legal issues involved in the dispute over Cyprus. Most particularly, it declined to answer the key issue raised by the Cypriot representative: whether Turkey had a unilateral right of military intervention under Article IV of the treaty of guarantee. The council could, and perhaps ideally should, have referred this and other legal issues to the International Court of Justice for an advisory opinion—in spite of the allegation by the Cypriot representative to the council that no such action was necessary because of the Charter's clear language precluding unilateral military intervention. Alternatively, the council might have requested the parties to the treaty of guarantee to refer the legal aspects of their dispute to the International Court of Justice for a binding judgment.

The fact is, however, that these were legal issues that neither party to the dispute, in the absence of certainty that it would win, wished to have decided authoritatively by a judicial tribunal. The Greek Cypriots did not wish to risk a court decision that, at least under certain circumstances, would have entitled Turkey to legally intervene militarily in Cyprus. Conversely, Turkey would not welcome a decision that it had no such right, at least if other efforts to protect the Turkish Cypriot minority proved unavailing. Rather, instead of a conclusive court decision, the parties wished to preserve their legal cases for use in the political organs of the United Nations, especially in the Security Council.

The legality of the Turkish use of force has been debated extensively in other forums.[89] It suffices for present purposes to note that, regardless of the legalities, Turkey could not be dissuaded from the use of force when it became persuaded that the Turkish Cypriot minority was in grave danger and that the United Nations was unable to afford them adequate protection. Under such circumstances, the absence of Security Council capacity to *enforce* the peace becomes the crucial factor in the decision-making process. It is unreasonable to expect the Security Council to do much more than it did during the Cyprus crisis unless it is given the tools to do the job.

ISRAEL-LEBANON

As we have previously noted, Israel suffered a variety of guerilla attacks from Egypt, Jordan, and Syria before and after the 1967 war. With the overwhelming defeat of the Arab armies in 1967 and Israel's occupation of the West Bank, the Gaza Strip, and the Golan Heights, Lebanon became a refuge for the Palestine Liberation Organization and a jumping-off place for guerrilla attacks into Israel. Israel complained about these attacks to the Security Council on several occasions but, as had been the case with earlier incidents, to no avail.[90] The presence of the Soviet veto precluded any possibility that the council would act on Israel's complaints.

The situation came to a crisis point when, on December 26, 1968, two Arabs attacked an El Al passenger plane at the Athens airport.[91] The attackers were members of the Popular Front for the Liberation of Palestine, a splinter group of the PLO, which had been operating openly in Lebanon since the 1967 war. They used gasoline bombs and submachine guns to attack the El Al plane as it was preparing to take off with forty-one passengers and a crew of ten on a flight bound for New York City. One Israeli passenger was killed by machine gun bullets that penetrated his plane window. There were reports of eighty-six piercings of the fuselage from the cockpit to the tail, with many of the bullet holes through the passengers' windows. The two Arabs had traveled from Beirut to Athens on travel documents provided to stateless persons by the Lebanese government.

This time Israel did not turn first to the Security Council. Rather, on the night of December 28, 1968, two days later, eight Israeli helicopters took part in an attack on the Beirut International Airport. The attack resulted in the destruction of thirteen planes, worth an estimated $43.8 million, which belonged to Arab airlines, as well as some damage to hangars and other airport installations. Two Israeli commandos were injured by gunfire from airport guards, but there was no loss of life.

On December 29, both Israel and Lebanon requested an urgent meeting of the Security Council. Lebanon requested the council to consider its charge that Israel had committed a "wanton and premeditated attack",[92] and Israel countercharged that Lebanon was "assisting and abetting acts of warfare, violence, and terror by irregular forces and organizations"[93] against Israel.

After considerable debate, on December 31, the Security Council, by a vote of fifteen to zero, unanimously adopted a resolution[94] censuring Israel for the Beirut raid. The four operative paragraphs of the resolution indicated that the council:

1. Condemns Israel for its premeditated military action in violation of its obligations under the Charter and the cease-fire resolutions;
2. Considers that such premeditated acts of violence endanger the maintenance of the peace;
3. Issues a solemn warning to Israel that if such acts were to be repeated, the Council would have to consider further steps to give effect to its decisions;
4. Considers that Lebanon is entitled to appropriate redress for the destruction it suffered, responsibility for which has been acknowledged by Israel.

Analysis of the legal and political validity of this resolution is complicated by a dispute over the factual context of Israel's attack. There was no dispute over the facts of the terrorist attack at the Athens airport; nor over those of Israel's attack at the Beirut airport. But there was considerable disagreement over the extent of the Lebanese government's involvement, not only in the attack at Athens, but also in the fedayeen attacks in Israel itself.

The prevailing perception in the council debates was that Lebanon was not responsible in any way for the Athens attack or for fedayeen raids in Israel. The United States representative to the council, for example, stated that there was no justification for a retaliation of any kind against Lebanon because its government had made efforts to control the actions of fedayeen groups within its territory and because Lebanon was a country that had clearly been doing its best to live in peace with all other states in the area.[95]

Israel's perception of the Lebanese government was strikingly different.[96] In its view, terrorist groups were operating quite openly in Beirut with the full knowledge and blessing of the Lebanese government. Israel's representative to the council contended that the attack in Athens was the culmination of a sustained and officially encouraged campaign, that throughout 1968 Lebanon had failed to heed Israel's protests and had played an increasingly active role in the overall Arab belligerency against Israel, that there had been twenty-two sabotage raids conducted in the area of the Israel-Lebanon cease-fire line between August and September, and that the Lebanese authorities were obviously aware of this concentration of raiders since they had appointed liaison officers to the commando units.

Assuming that Israel's version of the facts is correct, it does not necessarily follow that its attack on the Beirut airport was in accord with international law. Before the council Israel defended its raid as an exercise of self-defense. However, while violent acts of reprisal were legal in certain circumstances under rules of cutomary international law, they are prohibited by the United Nations Charter. The Israeli attack on the Beirut airport was clearly an act of reprisal rather than an act of self-defense against an armed attack.

Nonetheless, the Charter's prohibition against armed reprisals is premised on the understanding that it is necessary to reserve to the Security Council the authority to use armed force to punish (as compared to defend against) an attacker, and then only if the council determines that there is a threat to the peace. The council has been unwilling or unable to take any action against states tolerating or even actively supporting guerrilla attacks against Israel. Because of this and the failures of the council to act in similar situations, the proposition has been advanced that, in the event of council failure to fulfill its responsibility to enforce the peace, the customary law regarding reprisals revives, allowing states to engage in self-help exercises.[97] The practice of the United Nations—as illustrated by the council's resolution on Israel's attack at the Beirut airport—as well as the great majority of writers[98] rejects this proposition.

The reasons supporting rejection of this proposition are compelling. Acceptance of the proposition would be the death knell of Article 2(4) of the United Nations Charter. Pre-Charter restraints in international law on the unilateral use of force by states were few, and their absence helped to contribute to a milieu leading to two world wars. Express authorization permitting states to resort to force in any instance where the United Nations fails to redress a past armed attack or violation of an international obligation would create a chaotic and highly dangerous situation. It was to prevent such situations that the norms of the Charter limiting unilateral use of armed force were drafted.

At the same time, it must be acknowledged that a state like Israel will resort to its own devices if the United Nations fails to act against attacks on its territory or citizens. Hence the Security Council's failure to take any action with respect to Arab states' support of terrorist attacks against Israel, while condemning Israeli attacks in reprisal, amounts to an unfortunate double standard that inevitably heightens tensions in the Middle East and undermines chances for peace.[99]

For about two years after the Security Council's condemnation of Israel's attack at the Beirut airport, the Israel-Lebanon border was relatively quiet and peaceful. In September 1970, however, when it failed to overthrow King Hussein of Jordan, the PLO moved in force into southern Lebanon. Further complicating the situation was the outbreak in 1976 of communal violence in Lebanon between Christians and Muslims, the deployment of a Syrian peace-keeping force under an Arab League mandate, and the intervention by Israel on the side of the Christians in southern Lebanon.

Finally, in 1978, Israel went beyond reprisal raids into Lebanon.[100] On March 11, PLO terrorists attacked Israeli civilians on the Haifa-Tel Aviv highway, killing thirty-seven and wounding seventy-six, some critically. In response, at midnight of March 14, Israeli troops crossed into southern Lebanon from several areas, and Israeli patrol boats penetrated Lebanese territorial waters along the coastline. These troops did not merely attack PLO Camps; they attacked whole sections of southern Lebanon. On March 17, Israel and Lebanon requested by letter an urgent meeting of the Security Council.

In debate, Israel severely castigated the council.[101] The Israeli representative claimed that the council, having failed for thirty years to adopt a single resolution condemning the murder of innocent Israeli civilians, had long ago forfeited its right to pass judgment on actions caused by terrorist attacks. He claimed further that southern Lebanon harbored the largest concentration of terrorists in the world, and that they, in effect, were the governing authority in that area. At the same time he stated that Israel had no wish to acquire even one inch of Lebanese soil; rather, its sole purpose was to remove the terrorist forces and allow the official Lebanese authorities to return to the area and take over control with adequate force to back their mandate.

On March 19, the Security Council adopted a resolution[102] that demanded strict respect for Lebanon's territorial integrity, called upon

Israel immediately to cease its military activity and withdraw its troops, and established a United Nations Interim Force for Southern Lebanon (UNIFIL) "for the purpose of confirming the withdrawal of Israeli forces, restoring international peace and security and assisting the Government of Lebanon in ensuring the return of its effective authority in the area."

UNIFIL's mandate was renewed by the Security Council at regular six-month intervals, and it grew in size to 7,000 troops. The force did not, however, enjoy great success in maintaining peace in southern Lebanon. Terrorist attacks into Israel from this area continued, as well as Israeli reprisal raids. In addition, there was the persistent violence between Lebanese Christians, supported by Israel, and Syrian and PLO forces.[103] This escalation of violence resulted, perhaps inevitably, in a second massive invasion of Lebanon by Israel on June 5, 1982.

Fighting between Israeli and PLO forces began on June 4, when Israeli warplanes raided PLO camps in Beirut in response to the shooting in London of the Israeli ambassador to the United Kingdom, Shlomo Argov, even though the PLO denied any responsibility for the attack. When the PLO in turn reacted to the air raid by shelling northern Israeli settlements from bases in southern Lebanon, Israel retaliated with a massive invasion of Lebanon.[104] In doing so, the Israelis simply bypassed UNIFIL's "nonviolent tactics" to block their advance.[105]

The response of the Security Council was to adopt unanimously a resolution[106] calling for a halt in the hostilities, after hearing the secreatary-general's report on his unsuccessful efforts to achieve a cease-fire in southern Lebanon. Israel paid no heed to the resolution. The council adopted a more strongly worded resolution[107] on June 6, in which it demanded that "Israel withdraw all its military forces forthwith and unconditionally to the internationally recognized boundaries of Lebanon" as well as that "all parties . . . cease immediately and simultaneously all military activities within Lebanon and across the Lebanese-Israeli border." Hostilities continued unabated.

Israel's drive north brought it into conflict not only with PLO guerrillas but also with Syrian armed forces in Lebanon. After numerous unsuccessful diplomatic initiatives by various parties, Israel agreed to a cease-fire with Syrian forces on June 11, but continued its pursuit off the PLO all the way to the outskirts of west Beirut, where, a day and half later, Israel agreed to a second cease-fire with the guerrillas.

These cease-fires were short-lived. As reports of large-scale civilian casualties mounted, the council adopted resolutions[108] that authorized UNIFIL to take on the task of "extending their protection and humanitarian assistance to the population of the area" and appealed to combatants in Lebanon to refrain from violence against civilians.

The council also extended UNIFIL's mandate, but only for a two-month period instead of the customary six.

On June 26, the United States, the lone dissenter in a fourteen-to-one vote, vetoed a French resolution,[109] which, among other things, would have demanded the immediate withdrawal of Israeli forces to positions six miles from Beirut as a first step toward their complete withdrawal from Lebanon, and the simultaneous withdrawal of the Palestinian armed forces to refugee camps. It would also have requested the secretary-general to station, with the consent of the Lebanese government, military observers in Beirut to supervise the cease-fire and disengagement from Beirut and "to study any request by the Government of Lebanon for the installation of the United Nations force which could . . . take up positions beside the Lebanese interposition forces, or for the use of the forces available to the United Nations in the region." The reason for the American veto was reportedly that the draft resolution would have allowed the PLO to retain their arms rather than yield them to Lebanese security forces.[110] In demanding that the PLO surrender its weapons, the United States was supporting Israel's position that the PLO must be eliminated as a fighting force in Lebanon.

At this writing it is unclear what the final disposition of the crisis in Lebanon will be and whether the United Nations will play any role in it. There appears to be little chance that the Security Council will pass a resolution acceptable to all the parties to the conflict—in particular one calling for the departure of all foreign armed forces including those of the PLO. Israel may succeed in forcing the withdrawal of Syrian and PLO forces. Withdrawal of Israeli forces, however, may require the establishment of arrangements to ensure that southern Lebanon is never again used as a base for artillery attacks against northern Israeli settlements. To this end Prime Minister Begin and President Reagan have reportedly agreed that a twenty-five mile zone north of Lebanon's border with Israel should be secured free of PLO artillery.[111] Israel has demanded that a multinational peace-keeping force, with American troop involvement along the lines of the force in the Sinai, be established outside of the UN context. The United States has reportedly favored a strengthening of UNIFIL, but without American troops.

Were UNIFIL utilized for maintenance of such a zone, it is clear that it would have to be given a mandate different from the one it currently has. That is, UNIFIL would have to serve as an *enforcer* of the peace rather than a mere supervisor of cease-fire arrangements. It would have to be powerful enough to prevent military action either by the PLO or Syria or by Israel. Whether such a force could be established under UN auspices without the presence of the armed forces of the superpowers or those of their allies is problematic.

Israel's most recent invasion of Lebanon raises a host of questions.

For example, was Israel's invasion grossly disproportionate to PLO provocation and thus a violation of Article 2(4) of the Charter? Does the law of armed conflict apply to Israel's actions against the PLO in Lebanon, and, if so, are the widespread civilian casualties evidence of a violation of that law? An adequate discussion of these and many other issues would require a separate volume in itself. But as important as they are, they pale in comparison with the issue of what, if anything, can be done to bring to a close the seemingly endless violence in the Middle East. As has been demonstrated, and will be demonstrated again in later sections of this book, the United Nations, despite its uneven record in this area, has contributed to the main-tenance of peace in the Middle East and, if used wisely, can do so in the future.

Israel's efforts to exclude the United Nations from a meaningful role in resolving this conflict will ultimately prove self-defeating. There are simply too many interested parties in the Middle East to allow Israel, even with the United States support, to impose anything other than a temporary solution. The United Nations, with its worldwide focus, is still the most effective forum to seek an accom-modation of these interests.

VIETNAM-KAMPUCHEA-PEOPLE'S REPUBLIC OF CHINA

Vietnam's invasion of Kampuchea (formerly Cambodia) and the People's Republic of China's invasion of Vietnam raise issues re-garding possible exceptions to the UN Charter's prohibitions on the unilateral use of force by states, namely, self-defense and humanitarian intervention. These issues were examined, albeit only to a limited extent, during the Security Council's debates on the invasions.

The background to these invasions is long and complex and will be examined here only in brief outline. A salient fact of this back-ground, of course, is the victory of communist forces in South Vietnam and Cambodia and the installation of communist govern-ments in both countries.

As far back as the third century B.C., China had exercised suzerainty over Vietnam—sometimes ruling it directly, at other times exerting indirect influence.[112] This dominance ended in 1885 when France gained control of Indochina. At the end of World War II, however, pursuant to the Potsdam Agreements of 1945, Chinese Nationalist forces occupied northern Vietnam until May 1946. Despite their ideological differences, the Nationalists supported the Viet Minh, selling them captured Japanese weapons and American military equipment that had been provided to China. With the establishment of the People's Republic of China, the communists continued this support, declaring that the Viet Minh's struggle against other Viet-namese factions and the French was a "war of national liberation."

In 1950 the PRC became the first state to recognize Ho Chi Minh's Democratic Republic of Vietnam.

At the Geneva Conference of 1954, the PRC played a major role in negotiating the accords that divided Vietnam into northern and southern sectors and led to the incorporation of North Vietnam into the communist bloc. The PRC continued its strong support of North Vietnam during the 1960s when the war in South Vietnam intensified. By the early 1970s, however, relations between the two countries began to deteriorate. North Vietnam was displeased with the improvement in relations between the United States and the PRC, as evidenced especially by President Nixon's 1972 visit to Peking, at a time when North Vietnam was still the target of American bombing. Territorial disputes between Vietnam and the PRC also contributed to the deterioration of relations between the two countries.

As its relations with the PRC steadily worsened, North Vietnam drew closer to the Soviet Union, which provided massive support throughout the Vietnam War. Intensification of Soviet-Vietnamese relations after the end of the war in 1975 led to the conclusion of a treaty of friendship and cooperation[113] between the two countries on November 3, 1978. This treaty provided, among other things, that the parties would consult each other on all important international issues affecting their interests, and, in the event of either becoming the object of attack or threats of attack would "immediately begin mutual consultations for the purpose of removing that threat and taking appropriate effective measures to ensure the peace and security of their countries."[114] The treaty was viewed by many as being directed against the PRC.

For its part, the PRC became closely allied with the Pol Pot government in Kampuchea after its takeover at the end of the Vietnam War. The PRC therefore reacted strongly when, on December 25, 1978, Vietnam and Vietnamese-backed Kampucheans invaded Kampuchea with the intent of overthrowing the Pol Pot government. The president of Kampuchea, Khieu Samphan, immediately accused the Soviet Union of backing the Vietnamese action and called upon the United Nations and countries "far and near" to come to Kampuchea's assistance.[117]

Kampuchea also brought its complaint to the Security Council, where Vietnam sought to defend its invasion on two grounds: First, that it was a defensive border war "started by the Pol Pot-Leng Sary Clique," and second, that the Vietnamese invaders were volunteers assisting the "revolutionary war of the Kampuchean people against the dictatorial rule of that clique which was an instrument of the reactionary ruling circles of Peking."[108] The Soviet Union defended its Vietnamese allies by stressing conditions under the Pol Pot regime and alleged PRC complicity:

In a country with a population of 8 million, the rulers destroyed, according to statistics reported in the Western press, from two to three million people. The vocabulary used in normal international practice to describe mass violations of human rights was inadequate to describe those monstrous crimes.

Without outside help, the former regime would not have adopted a course of genocide against the people of its own country. That regime was a puppet of outside forces pursuing a policy of hegemonism, great-power chauvism and expansionism in Indo-China and in Aisa as a whole. The Kampuchea people was (sic) a victim of that policy.[117]

During the early days of the fighting, Deng Xiaoping, deputy prime minister of the People's Republic of China, reportedly indicated that China would probably not intervene to halt the Vietnamese invasion.[118] But China vehemently denounced the invasion before the Security Council. Its representative contended that the Vietnamese invasion constituted a flagrant military aggression against a small and weak neighbor, derided Vietnam's claim that it was assisting a people's insurgence against the Pol Pot government, and alleged that Vietnam's strategy was to establish a colonial empire under its armed control.[119]

The United States, as well as Great Britain and France, condemned Vietnam's invasion. While acknowledging the brutality of the Pol Pot government and the failure of the world community to take effective steps against it, they contended that this did not justify the invasion.[120] The French representative rejected the "notion that, because a regime was detestable, foreign intervention was justified and forcible overthrow was legitimate." In his view, acceptance of such a notion "could ultimately jeopardize the maintenance of international law and order and make the continued existence of various regimes dependent on the judgment of their neighbors."[121]

By January 7, 1979, Vietnamese troops had effectively occupied Kampuchea and installed Heng Samrin as president of the "Kampuchean People's Revolutionary Council."[122] On January 15, the Soviet Union vetoed a draft resolution that would have had the Security Council call on "all foreign forces involved in the situation in Democratic Kampuchea to observe scrupulously an immediate cease-fire, to put an end to hostilities and to withdraw from that country."[123]

After the Soviet veto, charges and countercharges between the PRC and Vietnam grew in intensity. On February 15, for example, Peking charged that mines planted by the Vietnamese on the Chinese side of the border had resulted in the death of twenty-two soldiers and civilians and injury to twenty more.[124] For their part, the

Vietnamese accused China of making "frantic war preparations against Vietnam."[125]

On February 17, Chinese troops crossed into North Vietnam. Chinese statements issued at the time asserted that Peking "did not want a single inch of Vietnamese territory," that the crossing of the border was in response to armed incursions by Vietnamese troops into China, that such incursions were part of Vietnamese attempts, with Soviet support, to dominate southeast Asia, and that Vietnam had cracked down on the 1.2 million ethnic Chinese in southern Vietnam—prompting an exodus of perhaps 180,000.[126] China limited its thrust into Vietnam to little more than twelve miles, halting its attack in part perhaps in response to a Soviet warning that China should pull out "before it is too late."[127]

The Security Council held five meetings on the situation, but adjourned the debate on February 28 without taking any action, while agreeing to meet again to address the problems. A draft resolution was submitted by the Soviet Union and Czechoslovakia that would have condemned China for aggression against Vietnam, demanded that it withdraw all its troops, and called upon all member states to cease supplying China with arms. By contrast, China proposed a resolution that would have condemned Vietnam for its armed aggression and military occupation of Kampuchea and demanded that Vietnam withdraw its military and other personnel from Kampuchea's territory. Neither resolution was pressed to a vote.[128]

On March 16, the Security Council completed its consideration of the situation in southeast Asia after being blocked by a Soviet veto from adopting a draft resolution which would have called upon all parties to cease hostilities immediately and withdraw their forces to their own countries.[129] China voted for the draft resolution and reportedly completed withdrawal of its troops from Vietnam on the same day.[130]

As indicated in Chapter 2, there is no agreement among scholars as to whether the doctrine of humanitarian intervention remains viable in light of the UN Charter's limitations on the use of force, although state practice—as illustrated by the debates in the Security Council on Vietnam's invasion of Kampuchea—strongly supports its demise. But even if one believes, as does this writer, that the doctrine of humanitarian intervention is incompatible with principles of modern public international law, Kampuchea may be the exception that proves the rule. As stated by Professor Franck:

> Yet we freely admit that we can imagine situations in which a humanitarian rescue would be highly desirable. With Churchill, we can visualize wanting our country to fight the menace of tyranny for years, and if necessary alone. Undeniably, there are circumstances in which the unilateral use of force to overthrow injustice

begins to seem less wrong than to turn aside. Like civil disobedience, however, this sense of superior necessity belongs in the realm not of law but of moral choice, which nations, like individuals, must sometimes make, weighing the costs and benefits to their cause, to the social fabric, and to themselves.[131]

Arguably, the slaughter in Kampuchea constituted "circumstances in which the unilateral use of force to overthrow injustice begins to seem less wrong than to turn aside." To be sure, the plight of the Kampucheans was not the dominant motive for the Vietnamese intervention. According to some scholars, this alone would negate the invasion being justified as a humanitarian intervention.[132] And one cannot say that the human rights record of the Vietnam government in dealing with its own citizens is exemplary. Nonetheless, the fact is that almost any alternative to the butchery of Pol Pot is an improvement.

The humanitarian intervention doctrine is even arguably applicable to China's invasion of Vietnam, because of Vietnam's persecution of the Chinese residents in its territory and the consequent exodus of some 180,000 of these residents to China. But the case is weak. Stronger, perhaps, is China's claim that it was acting in self-defense. According to the PRC, during 1978, the Vietnamese had made upwards of 1,100 armed incursions into China, resulting in 300 Chinese casualties during the latter half of the year.[133] China's warnings and appeals to Vietnam apparently went unheeded. These incursions and the injuries inflicted may have constituted an "armed attack" within the meaning of Article 51 of the United Nations Charter. If so, the Chinese would be entitled to respond with proportionate force. The thrust of the Chinese forces into Vietnam was limited in terms of distance, did not involve annexation of Vietnamese territory, and lasted only sixteen days. Therefore, it may have been proportionate to the Vietnamese incursions. There was little discussion of these factors in the council's debates.

One can understand and sympathize with the desire of most member states of the council to call for an end to the fighting and the withdrawal of armed forces. But the United Nations' inability to deal effectively with the brutality of Pol Pot or the tension along the Vietnam-China border contributed to a milieu in which self-help measures of armed force were likely to be used.

Parenthetically, it may be noted that the United Nations stood aside and failed entirely to respond to another instance of traditional international violence that arguably constituted humanitarian intervention: Tanzania's 1979 invasion of Uganda and its overthrow of President Idi Amin Dada.[134] Although President Amin had been responsible for earlier armed incursions into Tanzania prior to the invasions, the Tanzanian response could not be justified as an act of self-defense because it was greatly disproportionate to the Ugandan attacks. But the atrocities of President Amin were of the same nature (although not of the same magnitude) as those of Pol Pot, and the world community, in effect, approved *sub silencio* his overthrow by Tanzania. As in the case of Pol Pot, the United Nations had not been willing to come to grips with President Amin's barbarism.

IRAQ-IRAN

The September 22, 1980 invasion of Iran by Iraq presented the Security Council with a severe challenge to its capability for maintaining the peace. Unfortunately, the council failed dismally to meet the challenge.

Iraq's invasion of Iran illustrates *realpolitik* politics at their most pernicious. Viewing the weakness of Iran following the overthrow of the Shah and the confrontation with the United States over the taking of hostages as an opportunity to settle old grievances, Iraq invaded Iran and occupied the Shatt al Arab waterway which Iraq claims in a territorial dispute with Iran.

At this writing, the only action the Security Council has taken in response to the Iraqi invasion is to issue a resolution[135] merely calling for a cease-fire and for the secretary-general to lend his good offices to resolving the conflict. Not surprisingly, Iran has rejected any cease-fire while Iraq is illegally occupying its territory.[136]

The reasons for the council's inaction are several. Most of the Arab states, with the exception of Libya and Syria, which back Iran, approve of Iraq's invasion because of their opposition to the efforts of Ayatollah Khomenei's regime to stir up religious strife in the Muslim world. Great Britain and France reportedly stood aloof from efforts to draft a strong resolution because of their heavy investments in both Iraq and Iran and their desire to tread warily between the two countries.[137] For its part, the United States at first took no major initiative, but finally—over a month after the invasion began—the American representative spoke out in the council warning of the possible dismemberment of Iran because of the Iraqi invasion. He reportedly discussed in private with other members of the council the elements of a possible resolution that would include a call for an Iraqi withdrawal from Iran, with the evacuated territory converted to a cease-fire zone patrolled by UN observers. The resolution also proposed the mutual control of the Shatt al Arab waterway under the chairmanship of a neutral third nation, a mechanism or negotiating forum to settle Iraq's claims for land in Iran, and a pledge by both sides against interference in each other's internal affairs.[138] No resolution, however, was forthcoming from these efforts, and the council has taken no further action with regard to the conflict.

The American reaction to the Iraq-Iran war has been especially disappointing and has contributed to the failure of the Security Council to take forceful action. Although one can only speculate as to the precise reasons for the United States' failure to support forceful action in the council, there appear to be several primary reasons for the American position.

First, the United States wished to ensure that the U.S.S.R. would not use any action by the United States as a pretext for itself becoming involved in the conflict. But the United States would not be taking sides by supporting basic Charter norms against territorial aggression, and the Soviet Union could hardly use such action as a justification for supporting Iraq. On the contrary, had the administration pointed out the fact of Iraqi aggression early and forcefully in the council, it would have been more difficult for the Soviet Union to come to Iraq's aid.

In the same vein, the administration apparently did not wish to appear to be favoring Iran when Jordan and Saudi Arabia, friendly states, were supporting Iraq, and the unfriendly states of Libya and Syria were supporting Iran. The administration should have been especially concerned, however, about Jordan's expressed intent to aid Iraqi aggression, which would have greatly compounded the problem. Even one's friends should be firmly discouraged from engaging in such actions.

Another element was that Iran was still holding fifty-two American diplomats hostage, despite a call by the Security Council and a unanimous decision by the International Court of Justice that they should be released. But Iraq's invasion of Iran, a pure territorial grab, was in no way intended to secure the release of the hostages. Moreover, the Iraqi invasion rallied the people of Iran around the previously shaky regime of the Ayatollah Khomenei, caused even the moderates in Iran to believe that the United States was behind it, and made the release of the hostages more rather than less problematic.

Finally, 1980 was an election year, and the administration wished to appear to be taking a hard line against Iran. Nonetheless, any administration has a responsibility to educate the public in the reasons for controversial foreign-policy decisions. There is also a great need to educate the public (and the world community) about the importance of fundamental United Nations Charter norms against aggression.

The result of the Security Council's inaction was most unfortunate. Iraqi aggression continued unabated. Jordan and others threatened to join the fray. The United Nations appeared absurd in limiting its actions to a sure-to-be rejected call for a cease-fire. Most important, the failure of the council to act did a great disservice to the already endangered United Nations system for maintaining international peace and security. The message to other would-be aggressors is painfully obvious.

THE FALKLAND ISLANDS

The dispute between the United Kingdom and Argentina regarding sovereignty over the Falkland Islands dates back to 1833, when they were seized by the British. Argentina never recognized the validity of British sovereignty over the islands and rejected reference of the dispute to the International Court of Justice, or to other forms of third-party settlement, despite the opinion of some authorities, such as former Under Secretary of State Sumner Welles, that its claim to the Falklands was far stronger than Britain's.[139]

Britain virtually acknowledged the legitimacy of the Argentine claim in 1980 when it offered to turn the islands over to Argentina in return for a long lease. The United Kingdom ultimately failed to carry out the offer, however, when the 1,800 Falklanders on the islands protested vehemently.

The dispute moved toward the crisis stage on March 20, 1982, when fifty Argentine scrap metal dealers landed on South Georgia Island, which the British regard as not part of the Falkland Islands, to dismantle an unused whaling station. The Argentines had a contract with the British owner of the whaling station and had notified British officials of their intentions. However, they had not sought to obtain advance immigration clearance and were asked to leave, after raising an Argentine flag upon landing. The Argentine Foreign Ministry protested on the ground that the British had no authority to order the scrap metal dealers off Argentine territory. This resulted in both the United Kingdom and Argentina sending warships to the islands.[140]

The conflict escalated in intensity, and on April 1, 1982, having learned of Argentina's imminent invasion of the islands, the president of the Security Council, Lig Qing, the representative of China, formally appealed to Argentina not to invade.[141] This appeal fell on deaf ears as Argentina launched a massive invasion of the islands on April 2. Calling the invasion a "wanton act," the United Kingdom requested the Security Council to demand the immediate withdrawal of Argentine forces. Argentina's representative to the council defended the invasion as an act required to recover Argentine territory. He also argued that the requirement of the UN Charter to settle disputes peacefully did not apply to quarrels that arose before the Charter's adoption in 1945. The British representative pointed out that were this proposition true, "the world would be an infinitely more dangerous and flammable place than it already is."[142]

On April 3, the council adopted a resolution[143] under Chapter VII of the Charter that demanded an immediate cessation of hostilities as well as the immediate withdrawal of all Argentine forces from the Falkland Islands and called upon Argentina and the United Kingdom to seek a diplomatic solution to their dispute. In an explanation of vote on the resolution, the British representative to the council insisted that, if Argentina failed to withdraw, Britain retained the right under the Charter to exercise force in self-defense.[144]

The resolution was not carried out. Argentine forces remained on the islands, Britain proclaimed a 200-mile exclusion zone around the islands and sent a large fleet from the United Kingdom on an 8,000 mile journey of two weeks with the intent of retaking the islands by force if necessary, and diplomatic initiatives by American secretary of state Alexander Haig and UN secretary-general Pérez de Cuéllar (to be examined in a later chapter) were undertaken. When the British Navy sank the Argentine cruiser *Belgrano,* reportedly outside of the area of blockade, Ireland requested an urgent meeting of the Security Council. The United Kingdom resisted such a meeting on the ground that it would simply engender heated debate to no constructive purpose.

Discussions continued in the council until May 21, when British forces landed on the islands. The landing of British forces took place after mediation efforts by the secretary-general had ended in a stalemate. Finally, on May 26, the council adopted a resolution [145] calling on the secretary-general to negotiate "mutually acceptable terms for a cease-fire" in the Falklands and asking him to report back in seven days. Under threat of a veto, Britain had successfully opposed any resolution calling for an immediate cease-fire.

The United Kingdom made good on its threat when on June 4 it vetoed a resolution[146] introduced by Panama and Spain that would have called upon the parties to stop all warlike actions immediately, and to initiate, simultaneously with the cease-fire, all previous Security Council resolutions on the Falklands. Although these resolutions expressly called upon Argentina to withdraw its troops from the island, Britain regarded the resolutions as not specific enough on the connection between the cease-fire and Argentine withdrawal.

On June 14, Argentine forces on the islands surrendered. At this writing, British prime minister Margaret Thatcher has summarily rejected suggestions that the United Nations might play a role in negotiating a settlement with Argentina over the islands and has proclaimed that Britain will maintain a peace-keeping force on the islands by itself if it is not successful in setting up a multinational force with American participation. She has also stated that her government has no intention of permitting any Argentine role in the future of the islands and that the islands belong to Great Britain.

In this writer's view, the Security Council functioned about as well as anyone could reasonably expect during the crisis over the Falkland Islands. Immediately prior to Argentina's invasion of the island, the president of the council appealed to Argentina not to invade thus seeking to *prevent* the outbreak of international violence rather than just to control it. Although, in accordance with its usual approach, the council did not condemn the Argentine invasion as an act of aggression, it implicitly ruled on its illegality under the Charter when it demanded an immediate withdrawal of all Argentine forces from the islands. This judgment seems eminently correct. Argentina's case in support of its invasion was ludicrously weak. There is no support in law or logic for its position that the requirement under the Charter to settle disputes peacefully does not apply to quarrels that arose before the Charter's adoption in 1945.

Equally weak is Argentina's assertion that it was entitled to resort to force because of the strength of its legal claim to sovereignty over the islands and Britain's refusal to relinquish it. Under the Charter, the strength of a state's grievance with another state is not a justification for the use of armed force. The "just war" concept, widely utilized in the nineteenth century to support aggression, was rejected by the drafters of the Charter. In its place, self-defense is the only basis available under the Charter for the use of armed force by states in the absence of an authorization from the Security Council.

On the other hand, it is debatable whether the United Kingdom was justified in vetoing the draft resolution introduced by Panama and Spain. As noted above, the stated reason for the British veto was an alleged insufficiency of the link in the draft resolution between the request for a cease-fire and an Argentine withdrawal. However, the draft resolution referred specifically to previous resolutions by the council demanding an immediate withdrawal of Argentine troops and also requested that these resolutions be implemented simultaneously with the cease-fire. The unstated and questionable basis for the British veto appears to be Prime Minister Thatcher's change of heart regarding her willingness to negotiate with Argentina over the future status of the islands.

The legality of Britain's use of force to retake the islands has been challenged by some scholars. Professor Cornelius F. Murphy, Jr. (no relation to this writer) has contended that "[w]hen the Council assumed jurisdiction over the Falklands controversy on April 3, the principles of peaceful settlement enshrined in the Charter took precedence over coercive options"[147] and precluded the British from using force to retake the islands. In support of this contention, Murphy points out that Article 51 of the UN Charter preserves "the inherent right of individual or collective self-defense if an armed attack occurs against a member of the United Nations" only "until the Security Council has taken measures necessary to maintain international peace and security." But the issue is whether, under the circumstances of the Falklands crisis, the council's resolutions constituted "measures necessary to maintain international peace and security."

Argentina's refusal to withdraw its troops and the passage of time without a diplomatic solution made it abundantly clear that the council's resolutions were not measures necessary or sufficient to maintain international peace and security. This realization and an increasingly precarious military situation in the South Atlantic led the United Kingdom to conclude that it would have to exercise its inherent right to self-defense if the illegal occupation of the Falklands was to be ended.

The drafting history of Article 51 at the San Francisco conference demonstrates that those present were well aware that the Security Council might not be able to function as intended (i.e., as a collective security agency) because of disagreement among its permanent members. In such a case member states reserved to themselves their inherent right of individual or collective self-defense.

Aside from its correctness as a legal proposition, Murphy's contention that, once the Security Council assumes jurisdiction over a dispute, member states lose their right to use force in self-defense has dangerous implications for the maintenance of peace. Were Murphy correct, Great Britain would not have called for a meeting of the council and would have frustrated, by use of the veto, any attempt to have the council adopt a resolution regarding the crisis. Britain's insistence during discussion in the council on the resolutions that, if Argentina failed to withdraw, it reserved the right to exercise force in self-defense illustrates British concern to reserve options.

In contrast to Murphy's position, Professor Alfred P. Rubin has raised the interesting proposition that the lawfulness of Great Britain's use of force might be dependent upon Resolution 502. In Professor Rubin's words:

> There are legal and moral doubts regarding British sovereignty of the Islands. Thus, once the British garrison and governor had been removed by Argentina, it's doubtful than many impartial analysts would have accepted the British legal or moral right to react with force, even in "self-defense" under the Charter. So the British wisely sought and got another authority for action: Resolution 502 of the United Nations Security Council demanding that Argentina withdraw. As long as British actions are confined to the terms of that resolution, which does not prejudge ultimate sovereignty in the Falkland Islands, British actions raise no legal or moral issues.[148]

For the reasons given above, this writer disagrees with Rubin's thesis that legal and moral doubts regarding British sovereignty over the islands might preclude their right to use force against the Argentine invasion absent Resolution 502. Also, there is nothing in the terms of Resolution 502 that explicitly or implicitly authorizes the British to use force to expel Argentina from the islands. Resolution 502's demand that Argentina withdraw its troops from the islands hardly amounts to an authorization to Great Britain to use force, as an agent of the council, should Argentina fail to do so. Nothing in the debates on Resolution 502 indicated that Great Britain was seeking council authorization to use force. On the contrary, as noted above, Great Britain expressly reserved its inherent right to use force in self-defense if Argentina failed to carry out the council's demand.

Another point raised by Professor Rubin, however, is well taken. As he points out, "[i]f British actions exceed what was envisaged by Resolution 502, or if ultimate questions of sovereignty are raised, the United States would no longer be legally or morally obliged to support Great Britain."[149] This brings us to Britain's proclaimed, at this writing, intention to deny Argentina any role in the future of the islands and to maintain British sovereignty over them for the indefinite future. This position arguably contravenes Resolution 502, which, in addition to demanding that Argentina withdraw from the Falklands, calls upon Argentina and Great Britain to seek a diplomatic solution to their dispute and to respect fully the purposes and principles of the Charter of the United Nations. Britain's refusal even to discuss the future of the islands with Argentina hardly seems consistent with these provisions.

In support of its position, Britain has cited the principle of self-determination, pointing out that the Falklanders have strongly expressed their desire to remain under British rule. But the situation in the Falklands is highly unusual in this regard. It must be remembered that, in 1833, when the British occupied the island, they expelled the Argentines on the islands and established their own communities. These communities have lived under British rule ever since, albeit in the face of consistent Argentine protests, so it is hardly surprising that they should opt to continue current arrangements. However, their interests are not the only nor necessarily the paramount interests involved in this complex dispute. The appropriate way to accommodate these various interests would be through renewed negotiations. Alternatively, the issue of sovereignty might be referred to the International Court of Justice, as Britain has proposed in the past, or to international arbitration. It is unacceptable for Britain to arrogate to itself unilateral decision-making authority over the future of the islands.

CONCLUDING NOTE

There are, of course, some major instances of traditional international violence when the Security Council failed to act. Prominent examples would include the Soviet invasion of Czechoslovakia in 1968 and of Afghanistan in 1979. It would strain credulity to expect that, under the veto system of voting, the council would be able to act when a permanent member itself engages in blatant aggression. Even in these instances, however, the council served a role as a focal point for world reaction to the aggression and for exposure of the Soviet Union's weak defense. Initiatives in the council, moreover, as we shall see in later chapters, sometimes led to action by other UN organs, such as the General Assembly or the secretary-general.

Some of these observations apply as well to the council's role in the Cuban Missile Crisis—perhaps the most dire threat to world peace since World War II. Although the council passed no resolution during the missile crisis, it did provide a forum for a sharpening of the issues, and allowed the American representative, Adlai Stevenson, to present convincing evidence that, contrary to the Soviet denial, offensive missiles had indeed been installed in Cuba. The council also set the stage for the ultimately successful efforts of Acting Secretary-General U Thant to mediate an end to the crisis.[150]

NOTES

1. Advisory Opinion on Certain Expenses of the United Nations, [1962] I.C.J. 151.

2. Leland M. Goodrich, *The United Nations in a Changing World* (New York and London: Columbia University Press, 1974), p. 113.

3. Trygve Lie, *In the Cause of Peace* (New York: Macmillan, 1954), p. 166.

4. Ibid., pp. 169–70.

5. At least one prominent authority has contended that the mandate over Palestine was never terminated. Professor Eugene V. Rostow, former United States undersecretary of state for political affairs and currently, director, United States Arms Control and Disarmament Agency, has argued that General Assembly Resolution 181(II), which the assembly adopted on November 29, 1947, only recommended (and could only recommend) termination of the mandate. Actual termination could be effected only by the Security Council. Since the council failed to adopt the assembly's plan, Professor Rostow argues, the mandate remains in effect, at least for the West Bank and the Gaza Strip, the "Unallocated Territories of the Palestine Mandate." As to them, only the fact of British administration has ended. The mandate over the territories now comprised by Israel has ended, but only because of the world community's recognition of the state of Israel, not because of the General Assembly's resolution. See Eugene V. Rostow,"'Palestinian Self-Determination': Possible Futures for the Unallocated Territories of the Palestine Mandate," *Yale Studies In World Public Order* 5, no. 2 (spring 1979):147–72.

Professor Rostow's position is debatable. It is true that the General Assembly did not purport by Resolution 181(II) itself to terminate the mandate. But neither does that resolution recommend that the Security Council terminate the mandate. Rather, it recommends to the United

Kingdom, as mandatory, and to all other members of the United Nations, the adoption and implementation of the partition plan, which includes a statement that the mandate shall terminate not later than August 1, 1948. Then, in a separate paragraph, the resolution requests the Security Council to take the necessary measures as provided in the plan for its implementation. This request is made for the practical reason that only the Security Council has the authority to enforce the partition plan. The aid of the council, however, was not needed to terminate the mandate. This could be done by the mandatory accepting the recommendation of the General Assembly and declaring the mandate at an end. Hence, the General Assembly and the mandatory, acting together in tacit agreement, could terminate the mandate. The normal method of terminating trusteeships has been for the General Assembly and the administering authority to agree that the trust has ended. There has normally been no need for the Security Council to be involved.

6. Reprinted in John Norton Moore, *The Arab-Israeli Conflict* (Princeton University Press, 1974), vol.3, pp. 352–57.

7. The five include the war of 1947–48, the Suez Crisis of 1956, the Six Day War of 1967, the so-called "war of attrition" in 1969–70, and the conflict of 1973.

8. S.C. Res. 49, UN Doc. S/773 (1948).

9. S.C. Res. 50, UN Doc. S/801 (1948).

10. S.C. Res. 54, UN Doc. S/902 (1948).

11. See Count Bernadotte's Progress Report, UN Doc. A/648, Sept. 16, 1948.

12. Advisory Opinion on Reparation for Injuries Suffered in the Service of the United Nations, [1949] I.C.J. 174.

13. S.C. Res. 59, UN Doc. S/1045 (1948).

14. For a thorough discussion of the background to and the documents of UNTSO, see Rosalyn Higgins, *United Nations Peacekeeping 1946–1967, Documents and Commentary* (London, New York, Toronto: Oxford University Press, 1969), vol. 1, pp. 1–217.

15. To be fair, there is a serious question whether the partition plan, as originally drafted, set forth tenable boundaries for the proposed new Jewish and Arab states. See Frederick H. Hartmann, *The Relations of Nations* (5th ed. New York: Macmillan, 1978), pp. 244–45. Great Britain, however, did not base its objection to partition on this ground.

16. Trygve Lie, *In the Cause of Peace*, p. 167.

17. Ibid.

18. G.A. Res. 112, UN Doc. A/519, at 16–18.

19. G.A. Res. 195, UN Doc. A/810, at 25–27.

20. S.C. Res. 82, UN Doc. S/1501 (1950).

21. S.C. Res. 83, UN Doc. S/1511 (1950).

22. Trygve Lie, *In the Cause of Peace*, p. 333.

23. Ibid., p. 334.

24. Ibid., pp. 339–40.

25. G.A. Res. 376, 5 UN GAOR, Supp. 20 (A/1775), at 9(1950).

26. Trygve Lie, *In the Cause of Peace*, pp. 344–45.

27. Ibid., p. 345.

28. G.A. Res. 377A, 5 UN GAOR, Supp. 20(A/1755), at 10.

29. G.A. Res. 498, 5 UN GAOR Supp. 20A (A/1175/Add. 1), at 1.

30. As we shall see in later chapters, the Security Council has acted under Chapter VII of the Charter in imposing economic sanctions against Southern Rhodesia and an arms embargo against South Africa.

31. Trygve Lie, *In the Cause of Peace*, p. 328.

32. Michael Walzer, *Just and Unjust Wars* (New York: Basic Books, 1977), pp. 119-20.

33. Ibid., p. 121.

34. For a concise summary of the background to the Suez Crisis, see Rosalyn Higgins, *United Nations Peacekeeping*, pp. 222-27.

35. S.C. Res. 95, U.N. Doc. S/2322 (1951).

36. For an examination of many of these issues, see Carl F. Salans, "Gulf of Aqaba and Strait of Tiran: Troubled Waters," *United States Naval Institute Proceedings* 94, no. 12 (Dec. 1968):54-62; D.H.N. Johnson, "Some Legal Problems of International Waterways, with Particular Reference to the Straits of Tiran and the Suez Canal," *The Modern Law Review* 31 (1968):153-64; Majid Khadduri, "Closure of the Suez Canal to Israeli Shipping," *Law and Contemporary Problems* 33 (1968):169-82.

37. Report of the secretary-general to the Security Council pursuant to the council's resolution of 4 April 1956, 9 May 1956, reprinted in pertinent part in Rosalyn Higgins, *United Nations Peacekeeping*, pp. 179-80.

38. Ibid., reprinted in pertinent part in Rosalyn Higgins, *United Nations Peacekeeping*, p. 184.

39. S.C. Res. 114, UN Doc. S/3605 (1956).

40. S.C. Res. 118, UN Doc. S/3675 (1956). For further background, see Rosalyn Higgins, *United Nations Peacekeeping*, pp. 225-27.

41. These assurances were contained in a United States *aide-mémoire,* a copy of which may be found in John Norton Moore, *The Arab-Israeli Conflict* (Princeton: Princeton University Press, 1977), p. 1010.

42. This background information is taken largely from Charles W. Yost, "The Arab-Israeli War: How it Began," *Foreign Affairs* 46 (1968):304-20.

43. In 1974, in response to a suggestion by Professor Eugene V. Rostow that the United States endorse the right of reprisal under Article 51 of the UN Charter, Acting Secretary of State Kenneth Rush wrote:

[I]t is the established policy of the United States that a State is responsible for the international use of armed force originating from its territory, whether that force be direct and overt or indirect and covert. This equally is the announced policy of the United Nations, expressly reflected, . . . in the General Assembly's resolution 2625 on Principles of International Law concerning Friendly Relations and Cooperation among States. The definition of aggression recently forwarded by a UN Special Committee to the General Assembly also maintains this accepted principle of international law.

You would add a complementary principle, namely, that where a State cannot or will not fulfill its international legal obligations to prevent the use of its territory for the unlawful exercise of force, the wronged State is entitled to use force, by way of reprisal, to redress, by self-help, the violation of international law which it has suffered.

As you know, resolution 2625 also contains the following categorical statement: "States have a duty to refrain from acts of reprisal involving the use of force." That injunction codifies resolutions of the Security Council which have so affirmed.

The United States has supported and supports the foregoing principle. Of course we recognize that the practice of States is not always consistent with this principle and that it may sometimes be difficult to distinguish the exercise of proportionate self-defense from an act of reprisal. Yet, essentially for reasons of the abuse to which the doctrine of reprisals particularly lends itself, we think it desirable to endeavor to maintain the distinction between acts of lawful self-defense and unlawful reprisals."

See *American Journal of International Law,* 68 (1974):736

44. Quoted in Charles W. Yost, "The Arab-Israeli War," p. 305.

45. See Oran R. Young, "Intermediaries and Interventionists: Third Parties in the Middle East Crisis," in John Norton Moore, *The Arab-Israeli Conflict* (Princeton: Princeton University Press, 1974), vol. 3, pp. 22–43.

46. There appears to be little doubt that Israel made the first massive move of military force across international borders. But up to the time of the Israeli strike, Israel had been subjected to an almost continuous stream of border raids from Syria and Jordan.

47. See 22 UN SCOR (1361st mtg.) 13906 UN Doc. S/Res/237(1967) and 22 UN SCOR (1357th mtg.) 13575 UN Doc. S/Res/236(1967).

48. See Eugene V. Rostow, "Legal Aspects of the Search for Peace in the Middle East," *Proceedings of the American Society of International Law* 64, no. 4 (1970):64–71.

49. See Eugene V. Rostow, "The Illegality of the Arab Attack on Israel of October 6, 1973," *American Journal of International Law* 69 (1975):272, 276–86 (supporting the U.S.-Israeli position); Quincy Wright, "The Middle East Crisis," *American Journal of International Law* 64 (1970):271–77 (supporting the Arab position).

50. See Fayez A. Sayegh, "The Camp David 'Framework of Peace', An Agreement on Procedures or a Declaration of Principles?" in F. Zeady (ed.), *Camp David, A New Balfour Declaration* (New York: Arab Information Center, 1979), p. 17.

51. The text of the resolution may be found in Yonah Alexander and Nicholas Kittrie, *Crescent and Star* (New York & Toronto: AMS Press, 1973), pp. 427–29.

52. The text of the PLO Charter may be found in John Norton Moore, *The Arab-Israeli Conflict* (Princeton: University Press, 1977), p. 108.

53. Oran Young, "Intermediaries and Interventionists," p. 25.

54. Ibid., p. 26.

55. Ibrahim F. I. Shihata, "Destination Embargo of Arab Oil: Its Legality under International Law," *American Journal of International Law* 68(1974):591, 598–608.

56. See Eugene V. Rostow, "The Illegality of the Arab Attack."

57. 28 UN SCOR (1747th mtg.) 10 UN Doc. S/INF/29 (1974).

58. There is, to be sure, a question as to the scope of the Security Council's authority in the area of pacific settlement of disputes. See notes 12 to 14 and accompanying text in Chapter 2, supra. The binding nature of Security Council Resolution 338, however, has not, to this writer's knowledge, been challenged.

59. The phrase is taken from a paper by Professor M. Cherif Bassiouni entitled "An Analysis of the Egyptian Peace Policy Toward Israel: From Resolution 242(1967) to the 1979 Peace Treaty," presented to the Chicago Council on Foreign Relations by the author in April 1979.

60. The text of the agreement may be found in John Norton Moore,

The Arab-Israeli Conflict (Princeton: Princeton University Press: 1974), vol. 3, p. 1167.

61. Ibid., p. 1208.

62. *Early Warning System in Sinai: Hearings Before the Senate Committee on Foreign Relations,* 94th Congress, 1st Session 208 (1975) (statement of Secretary of State Kissinger).

63. The text of this agreement may be found in John Norton Moore, *The Arab-Israeli Conflict* (Princeton: Princeton Univeristy Press:1977), p. 1201.

64. Treaty of Peace, March 26, 1979, Egypt-Israel, reprinted in *International Legal Materials* 18 (1979):362.

65. Eugene V. Rostow, "The Illegality of the Arab Attack," p. 288.

66. A more extensive consideration of the historical background to the Cyprus crisis may be found in Thomas Ehrlich, *Cyprus 1958-67* (Oxford University Press, 1974).

67. 531 Parl. Deb. H.C. (5th Ser.) 507-508 (1954).

68. Article II, Treaty of Guarantee, Aug. 16, 1960, 382 U.N.T.S. 3.

69. Ibid.

70. Thomas Ehrlich, *Cyprus 1958-67*, p. 38.

71. 19 UN SCOR, Supp. January–March 1964, at 67, UN Doc. S/5543 (1964).

72. 19 UN SCOR, Supp. January–March 1964, at 69-70, UN Doc. S/5545(1964).

73. 19 UN SCOR, 1097th Meeting, at 27-28 (1964).

74. Ibid.

75. Ibid, p. 32.

76. UN SCOR, 1098th Meeting, at 10-12 (1964).

77. UN SCOR, 1098th Meeting, at 15-21 (1964).

78. S.C. Res. 186, 19 UN SCOR, Supp. January–March 1964, at 102-103, UN Doc. S/5575 (1964).

79. Letter dated March 1964 from the representative of Turkey to the secretary-general, 19 UN SCOR, Supp. January–March 1964, at 135, UN Doc. S/5596 (1964).

80. 19 UN SCOR, 1103d Meeting, at 2-9 (1964).

81. S.C. Res. 187, 19 UN SCOR, 1103d Meeting, at 30 (1964); 19 UN SCOR, Supp. January–March 1964, at 142, UN Doc. S/5603 (1964).

82. 19 UN SCOR, 1142 Meeting, at 11-12 (1964).

83. S.C. Res. 193, 19 UN SCOR, Supp. July–September 1964, at 152, UN Doc. S/5868 (1964).

84. Prominent among these were missions by Dean Acheson, United States secretary of state, and Galo Plaza, a former president of Ecuador, See Abram Chayes, Thomas Ehrlich, and Andreas Lowenfeld, *International Legal Process* (Boston: Little, Brown & Co., 1969), vol. II, pp. 1301–05.

85. *Yearbook of The United Nations,* 1974, p. 260.

86. Ibid., p. 266.

87. S.C. Res. 358, UN Doc. S/11448 (1974).

88. S.C. Res. 359, UN Doc. S/11449 Rev. 1 (1974).

89. For a survey of these arguments, see Thomas Ehrlich, *Cyprus 1958-67,* pp. 61-89.

90. See Yehuda Z. Blum, "The Beirut Raid and the International Double Standard," *American Journal of International Law* 64 (1970):73, 98-104.

91. The factual background to the Beirut raid is taken from Richard A. Falk, "The Beirut Raid and the International Law of Retaliation," *American Journal of International Law* (1969):415.

92. Ibid., p. 416.

93. Ibid., pp. 416–17.

94. S.C. Res. 262, UN Doc. S/P V. 1462, at 6 (1968).

95. *UN Monthly Chronicle*, January, 1969, pp. 6–7.

96. Ibid., pp. 5–6.

97. Myres S. McDougal, "Authority to Use Force on the High Seas," *Naval War College Review* 20(1967):19, 28–29.

98. See the survey of these writers in Ian Brownlie, "Humanitarian Intervention," in John Norton Moore (ed.), *Law and Civil War in the Modern World* (Baltimore: Johns Hopkins University Press, 1975), pp. 217–28. For a forceful dissenting position, see in the same volume Richard B. Lillich, "Humanitarian Intervention: A Reply to Ian Brownlie and a Plea for Constructive Alternatives," pp. 229–51.

99. This point is made most emphatically by Yehuda Z. Blum, "The Beirut Raid."

100. The summary of facts regarding the background to the Israeli raid is taken from *UN Chronicle*, April 1978, pp. 5–6.

101. Ibid., pp. 7–8.

102. S.C. Res. 425, UN Doc. S/12610 (1978).

103. See *New York Times*, December 24, 1980, p. A4, December 25, 1980, p. 3

104. See ibid., June 6, 1982, pp. A-1, 9, June 7, 1982, p. A–12. On June 6, British prime minister Margaret Thatcher announced that because a PLO London representative's name was on the "hit list" found on the suspects arrested after the shooting of Argov, Britain doubled Israel's assertion that the air strikes in Lebanon were justified. Ibid., June 7, 1982, p. A–13.

105. In a bulletin issued in Jerusalem, the UN commander said that the 7,000-man force "used a variety of [non-violent] tactics" on June 6 in an effort to curb the advance of the Israelis. Ibid., June 10, 1982, p. A–18.

106. S.C. Res. 508 (1982).

107. S.C. Res. 509 (1982).

108. S.C. Res. 511 and S.C. Res. 512 (1982).

109. For the text of the French draft resolution, see *New York Times*, June 27, 1982, p. A–12.

110. Ibid., p. A-1, 13.

111. Ibid., June 22, 1982, p. A-1, 10.

112. For more extensive discussion of China's relations with Vietnam, see Harold C. Hinton, *China's Relations with Burma and Vietnam* (Institute of Pacific Relations, 1958), pp. 1–64.

113. *Keesing's Contemporary Archives*, February 23, 1979, p. 29468.

114. Ibid.

115. *New York Times*, January 3, 1979, p. 9.

116. *UN Chronicle*, February 1979, p. 8.

117. Ibid., p. 9.

118. *New York Times*, January 5, 1979, p. 2.

119. *UN Chronicle*, February 1979, p. 8.

120. *New York Times*, January 4, 1979, p. 1.

121. *UN Chronicle,* February 1979, p. 11.

122. *New York Times,* January 8, 1979, p. 1.

123. *UN Chronicle,* February 1979, p. 5.

124. *New York Times,* February 16, 1979, p. 3.

125. Ibid.

126. *Beijing Review,* February 23, 1979, p. 3.

127. *New York Times,* February 19, 1979, p. 1.

128. *UN Chronicle,* March 1979, p. 5.

129. Ibid., April 1979, p. 46.

130. *Beijing Review,* March 23, 1979, p. 3.

131. Thomas M. Franck and Nigel Rodley, "After Bangladesh: The Law of Humanitarian Intervention by Military Force," *American Journal of International Law* 67(1973):275, 304.

132. Ibid., pp. 285–86. For a contrary view, see Thomas E. Behuniak, "The Law of Unilateral Intervention by Armed Force," *Military Law Review* 79 (1978):157–91.

133. *Beijing Review,* February 23, 1979, p. 8.

134. For a summary of the Tanzanian overthrow of Idi Amin, see *Facts on File, 1979,* April 11, 1979, p. 257A1.

135. S.C. Res. 479, September 28, 1980, *UN Chronicle,* November 1980, p. 5.

136. Ibid.

137. *New York Times,* November 5, 1980, p. A7.

138. *New York Times,* October 24, 1980, p. A7.

139. See the *Washington Post,* June 20, 1982, p. C-2, reprinting an article by Sumner Welles, first published in the *Post* on March 3, 1948.

140. *Washington Post,* April 1, 1982, p. A-21.

141. *New York Times,* May 21, 1982, p. A-8.

142. *Washington Post,* April 4, 1982, p. A-1, 17.

143. S.C. Res. 502 (1982).

144. *Washington Post,* April 4, 1982, p. A-1.

145. S.C. Res. 505 (1982).

146. UN Doc. S/15156/Rev.2, 4 June 1982. *New York Times,* June 6, 1982, p. A-1, 12.

147. Letter to the Editor, *New York Times,* May 19, 1982, p. A-26.

148. Letter to the Editor, ibid., June 17, 1982, p. A-26.

149. Ibid.

150. For a consideration of these efforts, and of the debates in the Security Council on the Cuban missile crisis, see Abram Chayes, Thomas Ehrlich, and Andreas F. Lowenfeld, *International Legal Process* (Boston: Little, Brown & Co., 1969), vol. II, pp. 1057, 1092–1107.

FOUR

The General Assembly

PEACE-KEEPING FORCES

As indicated in Chapter 2, by the terms of the United Nations Charter, the General Assembly is assigned a relatively subsidiary role in the maintenance of international peace and security. However, since the Security Council has often not been able to fulfill its "primary" responsibility in this area because of the Soviet Union's or other permanent members' employment of the veto power, in practice the assembly has assumed a greater role in the maintenance of international peace and security than a strict reading of the Charter would indicate.

The primary vehicle for this role has been the assembly's Uniting for Peace resolution.[1] By its terms, the resolution envisages the assembly making "appropriate recommendations to Members for collective measures, including in the case of a breach of the peace or act of aggression the use of armed force when necessary, to maintain or restore international peace and security."[2] It thus implicitly provides that the assembly may act as an agency to enforce the peace against a state deemed (by the assembly) to be an aggressor. As we have seen in Chapter 3, the Uniting for Peace resolution was so utilized against North Korea and the People's Republic of China. Since then, however, the assembly has assumed a more modest role and has confined its recommendations regarding the use of armed force to the establishment of peace-keeping forces.

Specifically, in 1956, the Security Council adopted a resolution, not subject to the veto because it dealt with a matter of procedure, that placed the question of the Suez crisis before the General Assembly.[3] Once the question was on its agenda, the assembly called upon the parties to the conflict to agree to a cease-fire and to the withdrawal of all forces behind the armistice lines, and passed a resolution establishing "a United Nations Command for an Emergency International Force [UNEF] to secure and supervise the cessation of hostilities."[4] Major General E. L. M. Burns of Canada was appointed chief of the UNEF, twenty-four member states offered forces to it, and forces from eleven were ultimately selected. With Egyptian approval, the UNEF was established on its territory, Israel having refused categorically to accept the stationing of any foreign force on its territory.

In abstaining on the assembly's resolution—the abstention rather than a negative vote was apparently due to a desire to avoid offending Egypt—the Soviet Union challenged the legality of the establishment of the UNEF. It argued, among other things, that the assembly had no jurisdiction in matters involving "action," and that all UN forces, whether their function was "policing" or "enforcement," were engaged in action. The authority to take "action," according to the Soviet view, was reserved to the Security Council under the terms of Article 11(2) of the United Nations Charter.[5] As we shall see below, this view was, in part at least, rejected by the International Court of Justice.

Somewhat surprisingly, the Soviet Union raised no such objections when the General Assembly established the United Nations Temporary Executive Authority (UNTEA), headed by a UN administrator and assisted by UN security forces, to oversee the transfer of West Irian, or Dutch New Guinea, from the Netherlands to Indonesia.[6] The United Nations had earlier been responsible in large part for the creation in 1949 of Indonesia out of territory that had been part of the Dutch colonial empire. Because of a failure to agree at the time on the disposition of Dutch New Guinea, it had remained under Dutch administration. Indonesia, however, had persisted in its claim and began to use armed force to back it up. A representative of the secretary-general helped to mediate the dispute, and Indonesia and the Netherlands reached an agreement on August 15, 1962, under which the United Nations would assume the administration of the territory temporarily, and then, in a manner and time to be decided later, would turn the territory over to Indonesia. The General Assembly approved the agreement on September 21. Pakistan provided the necessary military units with the costs of maintaining them being borne by Indonesia and the Netherlands. After seven months of UN administration, the territory was transferred to Indonesia on May 1, 1963. By the terms of the agreement, Indonesia was bound to hold a plebiscite, but was free to determine the time and method of doing so. A plebiscite of sorts was held in 1969, but it was less than a true act of free choice by the people of West Irian.[7]

Immediately upon the establishment of the UNEF, a disagreement arose as to the allocation of costs of the force not borne by members sending troops or met by donations.[8] In keeping with its legal position, the Soviet Union insisted that UNEF costs be borne by the United Kingdom, France, and Israel. The United States argued that the costs should be considered "expenses of the Organization" and financed on the usual scale of assessments. The General Assembly ultimately decided that assessments should be made on all members, but on a sliding scale with low-income members paying less than their usual share and the difference being made up by voluntary contributions.

The Soviet Union refused to accept the assembly's decision and withheld payment of its share of the UNEF's expenses. This, along with Soviet and French refusal to pay the assessed costs of the United Nations Peace-keeping Force in the Congo (ONUC), resulted by December 1961 in a financial crisis for the United Nations. In response the assembly passed two resolutions. The first authorized a $200 million bond issue. Despite substantial congressional opposition, the United States subscribed to approximately half of the issue. The second resolution asked the International Court of Justice for an advisory opinion on whether the cost of the UNEF and ONUC constituted "expenses of the Organization," and therefore subject to assessment by the General Assembly under Article 17 of the UN Charter.[9]

There was no expectation that a World Court decision on the question would end debate. But some nations in arrears did indicate that they would pay their assessments if the court advised that they had been properly authorized. Further, a favorable court opinion could be the first step toward imposing sanctions under Article 19 of the Charter against those member states which had refused to pay.[10]

Some twenty governments submitted materials to the court in the expenses case, including the United States and, for the first time, the Soviet Union.

In advising that the General Assembly had the authority to set up the UNEF, and that therefore costs incurred in connection with that operation constituted "expenses of the Organization," the court stressed that the force had been established with the consent of the nations concerned and that the assembly did not purport to entrust the UNEF with the power to engage in measures of enforcement.[11] The authority to establish a force to enforce the peace, the court indicated, was reserved to the Security Council. This was the kind of "action" referred to in Article 11(2) of the UN Charter.[12]

The clear implication of the court's opinion, then, is that the General Assembly does not have the authority it claims in the Uniting for Peace resolution to recommend the establishment of an armed force under its auspices to enforce the peace against an aggressor state. Member states of the United Nations retain the right, of course, to use armed force in individual or collective self-defense to meet an act of aggression. But, in light of the court's opinion in the expenses case, the authority of the General Assembly itself to recommend the establishment of a UN Force to meet such aggression is problematic.

Following the court's opinion, debate began in the General Assembly regarding what action, if any, the assembly should take in response to it.[13] The United States and other countries proposed that the assembly should formally accept the court's opinion. France, the Soviet Union, and various communist nations argued that, since the opinion was not binding, assembly acceptance would be tantamount to amending the Charter. Also, some member countries feared that accepting the opinion would lead to application of Article 19 sanctions against nations more than two years in arrears, which might result in a Soviet walkout.

The position of the United States prevailed, and on December 19, 1962, the assembly adopted a resolution in which it accepted the court's opinion.[14] The question then arose as to the application of sanctions against member states more than two years in arrears. According to the United States, loss of vote was automatic under Article 19 if a member state was the requisite two years in arrears on its payments.[15] Czechoslovakia, however, contended that only the General Assembly could decide to suspend the right of a member state to vote and that such a decision would be an "important question" requiring a two-thirds majority of those member states present and voting.[16]

When the General Assembly met for its nineteenth session in the fall of 1964, the United States pressed hard to have member states in arrears on their dues automatically deprived of their vote. However, the president of the assembly declined to rule that loss of vote was automatic, and the assembly decided to avoid an immediate confrontation on the issue by proceeding to do as much business as it could without taking any votes. Albania attempted to upset this arrangement by insisting on a formal vote over the question of returning to a normal voting procedure. The vote on the Albania motion (which was defeated) was ruled "procedural" and hence not relevant to the issue whether delinquent member states could vote on assembly business.

Between the nineteenth and twentieth sessions of the General Assembly, support for the United States position regarding the deprivation of vote for those member states in arrears on payments for the UNEF and ONUC eroded markedly, in part because of the developing countries' strong reaction to the joint American-Belgium airlift into the Congo in 1964. As a result, before the start of the twentieth session of the assembly in 1965, Arthur Goldberg, United States permanent-representative to the United Nations, announced that, while preserving its position on the legal issues, the United States would no longer press for adoption of its position and that the assembly could resume its normal business. At the same time, he noted, "the United States reserves the same option to make exceptions if, in our view, strong and compelling reasons exist for doing so. There can be no double standard among the members of the Organization."[17]

The dispute over the financing of United Nations peace-keeping operations remains unresolved, in spite of intensive efforts within and without the United Nations to reach a solution. In practice, some peace-keeping operations (e.g., Cyprus) have been financed entirely by voluntary contributions, while others (e.g., the UN force established to supervise the initial disengagements between Egypt and Israel, and Syria and Israel) have been created by the Security Council and their maintenance costs included as "expenses of the Organization" under Article 17 of the Charter.

Recently a new crisis over financing peace-keeping operations has arisen. The Soviet Union refuses to pay expenses to police the Second Sinai Agreement between Egypt and Israel negotiated by Secretary of State Henry Kissinger in 1975. It argues that, since this agreement was concluded outside of the United Nations, member states cannot be obligated to pay for it. Hence, in the Soviet view, the General Assembly resolutions approving the Second Sinai Agreement and authorizing the UN force established in connection with the initial disengagement agreements to help implement it are beyond the authority of the assembly.[18] The Soviet Union also opposed, and thereby defeated, a plan to have the Egyptian/Israeli peace treaty, concluded in 1979, monitored by UN forces.[19]

Ambassador Goldberg's statement, in the wake of the Article 19 crisis that the United States would reserve the right to make exceptions to the principle of collective financial responsibility, sounded the death knell for the role of the General Assembly as a creator of peace-keeping forces. Indeed, from 1960 onwards, the General Assembly has played a less and less prominent role on war and peace questions. The reasons for this have been aptly summarized by Evan Luard:

First, the outright opposition of the Soviet Union and France to the use previously made of the Assembly, their refusal to contribute to the costs of peacekeeping operations the Assembly had authorized, and the prolonged financial crisis which resulted from this constitutional difference of view, all served to induce some caution among other major powers in mobilizing the Assembly. Secondly, the increasing size of the Assembly, as well as the change in its composition (in which the Afro-Asian members came to hold more than two-thirds of the votes) meant that it came to be thought a less suitable instrument for use in such situations, by the US as much as by the Soviet Union. Thirdly, the far less frequent use of the Soviet veto in the Council reduced the need for an alternative agency. Finally, the desire of the other permanent members to retain the special influence which they held in the Security Council also encouraged the restoration of the Council's supremacy in Security questions.[20]

Aside from the creation of peace-keeping forces, the General Assembly's primary practice with respect to traditional international violence has been deliberation, debate, and, at times, condemnation. Examples of the latter would include the assembly's condemnations of Soviet invasions of Hungary (1956) and Afghanistan (1979). (Although, in the case of Afghanistan, the Soviet Union was not mentioned by name.) On the other hand, the assembly, as well as the Security Council, have ignored such incidents of traditional international violence as Ethiopia-Somalia (1977), Iraq-Iran (1979), and Ecuador-Peru (1980). Also, in 1968, after the Soviet Union vetoed a draft Security Council resolution that would have condemned its invasion of Czechoslovakia, no sustained effort was undertaken to have the General Assembly do so. Although condemnation by the assembly of acts of aggression are not likely to persuade the aggressor state to desist, they do serve to focus the attention of the world community on the offending act and to reaffirm the importance of fundamental UN Charter constraints on the use of force.

The chief stock in trade of the assembly with respect to traditional international violence, as with other areas, has been discussion, debate, and the passage of resolutions. It is here that the assembly has generated the most heated controversy. Let us briefly examine, as examples, three areas of assembly activity: the Arab-Israeli conflict; the definition of aggression; and friendly relations among states.

THE ARAB-ISRAELI CONFLICT

It is a fair statement that, at least in the last decade, the actions of the General Assembly with respect to the Arab-Israeli conflict have served to exacerbate tensions rather than resolve problems. The reason for this development is that the assembly has come under the control of a substantial pro-Arab majority and has accordingly acted with no pretense of impartiality.

The most striking example of the assembly's bias against Israel was its passage of the infamous Zionism resolution, in which the assembly proclaimed that "Zionism is a form of facism and racial discrimination."[21] The resolution was adopted after an emotionally charged debate and allegedly was the result of extremely heavy-handed lobbying by the Soviet Union and the Arab states. Daniel Patrick Moynihan, United States permanent representative to the United Nations, eloquently articulated the outraged reaction to the resolution: "The United States rises to declare before the General

Assembly of the United Nations, and before the world, that it does not acknowledge, it will not abide by, it will never acquiesce in this infamous act."[22]

While the Zionism resolution was the most dramatic example of the bias against Israel, it is unfortunately not the only instance when the assembly took action that undermined rather than contributed to a resolution of the Arab-Israeli conflict. Time and time again the assembly has adopted one-sided, polemical resolutions sponsored by the Soviet Union and the Arab states. On July 29, 1980, for example, the assembly adopted a resolution[23] calling for the formation of a Palestinian state and a pullout of the Israeli presence from *all* occupied territories, including Jerusalem, by November 19, 1980. No mention is made of Israel's territorial security or Palestinian terrorist attacks. The resolution is also contrary to the terms of Security Council Resolutions 242 and 338, the governing law on the matter, and amounts to little more than a PLO propaganda statement.

Under current circumstances, then, and indeed since the late 1960s and early 1970s, the assembly has become a forum incapable of taking constructive action on the Arab-Israeli conflict. The promise the assembly showed in its establishment of the UNEF has not been fulfilled.

THE DEFINITION OF AGGRESSION

As seen in Chapter 2, the United Nations Charter uses the term "aggression" only in Chapter VII, where it authorizes the Security Council to determine the existence of an act of aggression and to make recommendations or decisions on measures to be taken by member states in order to maintain or restore international peace and security. It is important to recognize, however, that the full range of its powers are available if the council merely determines the existence of a threat or breach of the peace. Exercise of the council's powers are in no way dependent upon or increased by a finding that a state has engaged in an act of aggression. Nowhere in the Charter is the concept of aggression defined.

This absence is deliberate, for many states, including the United States, opposed defining aggression. President Truman described such an effort as "a trap for the innocent and an invitation to the guilty" and noted that under the Charter system as adopted, "the appropriate U.N. organ, in the first instance the Security Council, would determine on the basis of the facts of a particular case whether aggression has taken place."[24]

This absence of definition notwithstanding, the United States had supported at the Nuremberg trials the concept of a "crime against peace," which the charter for the Nuremberg tribunal had defined in pertinent part as "planning, preparation, initiation, or waging of a war of aggression . . ."[25] During the drafting of the tribunal's charter, the United States representative attempted to have a specific definition of aggression included, but his efforts were unsuccessful. Nor did the tribunal in its judgment find it necessary to define aggression, accepting instead the argument that whatever the full scope of the concept, the acts perpetrated by the German leaders spoke for themselves and clearly constituted aggression.

Following the Nuremberg trials and the acceptance of the Nuremburg principles by the General Assembly,[26] the International Law Commission began work on a Draft Code of Offenses against the Peace and Security of Mankind.[27] In the course of its work, the commission listed aggression as a crime against the peace and security of mankind. Its definition of aggression, however, was limited to a statement that it was the use of armed force by one state against another other than for purposes of "national or collective defence", or pursuant to decisions or recommendations by competent United Nations organs.[28]

In 1952, partially in reaction to the conflict in Korea, the General Assembly declared that it was "possible and desirable" to define aggression further and appointed the first Special Committee of 15 States to do so. [29] This committee did substantial work from 1953 to 1956, as did the Second Special Committee of 19 States from October 8 to November 9, 1956, against the dramatic backdrop of the Suez crisis. Nonetheless, the primary thrust of the second special committee's report was that its members were unable to agree either on the question whether it would be desirable to define aggression, or whether it would be feasible to do so. These doubts were present also in the General Assembly, so when the assembly established its Third Special Committee in 1957, the task it imposed was essentially that "of determining when it shall be appropriate for the General Assembly to consider again the question of defining aggression."[30] At its meetings of 1959, 1962, 1965, and 1967, the committee found that the time was not yet ripe.

It was a Soviet initiative in 1967 that led to the establishment of the fourth and final special committee on defining aggression. This committee worked prodigiously until 1974 when it concluded its work and produced by consensus a draft resolution defining aggression. The General Assembly adopted (also by consensus) this resolution on December 14, 1974.[31]

The most serious questions regarding the assembly's definition of aggression arise with respect to unconventional violence, and we will consider these in later chapters. Some issues concerning the definition's treatment of traditional international violence are also worthy of note, however.

First, it is important to note that the effect of the definition is intended to be limited. Basically, the definition is designed for the guidance of the Security Council should it choose to refer to it; the council retains full discretion as to whether it will do so, and the definition notes that "nothing in this definition shall be interpreted as in any way affecting the scope of the provisions of the Charter with respect to the functions and powers of the organs of the United Nations."[32] The definition does state, perhaps overly optimistically, that "the adoption of a definition of aggression ought to have the effect of deterring a potential aggressor, would simplify the determination of acts of aggression and also facilitate the protection of the rights and lawful interests of, and the rendering of assistance to, the victim."[33]

Article 1 of the definition closely tracks Article 2(4) of the United Nations Charter in providing that aggression is "the use of armed force by a State against the sovereignty, territorial integrity or political independence of another State, or in any other manner inconsistent with the Charter of the United Nations, as set out in this definition." In a key provision, Article 2 of the definition provides that "the first use of armed force by a State in contravention of the Charter shall constitute *prima facie* evidence of an act of aggression although the Security Council may, in conformity with the Charter, conclude that a determination that an act of aggression has been committed would not be justified in the light of other relevant circumstances, including the fact that the acts concerned or their consequences are not of sufficient gravity."

Relevant circumstances that the council might take into account in determining that a first use of force did not constitute an act of aggression are nowhere specified in the definition. An earlier draft of Article 2 sponsored by six Western powers, including the United States, provided that the Security Council might conclude that the first use of armed force did not justify a finding that an act of aggression had occurred "in the light of other relevant circumstances, including, as evidence, the purposes of the states involved."[34] A draft six-power proposal had specified five objectives as examples of aggressive acts.[35] This provision was strongly opposed by Arab states, which was hardly surprising in light of the dispute over Israel's first use of massive force in the 1967 Arab-Israeli conflict.

In the final version of Article 2 relevant circumstances were left unspecified. But the requirement that the first use of force also had to be "in contravention of the Charter" appears to imply that there can be a legitimate first use of force that is not in contravention of the Charter. Several states objected to this language as encouraging a first strike as a purported preventive action. The language was finally agreed to on the understanding that the Security Council, and not the state engaged in the use of force, would determine whether the action was in contravention of the Charter.[36]

Unfortunately, the result of this effort at compromise is a provision that only the most unimaginative would-be aggressor will not be able to cite in support of its actions. Article 2 of the definition contains so many ambiguities and loopholes that it is rendered almost completely ineffectual. First, it clearly implies that a first use of armed force is permissible, although the language of Article 51 and the weight of scholarly opinion supports the proposition that "anticipatory self-defence" is not permitted under the UN Charter.[37] Second, the term "relevant circumstances" is so open-ended as to give the Security Council no guidance whatsoever. Arguably, it may be "relevant" that the use of armed force was undertaken for such pure motives as "humanitarian intervention" or in response to economic coercion. Third, the qualifying phrase "the acts concerned or their consequences are not of sufficient gravity" amounts to a *de minimis* clause designed to prevent minor incidents from being treated as acts of aggression. The unfortunate and clearly unintended implication is that there can be first uses of armed force in contravention of the UN Charter that need not be taken seriously. Such an implication hardly serves to enhance Charter constraints on the unilateral use of force by states.

Article 3 of the definition specifies, as an example of an act qualifying as aggression, "the invasion or attack by the armed forces of a State of the territory of another State, or any military occupation, however temporary, resulting from such invasion or attack, or any annexation by the use of force of the territory of another State or part thereof." This repeats an injunction in the preamble of the definition, and invasion or attack have long been regarded as a benchmark of aggression. However, as Professor Julius Stone has noted,[38] where one state's territory ends and another begins is often a matter of hot dispute, and a state utilizing force across a disputed frontier may argue that it is merely acting within its own territory and hence has not committed a *prima facie* act of aggression. The six-power draft had included as an act qualifying as an act of aggression the use of force in order to "alter internationally agreed lines of demarcation."[39] Such a provision would have had particular relevance to such areas as Germany, the Arab-Israeli conflict, and Korea. The definition, by contrast, "reduces not at all the problem of determining when there has been aggression in connection with disputes over boundaries."[40] Since these disputes are becoming ever more frequent, this is a serious failure. It is true that the definition, in Article 5(3), provides that "no territorial acquisition or special advantage resulting from aggression is or shall be recognized as lawful." But in light of the difficulty in determining under the definition when there has been aggression in connection with a dispute over boundaries, this provision adds little.

In this commentator's opinion, the assembly's definition of aggression is indeed, as predicted by President Truman, "an invitation to the guilty." The word "aggression" was included in the Charter as a result of a Soviet proposal at Dumbarton Oaks. The United States considered that the term "breach of the peace" was broad enough to cover aggression, but nonetheless acquiesed in the Soviet proposal.[41] The proposal should have been resisted; at the least the United States and like-minded states should have stuck fast to their initial inclination that no attempt should be made to define the term. Aggression is inherently an emotionally laden, politically charged term not susceptible to legal definition.

Evidence of the political nature of defining aggression may be found in the recent practice of the General Assembly. The resolution adopted by the assembly on January 14, 1980,[42] does not term the Soviet invasion of Afghanistan an act of aggression. On the contrary, the resolution never mentions the Soviet Union by name and merely calls for the immediate withdrawal of all foreign troops from Afghanistan. By contrast, both the Security Council and the assembly have declared that South Africa's raids into Angola in reprisal for Angola's allowing the South West Africa People's Organization to use its territory for staging guerrilla attacks into Namibia (itself a violation of international law[43]) are acts of aggression.[44] The double standard illustrated by these two cases is obvious.

FRIENDLY RELATIONS

A much more positive contribution by the General Assembly toward the control of international violence was its adoption, on October 24, 1970, of the Declaration on Principles of International Law Concerning Friendly Relations and Cooperation among States in Accordance with the Charter of the United Nations.[45] Although there is some dispute about the precise legal status of the declaration, it is generally regarded as an authoritative interpretation of broad principles of international law expressed in the UN Charter.[46]

The first principle of the declaration is that "States shall refrain in their international relations from the threat or use of force against the territorial integrity or political independence of any State, or in any other manner inconsistent with the purposes of the United Nations." The first paragraph developing this principle essentially restates Article 2, paragraphs 3 and 4 of the UN Charter, but addresses the rule to "Every State" rather than to "all Members." This reflects the perception that the rules of the Charter have become part of customary international law and are therefore binding on all states, even if they are not members of the United Nations.

The fourth and fifth paragraphs not only provide that every state "has the duty to refrain from the threat or use of force to violate the existing international boundaries of another State or as a means of resolving international disputes," they also require every state "to refrain from the threat or use of force to violate international lines of demarcation;" hence the arguable loophole found in the definition of aggression and discussed above is not present in the declaration.

The sixth paragraph categorically prohibits states from engaging in acts of reprisal involving the use of force. This prohibition is supported not only by the language of Article 2(4) of the Charter, but also by an express decision of the Security Council.[47]

The first sentence of the tenth paragraph provides that "the territory of a State shall not be the object of military occupation resulting from the use of force in contravention of the provisions of the Charter." This begs the issue of the validity of Israel's occupation of the West Bank and the Gaza Strip. However, the same paragraph goes on to say that "the territory of a State shall not be the object of acquisition by another state resulting from the threat or use of force. No territorial acquisition resulting from the threat or use of force shall be recognized as legal." These provisions greatly undermine the claim sometimes made that Israel has a right to be recognized as the legitimate sovereign over the West Bank and Gaza Strip.[48]

To be sure, the declaration does not resolve a host of disagreements among member states of the United Nations relating to the use of force. The final paragraph formulating the first principle of the declaration provides that "Nothing in the foregoing paragraphs shall be construed as enlarging or diminishing in any way the scope of the provisions of the Charter concerning cases in which the use of force is lawful." In the words of Robert Rosenstock, a chief American negotiator of the declaration, "the text thus accommodates those who support and those who oppose the residual peacekeeping role of the General Assembly in cases in which the Security Council is unable to act, those who regard regional organizations as able to authorize the use of force under certain circumstances and those who do not, those who subscribe to the notion of an inherent right of self-defence against colonialism and those who do not, those who read Article 51 restrictively and place their emphasis on the phrase 'if an armed attack occurs' and those who do not."[49] He further noted, "the generality of this paragraph diminishes the utility of the text as a whole."[50]

One other positive although modest accomplishment of the declaration with respect to the control of traditional international violence may be found in its elaboration of its second principle obligating states to settle their disputes by peaceful means. The second sentence of the penultimate paragraph under that principle provides that "recourse to, or acceptance of, a settlement procedure freely agreed to by States with regard to existing or future disputes to which they are parties shall not be regarded as incompatible with sovereign equality." This is a weak rejection of the Soviet argument that a state derogates from its sovereignty when it agrees to submit future disputes to binding third-party adjudication. Unfortunately, attempts to reach agreement on a general endorsement of third-party settlement, particularly by the International Court of Justice, were unsuccessful.[51]

NOTES

1. Nov. 3, 1950, U.N.G.A. Res. 377A(V), 5 U.N. GAOR, Supp. (No. 20)10, U.N. Doc. A/1775 (1951).

2. Section A, paragraph 1, of the resolution.

3. For a detailed discussion of the establishment of the UNEF, see Rosalyn Higgins, *United Nations Peacekeeping, 1946–1967 Documents and Commentary* (London, New York, and Toronto: Oxford University Press, 1969) vol. 1, pp. 221–529.

4. General Assembly Resolution 1000(ES-1), November 5, 1956, reproduced in ibid., pp. 233–34.

5. The Soviet argument is extensively examined in ibid., pp. 260–64.

6. Ibid., vol. 2, pp. 113–14.

7. See Arthur W. Rovine, *The First Fifty Years: The Secretary General in World Politics 1920–1970* (Leyden: A. W. Sijthoff, 1970), p. 36.

8. For discussion of this dispute, see Abram Chayes, Thomas Ehrlich, and Andreas Lowenfeld, *International Legal Process* (Boston: Little, Brown & Co., 1968), vol. 2, pp. 166–71.

9. Ibid., p. 167.

10. Article 19 of the Charter provides:

A Member of the United Nations which is in arrears in the payment of its financial contributions to the Organization shall have no vote in the General Assembly if the amount of its arrears equals or exceeds the amount of the contributions due from it for the preceding two full years. The General Assembly may, nevertheless, permit such a Member to vote if it is satisfied that the failure to pay is due to conditions beyond the control of the Member.

11. Certain Expenses of the United Nations [1962] I.C.J. 151.

12. Article 11(2) of the Charter provides:

The General Assembly may discuss any questions relating to the maintenance of international peace and security brought before it by any Member of the United Nations, or by the Security Council, or by a state which is not a Member of the United Nations in accordance with Article 35, paragraph 2, and, except as provided in Article 12, may make recommendations with regard to any such questions to the state or states concerned or to the Security Council or to both. Any such question on which action is necessary shall be referred to the Security Council by the General Assembly either before or after discussion.

13. Abram Chayes et al., *International Legal Process,* vol. 2, pp. 214–18.

14. U.N.G.A. Res. 1854A(XVII), 17 U.N. GAOR 1199, U.N. Doc. A/ PV. 1199 (1964).

15. Abram Chayes, et al., *International Legal Process,* vol. 2, pp. 219–26.

16. Ibid., pp. 218–19.

17. Ibid., pp. 240–42.

18. See note, "Financing Peacekeeping—Trouble Again," *Cornell International Law Journal* 11 (1978): 107–20.

19. *New York Times,* July 15, 1979, p. 8, and July 25, 1979, p. A1.

20. Evan Luard, *The United Nations* (New York: St. Martin's Press, 1979), pp. 46–47.

21. U.N.G.A. Res. 3379 (XXX), Nov. 18, 1975, 30 U.N. GAOR, Supp. (No. 34) 83, U.N. Doc. A/10034 (1976).

22. See Daniel Patrick Moynihan, *A Dangerous Place* (Boston: Little, Brown & Co., 1978), p. 197.

23. U.N.G.A. Res. ES-7/2, reproduced in *UN Chronicle,* (September-October 1980) p. 5.

24. Quoted in Majorie Whiteman, *Digest of International Law* (1965):740.

25. Article six of the Charter of the International Military Tribunal. The Charter of the Tribunal was annexed to the Agreement for the Prosecution and Punishment of the Major War Criminals of the European Axis (the London Agreement), 59 Stat. 1544, 82 U.N.T.S. 279.

26. G.A. Res. 95(2), U.N. GAOR, First Sess., Plenary 55, at 1144, Dec. 11, 1946.

27. U.N. GAOR, Supp. (No. 9), 11–12, U.N. Doc. A/2693 (1954).

28. See Article 2(1) of the Code, *1954 Yearbook of the International Law Commission,* vol. II, pp. 150–51.

29. This background description is taken from Julius Stone, *Conflict Through Consensus* (Baltimore: Johns Hopkins University Press, 1977), pp. 17–22.

30. Julius Stone, *Conflict Through Consensus,* p. 17.

31. U.N.G.A. Res. 3314 (XXXIX), 29 U.N. GAOR, Supp. (No. 31), 142, U.N. Doc. A/0631(1975), reprinted in *International Legal Materials* 13 (1974):710–14.

32. Fourth preambular paragraph.

33. Ninth preambular paragraph.

34. See Benjamin B. Ferencz, *Defining International Aggression* (Dobbs Ferry: Oceana, 1975), vol. 2, p. 527.

35. Op. cit. at note 32. The five objectives specified were: (1) Diminish the territory or alter the boundaries of another State; (2) alter internationally agreed lines of demarcation; (3) disrupt or interfere with the conduct of the affairs of another state; (4) secure changes in the government of another state; or (5) inflict harm or obtain concessions of any sort. Article IV, draft proposal submitted by Australia, Canada, Italy, Japan, the United Kingdom of Great Britain and Northern Ireland, and the United States of America (A/AC.134/L.17 and Add. 1 and 2), reproduced in ibid, pp. 428–29.

36. Op. cit. at notes 32 and 33.

37. See generally, Louis Henkin, *How Nations Behave* (New York: Columbia University Press, 1979), pp. 141–45.

38. Julius Stone, "Hopes and Loopholes in the 1974 Definition of Aggression," *American Journal of International Law* (1977):224, 226.

39. Article IV(2), Six-Power Draft, supra, note 35.

40. Julius Stone, "Hopes and Loopholes," p. 240.

41. Leland M. Goodrich, Edvard Hambro and Anne Patricia Simons, *Charter of the United Nations* (New York and London: Columbia University Press, 1969), p. 298.

42. U.N.G.A. Res. ES-612, reproduced in *UN Chronicle,* March 1980, p. 5.

43. The Declaration on Principles of International Law Concerning Friendly

Relations and Co-operation Among States in Accordance with the Charter of the United Nations, Oct. 24, 1970, U.N.G.A. Res. 2625 (XXV), 25 U.N. GAOR, Supp. (No. 28) 121, U.N. Doc. A/8028 (1971), which, as noted below in the text accompanying footnotes 43 to 50, is generally regarded as an authoritative interpretation of the United Nations principles regarding the use of force, provides in pertinent part:

> Every State has the duty to refrain from organizing, instigating, assisting or participating in acts of civil strife or terrorist acts in another State or acquiescing in organized activities within its territory directed towards the commission of such acts, when the acts referred to in the present paragraph involve a threat or use of force.

44. For a recent example of UN condemnation of South Africa's raids as acts of aggression, see S.C. Res. 454(1979), reproduced in *UN Chronicle,* January 1980, pp. 19–20.

45. See *supra,* note 42.

46. See Robert Rosenstock, "The Declaration of Principles of International Law Concerning Friendly Relations: A Survey," *American Journal of International Law* 65 (1971):713, 714.

47. S.C. Res. 188, April 9, 1964, U.N. Doc. S/5650 (1964).

48. See, e.g., Stephen M. Schwebel, "What Weight to Conquest?" *American Journal of International Law* (1970):344–47.

49. Robert Rosenstock, "The Declaration of Principles," pp. 723–24.

50. Ibid., p. 724.

51. Ibid., p. 725.

FIVE

The Secretary-General

At the outset of the drafting of the United Nations Charter, despite some reservations on this score by the Soviet Union,[1] it was understood that the secretary-general would be more than a high level administrative functionary. Article 99, which authorizes the secretary-general to bring to the attention of the Security Council any matter that in his opinion may threaten the maintenance of international peace and security, confers powers on the office that were denied to the secretary-general of the League. The comparable article of the Covenant[2] provided only that in case of war the secretary-general, "on the request of any Member of the League," should summon a meeting of the council. Hence the secretary-general of the United Nations, unlike his League counterpart, can act on his own initiative in regard to matters that threaten the peace. He need not wait for a request of a member state.

Although Article 99 contains the most expansive grant of authority in the Charter for the secretary-general, there are other bases for his competence to deal with matters threatening the peace. Under Article 98, the secretary-general is directed to act as the chief administrative officer of the organization at "all meetings of the General Assembly, of the Security Council, of the Economic and Social Council, and of the Trusteeship Council, and shall perform such other functions as are entrusted to him by these organs." In a number of instances the Security Council and other organs of the United Nations have entrusted wide-ranging responsibilities to the secretary-general. To be sure, the scope of the authority assigned him has sometimes been the subject of hot debate—as when the Soviet Union disagreed with the secretary-general's interpretation of his powers with respect to the introduction of United Nations forces into Katanga, the role of these forces in the civil war, and the extent to which support might be given to one or the other claimant to legitimate authority.[3]

The secretary-general is also required under Article 98 to make an annual report to the General Assembly on the work of the organization. Under the League, the report of the secretary-general was purely factual. The report of the UN secretary-general, by contrast, usually goes beyond a mere factual recounting and sets forth the views of the secretary-general regarding the achievements of the past year, the state of international affairs, and steps the organization and its members might take to promote the purposes of the United Nations more effectively. At times these reports have been quite critical of failures of member states to fulfill their responsibilities under the Charter.

Finally, it is significant that the secretariat is listed as one of the principal organs of the United Nations.[4] The comparable provision of the League Covenant[5] spoke merely in terms of "an Assembly and of a Council, with a permanent Secretariat."

As head of a principal organ of the United Nations, the secretary-general enjoys specific powers. For instance, the Statute of the International Law Commission provides: "The Commission shall . . . consider proposals and draft multilateral conventions submitted by . . . the principal organs of the United Nations."[6] The secretary-general has at his disposal a Division for the Progressive Development and Codification of International Law to take advantage of this authorization. The Genocide Convention was in large measure the product of a draft submitted by the secretary-general to an assembly committee that antedated the creation of the International Law Commission.[7]

Let us turn now to a consideration of how the five UN secretaries-general have utilized their powers.

TRYGVE LIE

Early in his tenure, the first secretary-general of the United Nations asserted substantial powers under Article 99 to deal with threats to the peace and, ironically in light of later developments, was supported in this stance by the Soviet Union and opposed by the United States. One of the first problems to come before the Security Council was an Iranian complaint that Soviet troops stationed in Iran during the war remained there in clear violation of treaty commitments to withdraw by March 2, 1946.[8] Soviet troops had stayed on in the province of Azerbaijan, and Iran was concerned that the Soviet Union would encourage an independence movement in the area.

Secretary-General Lie favored direct and quiet negotiations between Iran and the Soviet Union on the issue, and, in fact, such negotiations took place in March. At the end of the month, the Soviet Union announced that troop withdrawals would be completed in five or six weeks and claimed that the item should not be placed on the council's agenda. The United States disagreed, and when the Security

Council did discuss the problem, the Soviet delegate walked out. By April 15, Iran had formally withdrawn its complaint, but the United States, with support from eight council members, still argued that the question should be retained on the agenda.

At this point the secretary-general intervened on the side of the Soviet Union. On April 16, he submitted a legal memorandum to the president of the council in support of the proposition that, unless the council votes an investigation or recommends methods of adjustment, a request by both parties to a dispute for withdrawal of the complaint from the agenda should result in an automatic council decision to drop the item in question. The memorandum was submitted to the council's Committee of Experts, which rejected, by the same eight to three division between member states of the council, Lie's views on the substantive issue. The item therefore stayed on the council's agenda. However, although Lie lost on the merits, he won on the question whether the secretary-general had the right to intervene at all in meetings of the UN's political organs. The United States wanted a rule limiting the secretary-general's right to speak or to offer written presentations to situations where he had been invited to do so by the council's president. With the support of Moscow and a shift in the British position, Lie's position that the secretary-general should be able to intervene in the council's sessions as he wished prevailed. Also, the rule in the General Assembly was changed to allow the secretary-general to intervene at any time with oral or written statements. Since then, the secretary-general has often participated in political debates, offering his own position and recommendations on a variety of issues.

Lie continued to be an activist secretary-general. We have previously seen to some extent the role Lie played as mediator in seeking the creation of an international force to carry out the General Assembly's plan for the partition of Palestine, and his later efforts, as well as those of his representatives, to bring to a halt the fighting between Israel and the Arab states. Lie's experience with the Middle East convinced him that there was a great need for an international armed force in that area, and at a commencement address at Harvard University in June, 1948, he proposed the creation of a small armed force, which he called the United Nations Guard, under the UN secretariat with the secretary-general as its commander. His proposal called for a small army of some five to ten thousand men drawn from neutral nations, as a beginning. However, faced with substantial opposition from the major powers, especially from the Soviet Union, Lie was forced to water down his proposal and to request a much smaller force for narrower political purposes.

This he did in his 1948 report to the General Assembly, where he requested a guard of just 800 officials working for the UN secretariat—of whom only 300 would be permanent, with some 500 personnel in national sections available as reserve units. The primary function of this guard would be to protect the personnel of missions abroad and particular areas under truce arrangements or other UN intervention. The guard would not be a substitute for the kind of armed force envisaged under Article 43 of the Charter and would have only "personal emergency defensive weapons." Lie's proposal also specified that the guard would operate on a territory only with the consent of the sovereign and noted that its small size would preclude the guard's acting in an aggressive manner.

But the opposition to the secretary's plan persisted, and, in the event, there was established in 1949 what came to be known as the United Nations Field Service, a group of three hundred in the secretariat, unarmed but trained to carry out communications and transport services to UN missions in the field, as well as guard duties at headquarters. Although this modest operation was a far cry from the secretary-general's original proposed armed force of five to ten thousand, it was the forerunner of later UN forces that were established in the Middle East and elsewhere. Hence the idea of UN forces to be employed for purposes other than enforcement was essentially that of Trygve Lie.

Lie continued to engage in efforts at quiet diplomacy, such as during the Berlin blockade[9] and over the issue of Chinese representation,[10] but these efforts and Lie's delicate balancing act between the superpowers came a cropper when North Korea invaded South Korea in 1950. Lie was then forced to choose between a neutral role, with accompanying mediation attempts, which would perhaps have been acceptable to the Soviet Union but not to the United States, and strong support of Charter principles and the United States' efforts to defend South Korea. When he chose the latter course, Lie made himself unacceptable to the Soviet Union and, in effect, ended his usefulness as a neutral international civil servant. In speaking out against a clear violation of basic Charter principles, however, the secretary-general came out in support of the concept of collective security against aggression. It was the closest the United Nations has ever come to maintaining international peace and security in the manner envisaged by the framers of the Charter.

DAG HAMMARSKJÖLD

Totally unable to work with the Russians because of his actions on Korea, Lie submitted his resignation in 1952, and was succeeded in office by Dag Hammarskjöld in April, 1953. The Soviet Union agreed to the selection of Hammarskjöld in the belief that he would be much less of an activist than Lie had been and that he would limit his functions to those of a chief administrative clerk.[11] It could not have been more mistaken.

To be sure, during the early years of Hammarskjöld's tenure, there was little to indicate that the Soviet Union had been incorrect in its judgment. His speeches and statements on the United Nations had been largely conservative in tone with an emphasis on "quiet diplomacy" and little more.

All this changed with the Suez crisis in 1956 and the establishment of the UNEF. As we saw in Chapter 3, Hammarskjöld held private discussions in his office between the foreign ministers of Britain, France, and Egypt, the outcome of which was agreement on six basic requirements necessary for any permanent settlement of the Suez question. These in turn were adopted by the Security Council and formed a promising basis for peaceful settlement until the Biritsh and French decided upon recourse to force.

At a Security Council meeting called into session by the United States in response to reports that the British and French were bombing Egyptian airfields in the Suez Canal Zone and that troops from the two nations were on their way, Hammarskjöld stated that, had not the council been called into session by the United States, he would have called a meeting himself. He then made a statement that indicated his willingness to match and even go beyond the activist position of his predecessor regarding the scope of the powers and responsibilities of his office:

The principles of the Charter are, by far, greater than the Organization in which they are embodied, and the aims that they are to safeguard are holier than the policies of any single nation or people. As a servant of the Organization, the Secretary-General has the duty to maintain his usefulness by avoiding public stands on conflicts between member nations unless and until such an action might help to resolve the conflict. However, the discretion and impartiality thus imposed on the Secretary-General by the character of his immediate task, may not degenerate into a policy of expediency. He must also be a servant of the principles of the Charter, and its aims must ultimately determine what for him is right and wrong. For that he must stand. A Secretary-General cannot serve on any other assumption than that—within the necessary limits of human frailty and honest differences of opinion— all Member nations honor their pledge or observe all articles of the Charter. He should also be able to assume that those organs which are charged with the task of upholding the Charter, will be in a position to fulfill their tasks.

The bearing of what I have just said must be obvious to all without any elaboration from my side. Were the members to consider that another view of the duties of the Secretary-General than the one here stated would better serve the interests of the Organization, it is their obvious right to act accordingly.[12]

When the General Assembly decided to establish the UNEF, it set up an advisory committee to assist the secretary-general, and authorized Hammarskjöld to issue the necessary regulations and instructions for the force and "to take all other necessary administrative and executive actions."[13] Armed with this mandate, the secretary-general actively pursued negotiations towards the actual establishment of the UNEF, its deployment in the canal area, the withdrawal of the British, French, and Israeli troops, and the clearing of the Suez Canal itself, which had been blocked by Egypt at the commencement of hostilities. Arthur Rovine has aptly summarized the significance of this development:

For the Office of the Secretary-General, the Middle Eastern crisis was a striking turning point. For the first time in the history of the Office, the Secretary-General had delegated to him discretionary power over the organization and administration of an international armed force, thus initiating a development which was to establish the Office as a significant factor in international diplomacy. Essentially, Hammarskjold had turned the United Nations away from the impossible concept of collective security, the discredited foundation upon which its Charter still rests, and turned it forcefully toward the notion of a third party neutral intermediary that could serve as a buffer keeping hostile states apart while simultaneously insuring that great power intervention did not create a meaningful threat of world war. Given the conflict between the United States and the Soviet Union, Hammarskjold implemented new procedures and wrote new principles upon which international forces are still based, and he imparted a sense of direction to the UN that retains its validity today.[14]

Most of the other initiatives taken by Hammarskjöld to maintain international peace and security until his tragic death in the Congo in 1961 involved instances of revolutionary violence or civil war rather than traditional international violence, and some of these will be discussed in later chapters. For now it suffices to note that the Congo represented the peak of UN activity in peace-keeping. In reaction to Hammarskjöld's actions in the Congo, Premier Khrushchev demanded in the General Assembly that he resign and that the office of the secretary-general be abolished and replaced with a "troika" arrangement of three persons representing the Western powers, the socialist states, and the neutralist countries. The Soviet demands were rejected by the assembly, but they succeeded in severely damaging Hammarskjöld's position. The Soviet Union officially withdrew its recognition of him as secretary-general in February 1961, immediately after the death of Premier Patrice Lumumba in the

Congo. Hammarskjöld nonetheless continued his efforts to resolve the Congo crisis peacefully until he was killed in a crash there on September 17, 1961. With his death, both the United Nations and the office of the secretary-general entered a new era.

U THANT

The selection of U Thant as the third secretary-general of the United Nations reflected an enormous change that had taken place in the organization.[15] From the Western-dominated institution of the late 1940s and early 1950s, the United Nations had come to be controlled by a large bloc of countries from Africa and Asia, which were less interested in East-West issues and more in anticolonialism and neutralism. Thant, from the relatively small and nonaligned nation of Burma, became a leading spokesman for "third world" interests.

As the spokesman for the third world, Thant enjoyed an advantage not available to his predecessors and was less vulnerable to attack by the superpowers who were competing for influence in Africa and Asia. This was an especially valuable asset for Thant since the Congo crisis was still on the UN's agenda when he became acting secretary-general, and the Soviet Union's support was necessary if he was to be elected to serve a full term.

In the Congo, U Thant at first attempted to pursue, as had Hammarskjöld, a peaceful solution despite the Soviet's insistence that the United Nations should use force to bring Katanga's succession to an end, and although he was given a clear mandate by the Security Council in November 1961 to use force in Katanga against foreign advisers and mercenaries. In the face of indecision on the part of many Afro-Asian members of the United Nations as to whether force should be used against Tshombe's regime in Katanga, the Soviet Union was not in a position to withdraw its support from the secretary-general's efforts.

Thant's election to a full term as secretary-general was also helped by his performance during the Cuban missile crisis in 1962. Although the United Nations was not at center stage during the crisis, the organization and the acting secretary-general did play a role that permitted the Soviet Union to back down without too strong a loss of face by appearing to accede to UN appeals. The United States also greatly praised the work of Thant during the period.

Thant first intervened in the Cuba missile crisis on October 24, 1962, ten days after the United States government, through the use of U-2 reconnaissance planes, had discovered that the Soviet Union had begun to place medium and intermediate-range missiles in Cuba— thus securing a strategic base in the Caribbean from which an attack against the United States became feasible.[16] He did so at the request of a group of more than forty nonaligned countries by sending identical letters to President Kennedy and Premier Khrushchev appealing for a halt to the blockade by the United States and to arms shipments by the Soviet Union for a period of two to three weeks. Thant also appealed to Cuban Premier Fidel Castro to help find "some common ground" in the present "impasse," urging him to suspend the construction and development of military facilities during the negotiations.

In response, President Kennedy agreed to negotiations, but his letter made no mention of Thant's request for a suspension of the blockade. This, in the American view, would take the pressure off the Soviet Union, and Kennedy's letter stated that "the existing threat was created by the secret introduction of offensive weapons into Cuba, and the answer lies in the removal of such weapons."[17] The Soviet response, not surprisingly, was much more affirmative.

Thant addressed further appeals to the United States and the Soviet Union that they do "everything possible" to avoid direct military confrontation, and also held discussions in his office with American, Soviet, and Cuban representatives, especially regarding the possibility of UN inspection of the sites in Cuba to ensure removal of the missiles.

As the crisis mounted in intensity, Khrushchev and Kennedy communicated directly with each other and ultimately agreed that the Soviet Union would dismantle the missile systems it had constructed and return them to Soviet territory. The United States would pledge that it would not invade Cuba, and the United Nations would verify the dismantling of the missile sites.

Thant was unsuccessful, however, in his efforts to induce the Cuban government to agree to UN or any other system of site inspection. Even Soviet attempts to get Castro to change his mind were unsuccessful. The agreement regarding the dismantling of the missiles held together, nonetheless, because the United States decided it could adequately verify the dismantling of the missiles through aerial reconnaissance and naval checks on the high seas.

In sum, then, although the secretary-general played only a tangential role in the Cuban missile crisis, he did perform a crucially important if not indispensable function in facilitating the start of negotiations, urging that the parties to the conflict take steps to minimize the risk of direct military confrontation, and making the services of the United Nations available for verification purposes. Without the secretary-general and the United Nations available as a face-saving device, it would have been much more difficult for the Soviet Union to back down, and the resultant danger to world peace would have been substantially greater.

Thant also received high marks from member states for his efforts in resolving the dispute between the Netherlands and Indonesia over Dutch New Guinea (West Irian)[18] and the 1962 civil conflict in

Yemen, where the secretary-general's plan for the United Nations Yemen Observation Mission (UNYOM) was approved by the Security Council.[19] He was instrumental in settling the debate among Indonesia, the Philippines, and Malaya over whether Sarawak and North Borneo should be part of the Federation of Malaysia, where the secretary-general, for the first and only time in the history of the organization, served as an arbitrator whose decision the parties to the conflict regarded as binding.[20] He was praised as well for his role as chief administrator of the UNFICYP, the United Nations peace-keeping force in Cyprus.[21] Thant became a highly controversial figure, however, for his actions with respect to the 1967 Arab-Israeli war and the withdrawal of the UNEF. These raised serious general issues regarding the law and policy of peace-keeping.

The formal request from Egypt of the secretary-general for a total withdrawal of the UNEF came on May 18, 1967.[22] Thant convened the UNEF Advisory Committee and informed the members that he had no choice in the matter but to withdraw it as soon as possible. Although there was some disagreement in its ranks, the committee agreed. No one in the committee demanded a meeting of the General Assembly to discuss the Egyptian request.

Thant informed Egypt the same day that the UNEF would be withdrawn without delay. His fears for peace in the area were stated only after the troops were withdrawn and thus could not be part of any negotiations toward maintaining the UNEF's position. Four days after his statement on the withdrawal of the UNEF, a visit to Cairo was cut short when it was announced, while the secretary-general was still enroute, that President Nasser had decided to reinstitute the blockade against Israel in the Strait of Tiran. Despite efforts by the United States to gain support for a declaration and perhaps international action to open the Gulf of Aqaba, the blockade remained in effect. The conflict escalated quickly, and on June 5, Israel launched its attack on several airfields in surrounding Arab countries. The war had begun.

Reaction to the secretary-general's actions reflected a reversal in the traditional attitudes toward the scope of his powers. With the exception of its objections to Trygve Lie's initiatives over the Iranian issue, the United States had strongly supported an independent role for the secretary-general, while the Soviet Union had consistently insisted on strict control by the Security Council of all facets of peace-keeping. But it was the United States that was sharply critical of Thant for not seeking advice from a more representative political body than the UNEF Advisory Committee; for its part the Soviet Union, as well as France, raised no objection to Thant's precipitous withdrawal of the UNEF.

The legal issue revolved around whether Thant was bound by an understanding reached between Hammarskjöld and President Nasser in 1956 that the UNEF would not be withdrawn until its tasks had been completed and that, if there were a question as to whether the tasks had been completed, the issue would go to the General Assembly for discussion and an attempt to reach agreement. If, after such discussion, it proved impossible to reach agreement, the United Arab Republic's request would be controlling, but only after the issue had been subjected to public discussion.

The only evidence of this understanding, however, was an *aide-mémoire* drafted by Hammarskjöld after his discussions with Nasser. This memorandum, moreover, reflected only Hammarskjöld's interpretation of the understanding reached and was never made an official document or published in any form until June 1967, after the UNEF's withdrawal. At that time it was published by Ernest A. Gross, who had been Hammarskjöld's private attorney when the memorandum was drafted and had been given a copy.[23] It is not clear whether Thant had heard of the memorandum prior to its publication.

In any event, Thant argued that he was not bound by the memorandum because it was not an official UN document and because the UAR government knew nothing about it. The UNEF Advisory Committee had not called for a meeting of the General Assembly, although it was entitled to do so, and the consent of the host state was an indispensable legal basis for the continued functioning of a UN peace-keeping force. Thant contended further that the Hammarskjöld understanding could only apply to the tasks assigned to the UNEF in 1956 "to secure and supervise the cessation of hostilities." In 1957, the UNEF's mandate was broadened to oversee the "scrupulous maintenance of the armistice agreement." The latter tasks, according to Thant, had not been in Hammarskjöld's mind when he negotiated the understanding with Nasser.

To this writer, Thant's arguments that he was not legally bound by Hammarskjöld's *aide-mémoire* are persuasive. Far more cogent, however, are the criticisms of the secretary-general's actions based on political and strategic considerations. Reference of the dispute to the General Assembly, and perhaps to the Security Council, on the ground that withdrawal of the UNEF would create a situation threatening international peace and security would at the very least have bought some time and focused world attention on the seriousness of the developing crisis. This may have given Thant an opportunity to engage in meaningful discussions with Nasser over the matter. Thant argued at the time that delay would have served no useful purpose, that Nasser had warned him prior to withdrawal that appeals for the UNEF's remaining would be viewed as a hostile act, that India and Yugoslavia were determined to pull out their contingents regardless of Thant's decision, and that delay might have endangered the safety of UN forces. But these were risks the secretary-general should have been willing to take in light of the risk that the withdrawal of the force posed to world peace. It did not take extraordinary foresight to see that, with the withdrawal of the UNEF, war in the Middle East became inevitable.

The unfortunate, indeed tragic, consequences of Thant's precipitous withdrawal of the UNEF have been aptly pinpointed by Arthur Rovine:

> If the powers involved in a conflict want war, then obviously the UN and the Secretary-General are powerless to prevent it. It was never certain prior to UNEF's withdrawal, however, that the states concerned did prefer war, and thus the need for even the most marginal of possible restraints. The Secretary-General is obligated in any crisis to work to persuade the parties that peaceful settlement is preferable to violent change, but persuasion implies influence, and the shortcoming in Thant's response to Cairo was that he worked at peace-making only after he had been deprived of his best source of influence.
>
> The ultimate instruction to be derived from the UN's failure is the essential need for the Organization to devote far greater effort and resources to the functions of peace-making, as well as peace-keeping. This implies a greater use of the traditional diplomatic skills of mediation and negotiation by the Secretary-General. The UN should have been continually at work between 1956 and 1967 in the Middle East in terms of long-range settlement, rather than mere passive interposition. Perhaps here lies a fruitful path to development of the powers of the UN's chief executive.[24]

KURT WALDHEIM

Regardless of the soundness of his decision in law and policy, Thant's decision to withdraw the UNEF without reference to one of the political organs of the United Nations was in keeping with, and arguably even went beyond, the degree of independence exercised by his predecessors. His successor did not enjoy the same luxury.

Despite the objections of the Soviet Union, the standard practice during the tenures of Lie, Hammarskjöld, and Thant was for the secretary-general to receive a general mandate from a competent organ of the United Nations to establish a peace force. He then would negotiate largely on his own initiative the necessary agreement with the states involved, determine the composition of the UN force, appoint its commander, and issue political instructions for the conduct of operations. However, with the emergence of the Afro-Asian bloc at the United Nations, coupled with American displeasure over Thant's withdrawal of the UNEF and its perception he had been less than neutral over Vietnam and ineffective in dealing with the India-Pakistan conflict, the United States became more sympathetic toward the Soviet position. Partly because of this shift in position, when the UNEF was reestablished in the Middle East after the 1973 Arab-Israeli conflict, the force was established by the Security Council ·rather than by the General Assembly, and Waldheim was subject to close control by the council. His appointment of commander and his selection of units to compose the force, for example, were specifically endorsed by the council. In return for this endorsement of its views regarding peace-keeping, the Soviet Union raised no objection to the costs of the force being considered "expenses of the Organization" and funded as part of the General Assembly's budget.[25]

Although Waldheim did not enjoy the freedom of action his predecessors had with respect to the establishment and direction of peace-keeping forces, he nonetheless was an "activist" secretary-general. Even with respect to peace-keeping forces he was more than just an automaton carrying out the orders of the Security Council. This especially was the case with respect to the UNIFIL, the peace-keeping force in Lebanon. There, the Security Council's mandate was that the UN force should confirm the withdrawal of Israeli forces, establish the peaceful nature of its area of operations, ensure that the area was not used for hostile acts of any kind, and facilitate the restoration of the authority of the Lebanese government in the area.[26] The UNIFIL has had to operate, however, without a precise agreement between the opposing parties and in an area where there has been little or no exercise of authority by the Lebanese government. As a result, "the performance of these tasks required careful interpretation by the Secretary General and skillful handling by the commander in the field."[27]

Waldheim was also active in "quiet diplomacy," seeking to mediate armed conflicts in Cyprus, Yemen, and Indo-China, and between India and Pakistan, and North and South Korea. In May of 1969 he helped to bring about an agreement between the Greek and Turkish communities in Cyprus on a ten-point program to resume intercommunal talks, which, unfortunately, were unsuccessful in resolving the conflict.[28]

Waldheim also spoke out forcefully on occasion by way of critical comment. As a result of his public statement of July 24, 1972, disapproving of American bombing of dikes in North Vietnam, President Nixon publicly denounced him for bias regarding the conflict.[29] Statements he made on the Middle East and Northern Ireland, for example, also incurred the wrath of member governments of the United Nations. More generally, he decried the failure of states to refer disputes to the United Nations until they have broken out into armed conflict, and one side or the other is in danger of losing on the battlefield.[30]

In practice, then, Secretary-General Waldheim, like his predecessors, sought to fill vacuums left by the failure of member states to fulfill their responsibilities under the Charter regarding the peaceful settlement of disputes and the inability of the political organs of the UN, especially the Security Council, to maintain the peace. Waldheim, as we shall see in Chapter 15, even explicitly invoked the seldom-utilized powers of the secretary-general available under Article 99 in his efforts to resolve the Iran hostage crisis. The relative disuse of these powers, available when member states themselves decline to refer disputes threatening international peace and security to the United Nations, has been a common failing and one that should be remedied as a matter of high priority.

On December 15, 1981, the General Assembly appointed Javier Pérez de Cuéllar of Peru the fifth secretary-general of the United Nations.[31] Thus Waldeim's term came to a close after ten years of service.

JAVIER PÉREZ DE CUÉLLAR

Javier Pérez de Cuéllar did not have to wait long to receive his baptism of fire. His debut as a peacemaker was delayed, however, since, shortly after Argentina invaded the Falkland Islands, American secretary of state Alexander Haig, under directive from President Ronald Reagan, offered his "good offices" as a mediator. Pérez de Cuéllar defended his passive role in response to the crisis by stating that he wanted to avoid doing anything to damage Haig's "admirable" mediation efforts.[32]

With the collapse of the Haig mission, the secretary-general began an intensive effort to find a peaceful solution to the crisis.[33] To this end he reportedly proposed a plan that called for a cease-fire, withdrawal of Argentine troops from the Falklands and the British fleet from the area, and a temporary administration of the islands by the United Nations while negotiations between Argentina and Great Britain were conducted under UN auspices. The secretary-general undertook his mission despite the absence of a formal mandate or a request from the Security Council that he do so.[34]

As indicated earlier in Chapter 3, the secretary-general's mission ended in a stalemate, and the British launched their invasion to retake the islands. According to reports,[35] however, this mission very nearly resulted in a peaceful resolution of the dispute. In private negotiations with the parties, the secretary-general apparently succeeded in obtaining their agreement on a cease-fire, joint withdrawal in stages by both sides, temporary United Nations administration of the islands, and direct bargaining by the two sides without advance conditions until the end of 1982 to settle definitively which flag should fly over the Falklands. Disagreement still reportedly existed regarding certain aspects of the temporary UN administration; pro-visions for extending the direct talks if they were deadlocked on December 31, 1982; how far the two forces should withdraw; and whether South Georgia Island and the South Sandwich Islands, now under British control, should be included in the agreement, a provision Argentina sought and Britain resisted.[36]

However, according to the secretary-general's report, the final Argentine and British responses to his proposals received on May 17, only four days before the British invasion of the Falklands, represented a return to earlier, and less flexible, positions. The secretary-general did not specify precisely how the written replies he had received differed from the tentative accord he thought had been reached. But it appears that the negotiations ultimately broke down over the issue of sovereignty over the islands. Argentina demanded some form of assurance before withdrawal that Britain would recognize its sovereignty over the islands, while Britain insisted the principle of self-determination required that the wishes of the islanders should be paramount.[37]

As noted in Chapter 3, the Security Council called upon the secretary-general, five days after the British invasion of the islands, to renew his mission and to negotiate a mutually acceptable cease-fire.[38] The inability of the secretary-general to do so appears to have been due largely to a change in the British position that denied the possibility of an interim UN administration and insisted instead on unilateral withdrawal of Argentine troops and unfettered British control of the islands.[39]

From the record, it is difficult to fault Pérez de Cuéllar's performance as a mediator during the Falklands crisis. His task was made more difficult by Secretary of State Haig's mission, which delayed and denigrated the secretary-general's efforts. Despite this difficulty, Pérez de Cuéllar succeeded in obtaining the tentative agreement of the parties to a peaceful settlement of their dispute, only to be frustrated by a last-minute return to prior, inflexible positions.

The secretary-general may yet be able to bring about a peaceful settlement of the dispute over the Falklands, if the British government backs away from its current refusal to engage in discussions with Argentina over the future of the islands. One may fervently hope so. Indeed, more generally speaking, the performance of the United Nations in maintaining the peace over the next decade may largely turn on the ability of the new secretary-general to utilize the powers of his office with maximum effectiveness.

NOTES

1. See Leland M. Goodrich, Edvard Hambro, and Anne Patricia Simons, *Charter of the United Nations* (New York and London: Columbia University Press, 1969), p. 574.

2. Article 11(1).

3. See generally, Georges Abi-Saab, *The United Nations Operation in the Congo 1960–64* (Oxford and New York: Oxford University Press, 1978).

4. Article 7(1) of the UN Charter.

5. Article 2 of the Covenant of the League.

6. Statute of the International Law Commission, Article 17, Doc. A/CN. 4/4.

7. Stephen M. Schwebel, *The Secretary-General of the United Nations* (Cambridge: Harvard University Press, 1952), p. 47.

8. The following discussion of Trygve Lie's tenure is taken largely from Arthur W. Rovine, *The First Fifty Years: The Secretary General in World Politics 1920–1970* (Leyden: A. W. Sijthoff, 1970), pp. 201–69.

9. Ibid., pp. 226–29.

10. Ibid., pp. 230–36.

11. The following discussion of Dag Hammarskjöld's tenure as secretary-general is based largely on ibid., pp. 271–340.

12. Ibid., p. 287.

13. G.A. Res. 1001 (ES-I), 7 November 1956.

14. Arthur W. Rovine, *The First Fifty Years,* p. 294.

15. The following discussion of U Thant's tenure as secretary-general is based largely on ibid., pp. 341–414.

16. Ibid., p. 370.

17. Quoted in ibid., p. 371.

18. Ibid., pp. 362–68.

19. Ibid., pp. 375–77.

20. Ibid., pp. 377–81.

21. Ibid., pp. 375–77.

22. Ibid., p. 395.

23. Ibid., p. 398. Gross referred to the memorandum in a letter to the *New York Times* challenging the legal right of the UAR to withdraw the UNEF unilaterally and the propriety of the secretary-general's compliance. *New York Times,* May 26, 1967, p. 46. The memorandum was published in the *New York Times,* June 19, 1967, p. 12.

24. Arthur W. Rovine, *The First Fifty Years,* pp. 399–400.

25. See Max Jakobson, "Detente Nourishes a new UN," *Saturday Review World,* March 23, 1974, pp. 10–14.

26. Kurt Waldheim, *Building the Future Order,* (New York and London: The Free Press, 1980), p. 45.

27. Ibid., p. 46.

28. Ibid., p. 42.

29. See Milton Viorst, "Kurt Waldheim: Embattled Peacemaker," *The Saturday Review,* Sept. 23, 1972, pp. 39–44.

30. See *UN Monthly Chronicle,* May, 1975, pp. 36–8.

31. *UN Chronicle,* February, 1982, p. 5

32. *New York Times,* April 16, 1982, p. A–10.

33. Ibid., May 3, 1982, p. A–13.

34. Ibid., May 6, 1982, p. A–17.

35. See. e.g., ibid., May 8, 1982, p. A–5.

36. Ibid., May 22, 1982, p. A–1, 9.

37. See ibid.

38. S.C. Res. 505 (1982).

39. *Washington Post,* June 4, 1982, p. A–23.

SIX

The International Court of Justice

There have been a number of substantial recent studies devoted to determining why the International Court of Justice has not lived up to the expectation of its creators that: "The judicial process will have a central place in the plans of the United Nations for the settlement of international disputes by peaceful means."[1] Among the reasons most often advanced for the court's modest accomplishments in this area are: (a) adjudication necessarily involves a clear winner and loser, and states are unwilling to risk a loss in a case involving their vital interests as they perceive them; (b) in the atmosphere of the cold war, and because of the Marxist-Leninist ideology, communist states refuse to believe that third-party decision makers can be neutral; (c) third world states believe that international law was developed by the colonial powers as a tool designed to aid in the exploitation of their colonies; (d) the United States failed to support the court when it incorporated the so-called "Connally Amendment" into its acceptance of the court's compulsory jurisdiction, reserving to itself the right to determine whether a matter was "essentially within its domestic jurisdiction;" (e) many states perceive that the court has based certain decisions on political rather than legal considerations; and (f) the vague and fragmentary nature of international law discourages recourse to the court.

From the outset, states demonstrated their distrust of the International Court of Justice. Although the court was designated as "the principal judicial organ of the United Nations,"[2] the drafters of the Charter declined to accept proposals to make the court "a supreme court within the international administrative system" with "the power to settle conflicts of competence between international bodies" or decide the boundaries between international and domestic jurisdiction.[3] They also rejected proposals to make the jurisdiction of the court over legal disputes compulsory.[4]

Not everyone has decried the limited use that the United Nations or member states have made of the court as a means of controlling international violence. Inis Claude, an eminent authority on the United Nations, has put the case most cogently:

> The United Nations has clearly contributed little to establishing the sanctity of the principle of judicial decision. Its political organs have been little inclined to emphasize the legal approach to accommodation, a tendency which I think is sound even though it may not have been motivated by the right reasons. In at least one contentious case, the World Court has made it clear that judicial settlement may be virtually useless because of deficiencies in the law which the Court may apply. Ruling on the Asylum Case involving Colombia and Peru, the tribunal could do little more than state the indecisive conclusions dictated by the relevant international law, and advise the parties that they must look to political processes for a means of escape from the impasse in which they found themselves. More generally, the judicial approach is limited by the fact that, given the fundamental nature of the major disputes that arise in international relations, a judgment does not constitute a settlement. One can admit that the much-disputed line between legal and political questions is purely a subjective phenomenon of the minds and wills of the disputants, but the conclusion still emerges that many issues will be as far from settlement after a judge has said all that a judge can properly say as they were before such pronouncement. Indeed, the authoritative statement of legal rights and wrongs may even impede settlement, by encouraging self-assertive rigidity on one side and self-defensive rigidity on the other; the combination of an emboldened and a beleaguered party is not conducive to the political compromise that is required for the solution of critical problems in the relationships of states. When the International Court of Justice ruled that Ethiopia and Liberia were not legally competent to invoke a judicial evaluation of South Africa's policy in South-West Africa in the judgment of 1966 pertaining to that territory, this certainly contributed nothing to the diminution of the passions and prejudices on either side of the controversy. South Africa, relishing a limited but significant judicial victory, has disdained to make concessions to its antagonists, while the latter, smarting with anger at the frustration inflicted upon them by the Court, have renewed their emphasis upon political means for conducting the campaign against South Africa. If, on the other hand, the case had resulted in a victory for the applicants, there is every reason to suspect that the effect would have been to add judicial fuel to the political fire rather than to turn a judicial fire extinguisher upon the flames of political antagonism. Black African states, feeling vindicated, would surely not have been inspired to reduce

their pressure upon South Africa, and it is doubtful that the latter, feeling more persecuted than ever, would have been inclined to reduce its resistance. The United Nations may not have achieved the ideal balance between legal and political approaches to pacific settlement, but it has been on sound ground in rejecting primary reliance upon the device of adjudication.[5]

With respect to South-West Africa, or Namibia as it is now called, the court in 1971 "redeemed" itself in an advisory opinion by indicating, among other things, that the General Assembly had the authority to terminate South Africa's mandate over South-West Africa, and that the application of South Africa's *apartheid* policies to the territory violated international norms of human rights.[6] Indeed, as predicted by Claude, black African states have increased their pressure on South Africa. However, although initially South Africa's reaction was to reject the opinion as politically motivated and to harden its resistance, it has recently shown some signs of being willing to reach a settlement on the issue. It is at least arguable that the common perception that South Africa's continued occupation of Namibia is illegal—based on the court's opinion—may have contributed in some measure to a change in South Africa's posture, although, to be sure, increased guerrilla activity in the territory has surely been the most important factor.

In any event, Claude's basic point that primary reliance should not be placed on international adjudication as a means of controlling international violence is sound. Moreoever, while Claude is a political scientist, international lawyers have made a similar point. Abram Chayes, a former Legal Adviser of the United States Department of State, has warned against a "court-centered view, in which the health of international law is measured by the congestion of the World Court's docket...."[7] He has suggested further that this view "created the wrong kind of expectations about interntional law, expectations that are bound to be disappointed."[8] The same may be said of expectations that the International Court of Justice should play a major role in maintaining international peace and security.

On the other hand, the Claude view may be a bit of an exaggeration. Let us examine a few illustrative cases to determine what contributions the court has made to maintaining international peace. Ironically, these are cases where, at first blush, recourse to the court appears to have been a failure: where the judgment of the court has not been carried out or where the respondent state has refused to recognize the court's jurisdiction.

CORFU CHANNEL CASE *(UNITED KINGDOM v. ALBANIA)*

Shortly after its creation in 1946, the International Court of Justice had an opportunity to hand down a decision that greatly clarified the law of passage through international straits, as well as the obligation of states not to allow their territory to be used for acts of force violating the rights of other states.[9] In that case, on May 15, 1949, two British cruisers, while passing southward through the North Corfu Channel, were fired upon by an Albanian battery. Neither of the ships was hit, but the British government filed an immediate protest with the Albanian government. The Albanian government responded that foreign warships and merchant vessels had no right to pass through Albanian territorial waters without prior notification to, and the permission of, Albanian authorities. Great Britain, however, maintained its view that there was a right of innocent passage through straits forming routes for maritime traffic between two parts of the high seas and warned that if Albanian coastal batteries in the future opened fire on any British warship passing through the Corfu Strait, the fire would be returned.

On October 22, a squadron of British warships left the port of Corfu and proceeded northward through a channel previously swept for mines in the North Corfu Strait. During passage through the strait two of the British ships struck mines with consequent heavy damage and loss of life.

Three weeks later, on November 13, the North Corfu Channel was swept by British minesweepers and twenty-two moored mines were cut. Two of these mines were taken to Malta for examination.

In its action before the International Court of Justice, Great Britian alleged that Albania was responsible under international law for the explosions and for the damage and loss of life that resulted from them, and was therefore obligated to pay compensation. By way of counterclaim, Albania alleged that Great Britian had violated its territorial sovereignty by its passage through the channel on October 22 without obtaining permission from Albania and by its mine sweeping operation on November 13.

The court rejected Albania's contention that the British government violated Albanian sovereignty by sending its warships through the channel without Albania's previous authorization. According to the court, states in time of peace have a right to send their warships through straits used for international navigation between two parts of the high seas without the previous authorization of the coastal state provided the passage is innocent.

The court then ruled that the laying of the minefield could not have been accomplished without Albania's knowledge and that therefore Albania was under an obligation to warn Great Britain of the danger. It stated that this obligation was based on "certain general and well-recognized principles; namely: elementary considerations of humanity, even more exacting in peace than in war; the principle of the freedom of maritime communication; and every state's obligation not to allow knowingly its territory to be used for acts contrary to the rights of other states."[10] In light of its failure to fulfill this obligation and the consequent damage, Albania was obliged to pay compensation to Great Britain.

On the other hand, the court also held that the United Kingdom had no right to reenter Albania's waters in search of mine fragments, either as a means of preserving evidence regarding the earlier explosions or as a measure of self-help.

The court found that Albania owed the United Kingdom 843,947 pounds, but attempts to reach a compromise figure between the parties failed, and Albania never paid the judgment. Nonetheless, by its judgment, the court reaffirmed two important principles relating to the control of traditional international violence. First, that a state is under an obligation not to allow its territory to be used by others to commit acts that violate the rights of other states; and second, that a state has no right to use force by way of self-help, to violate the territorial integrity of another state. These two principles, tenuous though they may be under current circumstances, are fundamental to the maintenance of international peace and security.

CERTAIN EXPENSES CASE

As we have seen earlier, in the Certain Expenses case,[11] the International Court of Justice advised that the General Assembly acted within its authority in establishing the UNEF in 1956, and that the Security Council could authorize the use of force in the Congo despite the absence of Article 43 agreements so long as the force was utilized in accordance with the consent of the government in power and the entity against which the force was utilized (the province of Katanga) did not constitute a state. In the opinion of the court, both operations were peace-keeping rather than enforcement actions requiring the presence of Article 43 arrangements.

The opinion has been criticized as "wallowing in politics and giving it the name of law,"[12] and some have argued that the court should have declined to answer the General Assembly's question on the ground of its ambiguous language.[13] However, although inelegantly phrased, the question raised profound issues of the constitutional allocation of responsibility between the General Assembly and the Security Council for maintaining the peace; these were legal issues appropriate for consideration by the principal judicial organ of the United Nations.

In the event, the court upheld the legality of two of the most important efforts in United Nations history in maintaining the peace and ensured that the organization would not be powerless to act in situations where the Security Council was blocked by the veto of a permanent member. The court did so, moreover, in a majority opinion that, in this writer's opinion, was closely reasoned and aptly supported by citation to Charter provisions and UN practice. Although it is probably true that the drafters of the Charter did not envisage peace-keeping operations like the UNEF or ONUC, neither did they so limit the powers of organs other than the Security Council as to preclude their creation of peace-keeping forces.

To be sure, as we noted in Chapter 4, for political reasons the views of the United States and the Soviet Union on peace-keeping have tended to converge, the General Assembly is unlikely to establish a peace-keeping force in the near future; nor is the secretary-general likely to enjoy the relatively freewheeling independence that Dag Hammarskjöld enjoyed in the Congo. Nonetheless, in the Certain Expenses case, the court established the principle that the Security Council enjoys only primary and not exclusive authority in maintaining international peace and security, and, if the political situation shifts, this residual authority of organs other than the council to act may again become important. Legal constraints on the United Nations actions, if confirmed by the court, would have been a near-insurmountable barrier to the organization taking effective action with respect to the control of international violence.

FISHERIES JURISDICTION CASE
(UNITED KINGDOM v. ICELAND)

The so-called "Cod War" between Great Britain and Iceland can trace its origins, in a sense, all the way back to the Anglo-Danish Convention of 1901, which established a three-mile fisheries zone around Iceland in which foreign fishing was prohibited.[14] When Iceland became an independent republic on June 17, 1944, the 1901 treaty was maintained in force.

In 1948, however, the Icelandic parliament enacted a law that gave the Ministry of Fisheries authority to issue regulations establishing conservation zones within the limits of the continental shelf of Iceland, wherein all fisheries would be subject to Icelandic rules and control, provided that such regulations would be enforced only to the extent compatible with agreements with other countries. The reasons given for enactment of the law were that the island's economy depended almost entirely on coastal fishing and the growing efficiency of fishing equipment required action to conserve the available stocks of fish. Passage of the law was followed, on October 3, 1949, by denunication of the 1901 convention, which as a result expired on October 3, 1951. When Iceland then tried to regulate fishing off its shores beyond the three-mile limit, it came into conflict with the United Kingdom, the Federal Republic of Germany, as well as other states.

The parties to this conflict hoped that it might be settled by the 1958 Conference on the Law of the Sea. When the conference failed to settle the issue, Iceland issued regulations establishing an exclusive twelve-mile fishing zone around its coastline. This led to further incidents, and, when the second Law of the Sea Conference in 1960 failed to resolve the matter, Iceland, the Federal Republic of Germany, and the United Kingdom entered into negotiations.

On March 11, 1961, the United Kingdom and Iceland exchanged notes, under which the United Kingdom agreed that it would drop its objections to a twelve-mile fishery zone around Iceland, measured from certain specified baselines. For its part, Iceland would not object to United Kingdom fishing within certain areas of the twelve-mile zone at specified times during the year for a period of three years, beginning on March 10, 1964. Iceland indicated it would continue to work for implementation of the resolution regarding extension of fishing jurisdiction, but that it would give to the United Kingdom six months notice of any extension beyond the twelve-mile zone. In the event of a dispute regarding any such extension, either party might refer the matter to the International Court of Justice. Substantially identical provisions were included in notes exchanged between Iceland and the Federal Republic of Germany on July 19, 1961.

On July 14, 1971, Iceland announced that the 1961 agreements were terminated and that it was extending its fisheries jurisdiction to fifty nautical miles effective as of September 1, 1972. Iceland also claimed that the objectives and purposes of the 1961 provision for recourse to judicial settlement concerning the extension of fisheries jurisdiction were no longer valid. In response, the United Kingdom and the Federal Republic of Germany instituted proceedings against Iceland during the first half of 1972 and later asked for an indication of interim measures of protection from the court.[15] Iceland advised the court that it had no basis to exercise jurisdiction, that the issue involved "the vital interests" of Iceland, and that therefore it was unwilling to concede jurisdiction and appoint an agent.

The court nonetheless proceeded to indicate on August 17, 1972, interim measures of protection that imposed ceilings on annual catches of the United Kingdom and the Federal Republic of Germany. On February 2, 1973, in the absence of Icelandic pleadings, representation, and submissions, the court delivered two judgments, which held that it possessed jurisdiction to entertain the case and deal with the merits of the dispute. Pending its final decision, by eleven votes to three, the court issued, on July 12, 1973, two orders that confirmed the interim measures indicated in the orders of August 17, 1972. But Iceland's response was the same as it had been in 1972; it would not consider the orders binding and would continue to extend its fisheries jurisdiction.

This refusal precipitated conflict, particularly between British and Icelandic vessels, but at times involving German ships as well. The conflict lasted for over a year. It ended with an interim agreement of November 13, 1973, that did not affect the legal position or rights of either party with respect to the substantive issues.

In its Judgment on the Merits of July 25, 1974,[16] the court, as a preliminary matter, concluded that its jurisdiction of the case had not been affected in any way by the November 13 agreement. Turning to the merits, however, the court declined to rule on whether Iceland's extension of its exclusive fishing zone to fifty miles was in accordance with international law. Rather, it found that, while Iceland enjoyed "preferential rights for a coastal state in a situation of special dependence on coastal fisheries,"[17] its regulations of 1972 went beyond this concept and attempted to establish an exclusive fishing zone in disregard of the rights of other states, particularly the United Kingdom's, which had been fishing in the area for many years and whose rights Iceland had previously recognized. Thus the court ruled that "Iceland's extension of its exclusive fishery jurisdiction beyond twelve miles is not opposable to the United Kingdom."[18]

The court was then faced with the question of how to effect a reconciliation of the preferential rights of Iceland and the historical rights of the United Kingdom. It concluded that the most appropriate way to do so would be through negotiation between the parties, and that they should therefore be directed to "undertake negotiations in good faith for the equitable solution of their differences concerning their respective fishery rights in the areas...."[19] Although Iceland never recognized the ruling of the court to be binding, negotiations with the United Kingdom did take place and resulted in 1976 in an agreement concerning British fishing in Icelandic waters.[20]

At first blush, the International Court of Justice may appear to have been of little use in resolving the "Cod War." Iceland refused to acknowledge the court's jurisdiction, even declining to appoint an agent to argue the issue. It similarly announced that it regarded the orders and judgments of the court in the case as having no binding effect. However, the Icelandic government did not take the court's proceedings lightly and argued its case to some extent in various communications to the court.

Moreover, in the result the court did not hand down a judgment that threatened Iceland's "vital interests." On the contrary, it recognized Iceland's "preferential rights" based on its position as a coastal state with a special dependence on coastal fisheries. The court only denied that Iceland had exclusive fishing rights in the fifty-mile zone vis-à-vis the United Kingdom and ruled that Iceland's preferential rights had to be balanced against the traditional fishing rights of the United Kingdom. At the same time, the court ruled that the precise balance would have to be reached in good faith negotiations between the parties to the conflict based on equitable considerations as well as law. These good faith negotiations, in fact, took place and resulted in an agreement.

The effect of the Court's proceedings, orders, and judgments in resolving the "Cod War" may be regarded as indirect. Although Iceland denied the court's jursidiction, it proceeded to negotiate as if it believed it was bound by the court's decision that it should do so. The court's sensitivity to the major concerns of the parties to the dispute helped it to hand down a decision that served as a framework for the ultimate settlement of the conflict.

NUCLEAR TESTS CASES *(AUSTRALIA AND NEW ZEALAND v. FRANCE)*

In the Nuclear Tests cases,[21] France had conducted a number of atmospheric nuclear tests that Australia and New Zealand claimed resulted in some radioactive fallout being deposited on their territories. Alleging that further tests might cause irreparable damage, Australia and New Zealand, in separate submissions to the court, sought an interim measure ordering France to cease nuclear tests that could have such an effect.

France, however, contended that the court was manifestly without jurisdiction and that it should therefore drop the case from its docket. For these reasons, France refused to participate in any of the proceedings before the court relative to the dispute.

The court found that there was a *prima facie* basis for its assuming jurisdiction and issued an Interim Order of Protection. Ignoring the order, France conducted further tests. Shortly thereafter, however, the French government completed its testing program and indicated that it would conduct no further atmospheric tests. Australia and New Zealand nonetheless pursued their claims before the court, seeking a judgment declaring that the French tests had violated their rights under international law. The court declined to do so. Noting the applicants' prior assertions that they would be satisfied if France were to cease its testing, the court dismissed their claims as moot. At the same time, the court introduced a point not argued by the parties when it stated that France was bound by its unilateral declaration not to resume atmospheric nuclear testing in the future.

Only a plurality of the judges supported the court's dictum regarding the binding effect of France's unilateral declaration not to resume atmospheric nuclear testing,[22] and the dictum rests on an uncertain legal basis.[23] Nonetheless, as in the Fisheries Jurisdiction case, the court may have played a useful role in defusing a potential threat to the peace. To be sure, one can only speculate about cause and effect in this situation. But it is a fact that, although rejecting the court's interim order, France discontinued its atmospheric nuclear tests shortly after the order was issued. By doing so, France avoided the risk that the court would find that its tests had violated Australia's and New Zealand's rights under international law. Moreover, France did not reject the court's suggestion that it was bound by its unilateral declaration. Perhaps the same scenario would have taken place if no case had been brought before the International Court of Justice, but this is doubtful. At the least the case increased the pressure on France to stop its atmospheric testing, and the court's statement on the binding effect of the French declaration made it more difficult for France to resume such testing.

IRAN HOSTAGES CASE

One could easily conclude that the International Court of Justice played no useful role in controlling international violence during the Iran hostage crisis. Iran refused to participate in the proceedings and ignored an interim order[24] as well as a final judgment[25] of the court that it release the American hostages. After Iran rejected the interim order and while the judgment was pending, the United States launched its abortive rescue mission into Iran, despite a directive in the court's interim order that neither party should do anything pending final judgment that would aggravate the tensions between them. No effort was made in the Security Council to enforce the court's judgment, and there is no evidence that the court's decision in any way influenced the final agreement reached between the United States and Iran regarding release of the hostages.[26]

At a minimum, however, the presence of the court and its assuming jurisdiction over the dispute delayed American recourse to force. It was only after Iran had rejected the interim order of the court, the Soviet Union had vetoed a resolution of the Security Council that would have imposed economic sanctions against Iran for its refusal to release the hostages, and Iran had again threatened the lives of the hostages that the United States decided on the military option.

More important, the court conducted its proceedings in such a way as to obviate any charge that it was biased or that Iran would not enjoy full due process of law were it to decide to appear before the court. In its interim order of December 15, 1979, the court, while declining to accept Iran's contention that the seizure of the hostages was merely a "secondary" or "marginal" matter, noted that it was open to an appearance by Iran before the tribunal to raise, by way of either defense or counterclaim, its charges of alleged United States violations of international law. Iran declined the court's invitation to do so.

The court's impartial and professional handling of the Iran hostages dispute may encourage other states to consider seriously submitting their disputes to settlement by adjudication. Be that as it may, in its order and judgment the court unanimously upheld the inviolability of a diplomat's person and of diplomatic premises—cardinal principles of international law indispensable to maintaining global peace and security. Also, in the wake of the court's decisions there are some encouraging signs that states may redouble their efforts to uphold these principles and to minimize the risk of international violence that violation of them poses.[27]

CONCLUSION

None of the foregoing cases, of course, indicates that the court has played or is likely to play a major role in maintaining the peace. The court's contribution in this area has been much less than was originally expected, while its contribution to the development of legal principles has somewhat exceeded expectations.[28] This situation is unlikely to change. What should be avoided, however, is a conclusion that the court has no meaningful role to play in the control of international violence. As we have seen above in the Fisheries Jurisdiction, Nuclear Tests, and Iran Hostages cases the court may be able to make a contribution to the control of international violence even where the defendant state refuses to acknowledge the court's jurisdiction. At a minimum, the court remains one of the means of peaceful settlement that states may turn to as an alternative to the use of armed force. Efforts should continue to induce states to make greater use of it.

NOTES

1. Statement made by the Rapporteur of the First Committee in presenting the Statute of the Court to the Fourth Commission at the United Nations Conference on International Organization, quoted in Leo Gross, "The International Court of Justice: Consideration of its Role in the International Legal Order," Leo Gross (ed.), *The Future of the International Court of Justice* (Dobbs Ferry: Oceana, 1976), vol. 1, p. 22.

2. Article 92 of the United Nations Charter.

3. See *The United Nations Conference on International Organization: Selected Documents,* pp. 162, 179–181.

4. Leland M. Goodrich, Edvard Hambro, and Anne Patricia Simons, *Charter of the United Nations* (New York and London: Columbia University Press, 1969), p. 545.

5. Inis L. Claude, Jr., *Swords into Plowshares* (New York: Random House, 4th ed., 1971), pp. 234–35.

6. Advisory Opinion on the Continued Presence of South Africa in Namibia (South West Africa) [1971] I.C.J. Rep. 16.

7. Abram Chayes, "A Common Lawyer Looks at International Law," *Harvard Law Review* 78 (1965):1396.

8. Ibid.

9. Corfu Channel Case [1949] I.C.J. Rep. 4.

10. Ibid.

11. Certain Expenses of the United Nations (Advisory Opinion) [1962] I.C.J. Rep. 151.

12. Stanley Hoffmann, "A World Divided and a World Court Confused: The World Court's Advisory Opinion on U.N. Financing," Robert S. Wood (ed.) *The Process of International Organization* (New York: Random House, 1971), pp. 137, 150.

13. Ibid.

14. This background to the fisheries dispute is taken largely from Richard D. Kearney, "Sources of Law and the International Court of Justice," Leo Gross (ed.), *The Future of the International Court of Justice* (Dobbs Ferry: Oceana, 1976), vol. 2, pp. 610, 681–96.

15. Ibid., p. 683.

16. Fisheries Jursidiction (*United Kingdom v. Iceland*) [1974] I.C.J. Rep. 5.

17. Ibid., p. 25.

18. Ibid., p. 29.

19. Ibid., pp. 34–35.

20. "Iceland-United Kingdom Agreement on British Fishing in Icelandic Waters, June 1, 1976," *International Legal Materials* 15 (1976):878–90.

21. Nuclear Tests Cases (*Australia v. France*) [1973] I.C.J. 99 and (*New Zealand v. France*) [1973] I.C.J. 135.

22. See Alfred P. Rubin, "The International Legal Effects of Unilateral Declarations," *American Journal of International Law* 71 (1977):1, fn. 3.

23. Ibid.

24. "Case Concerning United States Diplomatic and Consular Staff In Tehran, Interim Order," *International Legal Materials* 19 (Dec. 15, 1979):139–47.

25. "Case Concerning United States Diplomatic and Consular Staff In Tehran, Judgment," *International Legal Materials* 19 (May 24, 1980):553–84.

26. For the texts of the official documents relating to the settlement of the Iran hostage crisis, see *American Journal of International Law* 75 (1981):418–32.

27. See Francis A. Boyle, "International Law in Time of Crisis: From the Entebbe Raid to the Hostages Convention," *Northwestern University Law Review* 75 (1980):769–856.

28. Guenter Weissberg, "The Role of the International Court of Justice in the United Nations System: The First Quarter Century," Leo Gross (ed.), *International Court of Justice*, vol. I, pp. 131, 189.

SEVEN

Traditional International Violence: Overview, Conclusions, and Recommendations

OVERVIEW AND CONCLUSIONS

In evaluating the response of the United Nations to traditional international violence, one has first to determine the appropriate standard to employ. If one adopts an ideal standard—for example, the expectations of the drafters of the UN Charter—there is no question that the United Nations has failed abysmally to cope satisfactorily with traditional international violence. On the other hand, if the standard is the best that could be expected of the United Nations considering the difficult economic, political, and social milieu in which it has had to operate since World War II, the evaluative process becomes more complex.

It is also important to note that the United Nations is not a supranational agency capable of taking action with respect to traditional international violence independently of its member states. Unless member states, especially the permanent members of the Security Council, have the will to utilize the United Nations as an instrument to maintain international peace and security, the provisions of the Charter and organs of the organization designed to this end are of no practical utility.

By now the observation that the breakdown in American/Soviet cooperation following World War II prevented the United Nations from acting as a collective security agency has been so often repeated as to become a cliché. Moreover, like many clichés, it is at best a half-truth. Inis Claude points out that collective security as an approach to peace is difficult to carry out in practice even among allies,[1] and goes on to question the general desirability of collective security on the ground that it ignores "the infinite variety of circumstances, the flux of contingency, the mutability of situations," and that it constitutes an abdication of "the function of applying statesmanlike rationality to problems as they arise."[2]

One must further guard against concluding that the inabilty of the United States and the Soviet Union to agree on the terms of Article 43 agreements rules out cooperation between them in the United Nations with respect to the control of traditional international violence. To be sure such cooperation is not possible in cases where the Soviet Union is itself engaged in aggression or threatening the peace, such as the invasions of Hungary and Afghanistan. But there are many other situations where traditional international violence is contrary to the interests of both superpowers, especially where it threatens to drag one or the other or both into the conflict. Hence the United States and the Soviet Union cooperated, at least ultimately, on the Suez crisis, Security Council Resolution 242, Cyprus, and the Declaration on Friendly Relations.

Even when the United States and the Soviet Union are in confrontation regarding traditional international violence, the United Nations may serve a useful role. At the least it may provide a forum for exposure of acts of aggression or threats to the peace (Hungary, Afghanistan) or for quiet diplomacy and mediation (the Cuban missile crisis).

United Nations actions with respect to Korea, of course, were an historical aberration, and it is unlikely that any future UN peace-keeping force (much less an "enforcement" mission like Korea) will be established without Soviet consent. However, during the 1970s the Soviet Union agreed to the Security Council establishing peace-keeping forces in Cyprus and in Lebanon, a new UNEF force to implement the 1975 Egyptian-Israeli Agreement on Disengagement of Forces, and a United Nations Disengagement Observer Force (UNDOF) for the Golan Heights. The Soviet Union's refusal to agree to an extension of the UNEF's mandate in 1979 was due not to any opposition to peace-keeping forces *per se*, but rather to the Soviet desire to support strong Arab opposition to the Camp David accords and the Egyptian-Israeli peace treaty.

Moreover, the views of the Soviet Union and the United States regarding the principles to govern peace-keeping have become largely congruent.[3] Both countries have agreed, tacitly if not explicitly, that peace-keeping forces are to be established and controlled by the Security Council rather than by the General Assembly. Indeed, the 1962 UN Temporary Executive Authority Force (UNTEA) in West Irian was the last peace-keeping force established by the assembly. Similarly, the secretary-general's actions regarding peace-keeping forces are to be subject to the close scrutiny and control of the council. Although a General Assembly Special Committee on Peace-keeping Operations has been working on the subject of guidelines for peace-keeping forces since 1965 without reaching formal agreement, tacit agreement has been reached on a number of points. Perhaps it is just as well that agreement on formal guidelines has not been reached. Formal guidelines might introduce an undesirable measure of rigidity into the peace-keeping process. Detailed guidelines agreed upon now in the abstract would not necessarily be appropriate for the future in an environment that changes rapidly and unpredictably. It is difficult if not impossible to write guidelines that provide for all eventualities. The variables are too many. Reliance on a kind of common law approach to peace-keeping may thus be preferable to the legislative model.

With respect to the performance of individual components of the United Nations, perhaps the secretary-general has come closest to fulfilling the ideal expectations of the organization's founders. Indeed, it is arguable that the secretary-general has exceeded these expectations in filling vacuums left by the failure of UN organs with primary responsibility for controlling traditional international violence to fulfill their responsibilities.

For their part, the Security Council and the International Court of Justice have clearly performed below expectations, but arguably they have done about as well as might be expected in the chaotic post-World War II environment. The record of the General Assembly is mixed, complex, and especially difficult to evaluate. During the early days of the assembly when the United States and the Western European democracies could control the vote, the assembly performed most satisfactorily, from a Western perspective, in adopting the Uniting for Peace resolution over the strong objections of the communist countries, in condemning the People's Republic of China's intervention in North Korea, and in establishing the UNEF in response to the Suez crisis. But in later years, with the influx of new member states from Africa and Asia as a result of the decolonialization process and the rise in influence of the Arab and communist countries, the assembly adopted resolutions and took other actions reflecting an anti-Western bias. Some of these actions inflamed passions and conceivably contributed to an atmosphere that supported traditional international violence. The notorious resolution on Zionism and others on the Arab-Israeli conflict are perhaps the best examples.

On the other hand, even in today's supercharged atmosphere, the record of the General Assembly is not all negative. As noted in Chapter 4, the Declaration on Friendly Relations is a useful affirmation of UN Charter principles regarding the control of traditional international violence. The work of the Special Committee on Peace-keeping Operations has helped to clarify the contending positions of member states and to facilitate a substantial measure of reconciliation between them. The assembly also condemned, although only indirectly, the Soviet Union's blatant aggression in Afghanistan. And there are some encouraging, although still tentative, signs that the heated rhetoric of the 1970s is beginning to abate and that states in the assembly may be willing to turn to a more cooperative and less confrontational style in the 1980s.

With respect to traditional international violence, the law of the United Nations Charter has proved equal to the task. Even if they are often honored in the breach, the prohibitions of Article 2(4) against the threat or use of force against the territorial integrity or political independence of any state have served the world community well. The drafters of the Charter have also been proven right in limiting the sole exception to the strictures of Article 2(4), excluding UN-sponsored use of force, to the inherent right of self-defense as set forth in Article 51. Exercises of "humanitarian intervention"— assuming for the sake of argument that they can be validly so classified—have been generally regarded as extralegal and have not received any formal UN imprimatur of approval. The intervention of India, and the resultant creation of Bangladesh, is not, as we shall see in a later chapter, evidence to the contrary.

It is true, of course, as we have seen and shall see again, that the exact scope of Article 51 has been the subject of debate and that aggressors have devised ingenious interpretations to support claims that their use of force was undertaken in self-defense. However, these states have had to make their arguments within the relatively narrow terms of Article 51. Although ideally one could envisage redrafting Article 51 in order to resolve ambiguities and to close "loopholes," in reality this would surely open a Pandora's box of crippling amendments that would weaken rather than strengthen that provision. Hence the temptation to engage in such an exercise should be resisted.

The record of United Nations efforts to interpret fundamental principles of the Charter regarding the control of traditional international violence has been mixed. If the General Assembly's resolution on the definition of aggression is indeed a "guidepost to the guilty," its Declaration on Friendly Relations may serve to make the journey more difficult. Reliance in UN deliberations on the latter rather than the former document would therefore seem highly desirable.

Because the United Nations has not been able to perform the functions of collective security set forth in Chapter VII of the Charter, forceful responses to traditional international violence will have to come from states acting in the exercise of individual or collective self-defense. The United Nations may still serve a useful role, however, in preventing outbreaks of violence, especially if the secretary-general plays an active role in this regard; in maintaining a ceasefire or implementing a peace treaty through peace-keeping forces; and, perhaps, in facilitating the final resolution of the dispute that precipitated the violence.

The record of the United Nations regarding peaceful settlement is difficult to judge. As Inis Claude has noted, "we cannot really know when any technique for preventing war works successfully. The evidence of failure is provided by the outbreak of war, but if the technique succeeds in averting hostilities the world may never know and scholars can never demonstrate that it was the effective cause of that negative result. In this as in many other realms, disproving is more feasible than confirming."[4] Despite these difficulties, one may conclude with some degree of confidence that the United Nations played a part in preventing or at least delaying the outbreak of traditional international violence during disputes over the Soviet occupation of the Azerbaijan region of Iran, the Berlin Blockade, West New Guinea, the Cuban missile crisis, and Cyprus.

The United Nations has been much less successful in helping to resolve disputes once they have erupted into traditional international violence. The Arab-Israeli conflict and Cyprus are perhaps the best although by no means the only examples. Nonetheless, even in these seemingly intractable cases, the United Nations has taken some useful actions. Examples with respect to the Arab-Israeli conflict would include the UNEF and UNDOF peace-keeping forces and Security Council Resolution 242. As for Cyprus, primary examples would be the UNFICYP, the UN peace-keeping force, and Secretary-General Waldheim's mediation efforts that resulted in the 1969 agreement between the Greek and Turkish communities in Cyprus on a ten-point program to resume intercommunal talks.

Moreover, it does not necessarily follow that, because a dispute remains unresolved, the United Nations has failed to fulfill its responsibilities. On the contrary, as Inis Claude, in his usual incisive fashion, has pointed out:

"Settlement", like "pacific", is a relative term. In some cases, the realistic ideal may be not to achieve the permanent settlement of a dispute, but to persuade the parties to settle down permanently with the dispute. The agenda of the Security Council and the General Assembly are liberally sprinkled with items that are beginning to seem like permanent fixtures, quarrels which the United Nations has managed to subject to peaceful perpetuation rather than peaceful settlement. This is not a cynical comment; many of life's problems are meant to be lived with rather than solved, and the urge to have a showdown, to settle the matter one way or the other, is often an unwise impulse in both personal and international affairs.[5]

RECOMMENDATIONS

As an initial observation, one must conclude that, with respect to traditional international violence, dramatic changes in UN law and institutional arrangements are neither necessary nor desirable. When the United Nations has failed to fulfill its responsibilities, this has not been because the organization has lacked the tools; it has been because member states, especially the superpowers, have been unwilling to use the UN or because, at times, they have actively sought to prevent it from becoming involved with the conflict. The fact noted at the beginning of this chapter, while commonplace, bears repeating: the United Nations is not a supranational organization with independent powers to control traditional international violence. If a significant number of UN members, especially if they enjoy the support of a superpower, decide that it is in their interest to support the use of armed force, there is nothing the United Nations can do.

Still, some modest steps toward reform should be taken. For example, if the secretary-general is to play an active role in preventing traditional international violence, he will need to have an early warning system. There is nominally in existence a UN Peace Observation Commission, which was set up in 1950.[6] But it is now merely a paper organization, nor would its resuscitation be desirable. Rather, a branch of the secretariat should be given primary responsibility for monitoring trouble spots around the world and for bringing especially dangerous situations to the attention of the secretary-general, who in turn should report on developments to the Security Council on a regular basis. The secretary-general should also be strongly encouraged, upon learning of an especially dangerous situation, to offer his good offices or to serve as a mediator for the parties to the conflict.

As we saw in Chapter 6, states have been reluctant to submit their disputes to the International Court of Justice as a means of peaceful settlement. In recent years a number of imaginative proposals for increasing the workload of the court have been advanced by scholars and in official reports.[7] These include expanding the jurisdictional capacity of the court through a "preliminary opinion" procedure, under which appellate national courts should refer any question of international law to the court for its advisory opinion whenever it was the judgment of the national court that such a reference would be desirable before it rendered its own final decision; granting the United Nations the right to appear before the court as a party in contentious proceedings, provided that two-thirds of the General Assembly and the Security Council, including its permanent members, have approved such an appearance; and enlarging the number of international organizations authorized to seek advisory opinions from the court. These proposals are worthy of being pursued for their own merits. None of them, however, is likely to persuade states to become more willing to submit disputes involving their vital interests as they see them to the court.

Of course, as we saw in the Fisheries Jurisdiction, Nuclear Tests, and Iran Hostage cases, the court, in certain circumstances, may decide it has jurisdiction and proceed to render a decision although the respondent state refuses to recognize such jurisdiction or even to appoint an agent to argue its case before the court. While such decisions have arguably contributed to the control of traditional international violence and the eventual settlement of the dispute, the costs of the court rendering decisions under such circumstances may be considerable. The respondent state may withdraw its declaration accepting the compulsory jurisdiction of the Court—as France did after the court's judgment in the Nuclear Tests cases. Also, states may become less willing to agree to the insertion in treaties of so-called compromissory clauses, under which disputes regarding the interpretation or application of a treaty may be referred to the court by either party to the dispute, and may generally become suspicious that the court is a "dangerous branch," which may threaten their vital interests by becoming a tool of their adversaries. Considering these possible costs, one might even conclude that no reference of a dispute to the court should take place except when both parties agree at the time of reference to the court's assuming jurisdiction. This *ad hoc* approach to the court would have the advantage of eliminating long and often legalistic disputes over jurisdiction and ensure compliance with the court's decisions.

The effect of this approach, however, would be to eliminate the compromissory clause in treaties and the court's compulsory jurisdiction under Article 36(2) of its Statute.[8] The jurisdiction of the court in the Fisheries Jurisdiction and Iran Hostages cases was based on compromissory clauses in applicable treaties, and the basis of the court's jurisdiction in the Nuclear Tests cases was the French, Australian, and New Zealand declarations accepting the court's jurisdiction pursuant to Article 36(2). If one believes, as does this writer, that the decisions in these cases contributed in some small measure to controlling traditional international violence, it would seem a mistake to limit access to the court so as to bar the possibility of such cases arising in the future.

Moreover, the fact is that these cases did raise complex and important legal issues deserving of consideration by the principal judicial tribunal of the world community. To eliminate the court's compulsory jursidiction, even in its current limited form, would be to hold law and the legal process hostage to the political currents of the moment.

Finally, although the political milieu is currently not supportive of increased reference of disputes to the court, this may change over time. Even the Soviet Union and Eastern European countries have agreed to third-party arbitration of international business disputes in recent years. The People's Republic of China is undergoing a revolutionary change in constructing a legal system, which includes an elaborate court structure and an emphasis on international law. Most important, as they gain confidence in international relations and in the impartiality of the International Court of Justice, third world countries may become more inclined to refer their disputes to the court. It is noteworthy that, at the time of writing, a case[9] before the court involves a dispute between Tunisia and Libya, two third world countries, over the delimitation of their respective continental shelves—a dispute with the potential to erupt into traditional international violence. The willingness of Libya to submit such a dispute to the court is particulary surprising, since that country is ordinarily known for its support of international violence rather than peaceful settlement. The United States should therefore continue to support, in both its bilateral and multilateral diplomacy, the thesis that the International Court of Justice can play an important role in the peaceful settlement of international disputes. To make the American position more credible, renewed efforts should be made to induce the Senate to repeal the Connally Amendment, which, in effect, negates the acceptance of the compulsory jursidiction of the International Court of Justice.

If the United Nations fails in its efforts to prevent the outbreak of traditional international violence, the problem then becomes one of damage control, i.e., to bring the fighting to a halt as soon as possible. During the Arab-Israeli conflict of 1967, and with respect to the Iraq-Iran war, the United Nations failed to take steps promptly to bring fighting to a halt. To be sure, the parties may ignore UN resolutions calling for a cease-fire. But at a minimum, the United Nations should be utilized as a forum in which the full pressure of publicity and public opinion is brought to bear on the parties to stop the fighting. *Realpolitik* maneuvers, as those employed in the Security Council upon the outbreak of the Iraq-Iran war, not only fail to bring about a cease-fire, but also undermine basic norms of the Charter.

Most important, perhaps, greater efforts should be made to utilize the United Nations as a forum for negotiation, conciliation, and mediation. Despite references by some international lawyers to the quasi-legislative quality of General Assembly resolutions,[10] the United Nations is not a world government with correlative police powers. As Evan Luard has noted,[11] less time should be spent in the drafting of resolutions and in making debating points, and more in promoting negotiations between the parties to a dispute. At the least, he suggests, efforts to draft a resolution as soon as a dispute is referred to the United Nations should be avoided. The wisdom of this advice is well illustrated by UN actions regarding the Arab-Israeli conflict. There the pattern has been to adopt resolution after resolution condemning Israel. These do nothing to resolve the dispute; rather they increase passions and thereby heighten the prospects for traditional international violence. Some have suggested that the passage of such resolutions constitutes "peacebreaking" rather than peacekeeping. This should be avoided.

NOTES

1. Inis L. Claude, *Swords into Plowshares* (New York: Random House, 4th ed., 1971), pp. 245–85.
2. Ibid., p. 278.
3. For a recent discussion of this development, see Richard W. Nelson, "Peacekeeping Aspects of the Egyptian-Israeli Peace Treaty and Consequences for United Nations Peacekeeping," *Denver Journal of International Law and Policy* 10 (1981):113–53.
4. Inis L. Claude, *Swords into Plowshares,* pp. 227–28.
5. Ibid., pp. 236–37.
6. See Evan Luard, *The United Nations* (New York: St Martin's Press, 1979), p. 164.
7. The most substantial scholarly study is the two volume, Leo Gross (ed.), *The Future of the International Court of Justice* (Dobbs Ferry: Oceana, 1976). See also "Study on Widening Access to the International Court of Justice", reprinted in McDowel (ed.), *Digest of U.S. Practice in International Law 1975* (Washington: Department of State, 1976) pp. 650–80.
8. Article 36(2) of the Statute of the International Court of Justice provides:

> The states parties to the present Statute may at any time declare that they recognize as compulsory ipso facto and without special agreement, in relation to any other state accepting the same obligation, the jurisdiction of the Court in all legal disputes concerning:
> (a) The interpretation of a treaty;
> (b) any question of international law;
> (c) the existence of any fact which, if established, would constitute a breach of an international obligation;
> (d) the nature or extent of the reparation to be made for the breach of an international obligation.

9. Case Concerning the Continental Shelf *(Tunisia v. Libyan Arab Jamahiriya).* For the application of the government of Malta to intervene in the case, see *International Legal Materials* 20 (March 1981):329–32.
10. See especially Richard A. Falk, "On the Quasi-Legislative Competence of the General Assembly," *American Journal of International Law* 60 (1966):782–91.
11. Evan Luard, *The United Nations,* p. 163.

PART TWO

The United Nations and Nontraditional International Violence

Not the least of the difficulties associated with revolutionary violence is the problem of determining the facts of the situation. As we have seen in previous chapters, it may be difficult enough to determine the facts in the case of traditional international violence. The problem is greatly compounded with revolutionary violence. There is unlikely to be an impartial third-party observer on hand at the site of the conflict, and even if there is, it may be next to impossible to determine such basic issues as the cause of the conflict, which side enjoys the support of the people, the truth as to allegations regarding gross violations of fundamental human rights, etc.

The aspects of revolutionary violence that pose the greatest challenge to UN law and practice are its ideological, political, and psychological dimensions. Especially strong contributors to the revolutionary milieu have been the forces of communism and nationalism (anticolonialism) as well as the heated reaction by blacks against racism in southern Africa. Hence revolutionary violence, or "wars of national liberation" to use the communist formulation, most often seeks to fulfill one or more of four goals: first, to separate a colony from rule by a colonial power; second, to overthrow a government deemed (by the rebels) to be oppressive; third, to allow minority "peoples" to secede from the territory of a state and establish their own country; and fourth, to overthrow a racist, minority government and install one governed by the majority. These goals are not necessarily mutually exclusive. In South West Africa, or Namibia, the South West Africa People's Organization (SWAPO), a Marxist organization, views South Africa as a colonial, racist, and oppressive power, which it seeks to drive from the territory and replace with a government dominated by blacks. Similarly, the Palestine Liberation Organization, as well as some Arab states, attempts to justify violence against Israel in part on the grounds that it is in colonial, or "settler," control of the West Bank and the Gaza Strip, that it is "racist" in its Zionist doctrine, and that its governance of the occupied territories is an oppressive denial of the inhabitants' right to self-determination.

As Firmage has pointed out,[4] doctrinal support for revolutionary violence bears a striking resemblance to the heavily theological concept of the "just war." Most particularly, as it developed from the Greeks to Saint Thomas Aquinas, the concept of the just war emphasized the justness of the cause of those who resorted to armed force against others. Emphasis was also placed on the identity of the participants. Thus war might be justified if it was undertaken by Roman against barbarian, Christian against infidel, or by Islamic faithful against the unfaithful. These two criteria—the justness of the cause and the identity of the participants—formed the primary bases for the doctrine of just war until Machiavelli shifted the focus to a more secular orientation by stressing state practice rather than the scriptures and declaring that any war was just that was necessary and that necessity was determined by the preservation of the state.[5]

Like their theological predecessors, today's supporters of revolutionary violence stress the justness of their cause and their identity as "freedom fighters" against oppressors, communists against capitalists, colonial people against colonialists, victims against racists, etc. They tend to have a Clausewitzian perception of violence as part of politics, to be used expressly for the accomplishment of political goals.

To be sure, revolutionary ideology is not always the primary precipitating factor of rebellion. Overwhelming social, political, and economic problems within the third world ensure the continuance of a high level of internal violence in those areas of the world. But revolutionaries react to these problems and attempt to exploit them in order to accomplish their own goals, which may have little or no relationship to social conditions within the state.

The norms of classic customary international law regarding foreign participation in internal conflict are, in the words of Professor Firmage, "few, tentative, and to a considerable extent contradictory. Norms governing intervention in civil wars generally veer between two opposite approaches: one stresses the legitimacy of outside support for the incumbent government against either internal political rebellion or secession—an approach that has been described by one author as 'Metternich legitimacy.' The other stresses that 'international law developed a stronger emphasis upon anti-intervention doctrine than upon doctrine favoring constitutional legitimacy.'"[6]

In practice, at least during the nineteenth and early twentieth centuries, the "Metternich legitimacy" approach was favored. Aid to an incumbent government to assist it in dealing with a rebellion was widely regarded as legitimate. If the rebellion grew in size and proved to have some staying power, the situation became more problematic. Under certain circumstances—when they developed a countergovernment, administered a substantial portion of national territory, and fielded a military force capable of doing battle for a considerable length of time—rebels might be accorded insurgent status by third-party states. But such recognition did not give rise to an obligation of neutrality on the part of these third-party states. They remained free to assist the incumbent government and precluded from assisting the insurgents.

Only if the civil war persisted did it become permissible and perhaps obligatory to recognize a condition of belligerency, and then only if certain objective factual conditions existed. These conditions were "the existence of a civil war accompanied by a state of general hostilities; occupation and a measure of orderly administration of a substantial part of national territory by the insurgents; observation of the rules of warfare on the part of the insurgent forces acting under a responsible authority; the practical necessity for Third States to define their attitude to the civil war."[7] Upon formal recognition of a belligerency, a duty of neutrality arose, and each side to the civil conflict was able to exercise belligerent rights.

The classic approach weakened in the early twentieth century as governments defined their relationship to insurgent factions largely in accord with their political preferences rather than on the basis of legal criteria; it collapsed with the Spanish Civil War. During that conflict, within ten days of the revolt by the army officers and before Franco had assumed leadership, both Germany and Italy were providing substantial aid to the Nationalist forces. The attempt of Britain and France to establish a generally accepted policy of neutrality, and their refusal, as well as that of the United States, to provide supplies to the incumbent Loyalist government contributed substantially to the eventual Nationalist victory. Although Mexico and the Soviet Union actively supported the Loyalists, the weight of intervention was heavily in favor of the Nationalist forces.[8] The Spanish Civil War dramatically illustrated what had already become apparent: customary norms of international law purporting to govern intervention in internal conflict had become impotent.

The impact of UN law and practice on the traditional norms governing intervention in internal conflict, as well as on efforts to control revolutionary violence, is uncertain and the subject of heated debate. We turn to this subject in the next section of this chapter.

UNITED NATIONS LAW AND PRACTICE;
DESCRIPTION AND ASSESSMENT

In analyzing United Nations law pertinent to revolutionary violence, one's focus should be on Article 2(4) of the Charter, which requires all member states to "refrain in their international relations from the threat or use of force against the territorial integrity or political independence of any state, or in any other manner inconsistent with the Purposes of the United Nations," and on Article 2(7), which precludes "intervention" by the organization itself in matters "essentially within the domestic jurisdiction of any state . . . ." During the early days of the United Nations, Western states, especially the colonial powers, resisted any UN consideration of colonial policies on the ground that it would be a violation of Article 2(7). Similar arguments were advanced by South Africa in its efforts to preclude the United Nations from critically examining *apartheid* practices at home and in the mandated territory of South West Africa. The arguments revolved around two basic issues: what actions by the United Nations might constitute "intervention," and whether *apartheid* or similar forms of racial discrimination and colonial practices were essentially domestic matters. Although there have been arguments that only "dictatorial interference" would constitute intervention within the meaning of Article 2(7), the generally accepted view is that the dividing line is between United Nations resolutions that make general recommendations and those that make specific recommendations regarding a particular state (or identifiable group of states).[9]

The debate in the United Nations continues over whether racial discrimination practices are essentially domestic matters and over whether forceful efforts to maintain such practices give rise to a right to use revolutionary violence in eradicating them on the part of the victims, as well as a right for third-party states to support such revolutionary violence with arms and material, the provision of safe-haven and bases, etc. The nature of the debate is best illustrated by the controversy surrounding UN actions with respect to southern Africa, i.e., South Africa, South West Africa (Namibia), and Southern Rhodesia (Zimbabwe). Southern Rhodesia is the paradigmatic case and will be explored in some detail in the following subsection. There will also be a brief examination of the situations in South Africa and South West Africa, which are the current focal points of revolutionary violence that promises to increase greatly in magnitude and intensity if the conflicts there are not peacefully resolved.

THE UN AND SOUTHERN AFRICA

The background to UN actions on Rhodesia may be briefly summarized. Southern Rhodesia (the name given Rhodesia when there was a Northern Rhodesia, now Zambia) was classified under the UN Charter as a nonself-governing territory rather than a British colony, although it enjoyed a substantial amount of autonomy within the British system.[10] However, the British had declined to grant the territory independence because it was governed by a white minority (about six percent of the population) that exhibited little willingness to share power with the black majority and that imposed a number of restraints on their economic, social, educational, and legal rights. Negotiations between the British and the governing regime in Southern Rhodesia, headed by Ian Smith, over the constitution to govern the territory when it became independent failed, and on November 11, 1965, Southern Rhodesia issued a "unilateral declaration of independence," (UDI). The declaration was rejected by the United Kingdom, and resolutions by the General Assembly and by the Security Council condemned the "usurpation of power by a racist settler minority."[11] As an initial step towards sanctions, the Security Council found that continuation of the situation caused by the UDI would constitute a threat to the peace and called upon states to cease sending military supplies, including oil and petroleum, to Southern Rhodesia. The council subsequently took more far-reaching steps. In

April 1966, it determined that the situation in Southern Rhodesia had become a current threat to the peace and authorized the United Kingdom to use force, if necessary, to prevent oil from reaching Rhodesia.[12] By December 1966, the council had decided to adopt limited mandatory economic sanctions under Article 41 of the Charter, and in its Resolution 253 of May 29, 1968, the council adopted more detailed and specific sanctions.[13]

Critics of the Security Council's resolutions focused their primary attack on the council's finding that the situation in Southern Rhodesia constituted a threat to international peace and security.[14] In their view actions taken by the Smith regime entirely within its own territory could not constitute a threat to international peace and security. Rather, the threat to international peace and security, if any, came from black African states that threatened to intervene militarily. Hence, they argued, if any sanctions were called for, they should be directed against these black African states and not against Southern Rhodesia. The critics also argued strenuously that the Security Council's action constituted a clear violation of Article 2(7).

In response, defenders of the council's sanctions contended that, under Chapter VII of the Charter, a threat to the peace could consist of a situation, as well as "the threat or use of force against the territorial integrity or political independence of any state" prohibited by Article 2(4).[15] The situation in Southern Rhodesia, the argument continued, threatened the peace in two ways. First, the threat of internal violence in Southern Rhodesia was so great that any outbreak of violence was likely to be of such intensity and magnitude that it would spill over onto the territory of adjoining states. Second, the "racist" actions of the white minority in Southern Rhodesia had so inflamed passions in neighboring black African states that indirect outside support of guerrillas and even direct military intervention was likely. It was also noted that the UDI represented an illegal rebellion against British authority and that nearly all member states of the United Nations regarded the regime as illegal and in flagrant violation of fundamental international human rights norms. Finally, the defenders of the sanctions pointed out that Southern Rhodesia was not a state but a territory and thus Article 2(7) was inapplicable by its terms.

Whatever their legal validity, the economic sanctions against Southern Rhodesia proved to be largely ineffective.[16] The neighboring countries of South Africa and the Portuguese territories openly refused to carry out the sanctions, and a special committee established by the Security Council reported that a number of countries were secretly violating the terms of the embargo. Also, for six years, starting in 1972, the United States began to breach the embargo by importing Rhodesian chrome and other minerals under the so-called Byrd Amendment, named after Senator Harry F. Byrd of Virginia. The

Carter administration obtained repeal of the Byrd Amendment in 1977.

The turning point for the Smith regime was in 1974 when the Salazar dictatorship was overthrown in Portugal, and the Portuguese government decided to grant independence to Portugal's African territories. Independence brought the formation of a black government in Mozambique on Rhodesia's eastern border and intensification of the guerrilla war inside Rhodesia. Under this military pressure, the Smith regime released black nationalist leaders who had been in prison for more than a decade and agreed to negotiate Rhodesia's future with them.

Negotiations proved to be long and arduous. In 1976, the Rhodesia regime, after an effort at mediation by Secretary of State Henry Kissinger, finally accepted in principle the idea of a two-year transition to majority rule with built-in safeguards for whites. However, several rounds of negotiations failed to result in agreement on the details of such an arrangement, and the Carter Administration inherited a disintegrating Rhodesian situation that threatened to bring about a large-scale racial war and intervention by the great powers in southern Africa.

Despite strenuous efforts on the part of the United States and Great Britain to negotiate an end to the fighting and a peaceful passage to majority rule, the situation continued to deteriorate. Apparently convinced that the regime would never surrender white power peacefully, two black leaders, Joshua Nkomo and Robert Mugabe, formed the Patriotic Front to wage a guerrilla war from bases in Zambia and Mozambique. In part because of this pressure, the Smith regime then negotiated an internal settlement with three other black leaders, Bishop Abel T. Muzorewa, the Reverend Ndabaningi Stihole, and Senator Jeremiah Chirau. The external nationalists did not participate in the settlement charging, along with other critics, that the arrangement would reserve real power to the white minority. After elections in 1979, in which the Patriotic Front did not participate, Bishop Muzorewa was installed as the first black Prime Minister of "Zimbabwe-Rhodesia."

Despite considerable pressure to do so, the Carter Administration declined to recognize the internal settlement as legitimate or to recommend that, pursuant to applicable legislation, Congress lift economic sanctions against Rhodesia. This was an important factor in persuading Margaret Thatcher, when she became Prime Minister of the United Kingdom in the spring of 1979, not to fulfill her campaign promise and unilaterally lift economic sanctions against Rhodesia.

Instead, the British government began a new round of consultations in an effort to reach a settlement acceptable to all the parties. These resulted in intense negotiations on a new constitution being held at

Lancaster House, London from September to December 1979 between the British government and the two Rhodesian delegations. As a result of these negotiations, the parties reached agreement on a new constitution that, among other things, instituted majority rule with protection for minority rights and, after a short transition period during which Rhodesia would be under British sovereignty, provided for free and impartial elections open to all political parties and supervised by the British government with observers from the Commonwealth countries.[17]

On December 16, 1979, President Carter lifted American economic sanctions against Rhodesia on the ground that their objective had been achieved, i.e., there had been a return to legality in Rhodesia and a process leading to self-determination and independence had begun. The Security Council followed suit on December 21 when it voted unanimously to call upon member states to lift the sanctions.[18]

Pursuant to the agreements, elections were held on February 27, 1980, and resulted in a landslide victory for Robert Mugabe's party. Six months later, on August 25, Rhodesia, as the state of Zimbabwe, became a member of the United Nations.

Although the proposition is debatable, it appears that, on the whole, economic sanctions had relatively little effect on Southern Rhodesia and that guerrilla activity played a much more substantial role in inducing the Smith regime to agree to the ultimate settlement— despite his earlier claim that "not in a thousand years would blacks govern Rhodesia." An important and perhaps crucial factor in the success of this guerrilla activity, moreover, was the safe haven and bases given the guerrillas by Zambia and Mozambique as well as the arms supplied to the guerrillas by a number of states.

The United Nations did not condemn Zambia and Mozambique for allowing the guerrillas to establish bases in their territory; nor did it express concern over the supply of arms to these guerrillas by member states. On the contrary, in 1976, for example, only four states, including the United States, voted against a General Assembly resolution on self-determination[19] that gave unqualified approval to the use of armed force in order to allow the people of Palestine, Namibia, Rhodesia, and South Africa to exercise their right to self-determination. Encouraged by this imprimatur of UN approval, active military support of revolutionary groups in these areas has been forthcoming from many countries.

The legality of such support and of the UN's approval of it must be analyzed in terms of Article 2(4)'s prohibition of "the threat or use of force against the territorial integrity or political independence of any state." Article 2(4), in turn, has been interpreted and applied with a degree of specificity by the General Assembly's Declaration on Friendly Relations and by its Definition of Aggression. In pertinent part the Declaration on Friendly Relations[20] provides:

Every State has the duty to refrain from organizing, instigating, assisting or participating in acts of civil strife or terrorist acts in another state or acquiescing in organized activities within its territory directed towards the commission of such acts, when the acts referred to in the present paragraph involve a use of force.

Every State has the duty to refrain from any forcible action which deprives peoples . . . of their right to self-determination and freedom and independence. In their actions against, and resistance to, such forcible action in pursuit of the exercise of their right to self-determination, such peoples are entitled to seek and to receive support in accordance with the purposes and principles of the Charter.

Nothing in the foregoing paragraphs shall be construed as authorizing or encouraging any action which would dismember or impair, totally or in part, the territorial integrity or political unity of sovereign and independent States conducting themselves in compliance with the principle of equal rights and self-determination of peoples as described above and possessed of a government representing the whole people belonging to the territory without distinction as to race, creed or colour.

Similarly, the assembly's Definition of Aggression[21] contains a provision that:

Nothing in this definition . . . could in any way prejudice the right to self-determination, freedom and independence, as derived from the Charter, of peoples forcibly deprived of that right and referred to in the Declaration on Principles of International Law concerning Friendly Relations and Cooperation among States in accordance with the Charter of the United Nations, particularly peoples under colonial and racist regimes or other forms of alien domination; nor the right of these peoples to struggle to that end and to seek and receive support, in accordance with the principles of the Charter and in conformity with the above-mentioned Declaration.

As Stephen Schwebel has pointed out, these provisions "appear to concede much to doctrines of wars of liberation, if not in terms, then in substance."[22] Their recognition of a right of internal revolution is simply a codification of traditional customary international law. More far-reaching and controversial is the Declaration on Friendly Relations' imposition of a duty on states not to suppress revolutions for self-determination and freedom and independence. In practice, these provisions are difficult to apply because of disputes over the definition of the terms self-determination, freedom, and independence.

The key issue, however, is whether these provisions support the proposition that peoples fighting for self-determination and freedom and independence have the right to seek and receive *armed assistance.* The position of the United States and other Western states is that they do not. In support of their view, they point out that these provisions do not specify "armed" support and that the support allowed must be "in accordance with the purposes and principles of the Charter." Since the overriding purpose of the Charter is the maintenance of peace and security, the argument continues, the Declaration on Friendly Relations in particular "does not constitute a license for gun-running."[23]

This interpretation of the declaration as categorically excluding armed support for rebels is opposed by the great majority of UN member states, or at the least it is opposed as applied to particular contexts, most especially in southern Africa. Under this view, although the maintenance of international peace and security may be the paramount principle and purpose of the UN Charter, it is not an absolute, and other primary goals of the United Nations must be taken into account. The right of people to self-determination, freedom, and independence must not be frustrated, and, if it is frustrated by forcible means, such people have a right to resist through armed force and to seek and receive outside assistance to this end.[24] The provision of such assistance by outside states does not violate Article 2(4) because it is consistent rather than inconsistent with the purposes of the United Nations. With respect to Rhodesia and Namibia, the argument adds, Article 2(4) is simply inapplicable by its terms since neither entity is a state under international law.

It should be noted that UN approval of revolutionary violence has been infrequent, highly selective, and serving of special interests. Indeed, as a general matter, the United Nations has been unwilling even to lend moral support for revolutionary violence, much less to approve the furnishing of armed support for it. This conservative approach to revolutionary violence is demonstrated by the organization's approach to Biafra's war of secession against the central government in Lagos, Nigeria, and to the conflict between West and East Pakistan, which resulted in armed intervention by India and the creation of Bangladesh. In the case of Biafra, the United Nations maintained a position of strict neutrality regarding the merits of the conflict and limited its efforts to humanitarian assistance and offers of mediation. The organization adopted a similar stance with respect to the fighting in East Pakistan until India's intervention with its own forces made the conflict impossible to ignore.

Recent formulations by the General Assembly of the right to self-determination also demonstrate the narrow focus of the UN's approval of revolutionary violence and third-party support. These formulations couple the "exercise of the right to self-determination and independence" with "peoples struggling against colonialism, alien domination, foreign occupation, racial discrimination, and *apartheid*."[25] This serves the political purposes of communist, third world, and Arab states in highlighting and perhaps limiting the exercise of the right of self-determination to southern Africa, the West Bank, and the Gaza Strip.

The double-standard aspects of this application of the right of self-determination raise a host of complex issues. These have been explored in other forums and need not detain us here. But concerning our immediate subject—UN law and practice with respect to revolutionary violence—the situation should be kept in proper perspective. First and most important, it must be emphasized that the United Nations has rejected the communist doctrine that armed support for "wars of national liberation" is legitimate. While the communist bloc has successfully aligned itself with black African state views and actions on southern Africa and with those of Arab states regarding Israel's occupation of the West Bank and the Gaza Strip, it has failed to enlist the great majority of UN members in any general campaign to support radical revolutionary activity along the lines of the Cuban model.[26] Rather, most member states of the UN regard the supply of arms to rebels in southern Africa or to the Palestinians as exceptions to a general norm prohibiting such assistance—a norm emphasized in the Declaration on Friendly Relations and in the assembly's Definition of Aggression.

To be sure, one cannot lightly dismiss the General Assembly's call for the support of armed force in southern Africa or the Middle East as a mere aberration of no major consequence. Even if the wording of the Declaration on Friendly Relations and the Definition of Aggression may be interpreted so as to support the legitimacy of third-party states providing armed support to rebels in these parts of the world, the terms of the UN Charter prevail over any inconsistent provisions of General Assembly resolutions—as the Declaration on Friendly Relations itself makes clear. And although this conclusion is debatable, the better view is that Article 2(4) precludes armed support being furnished for rebel groups—unless such support is authorized by the Security Council pursuant to its authority under Chapter VII of the Charter.

Assuming the illegality of this support, as well as of the assembly's attempted authorization of it, one must still consider the economic, political, and social context in which the support took place. This should be done not to excuse the assembly's action, but to try to understand the reasons for it with a view toward avoidance of similar assembly actions in the future and the development of a more constructive approach toward the control of revolutionary violence.

Simply put, the primary argument advanced by defenders of General Assembly resolutions calling for support of armed revolution in southern Africa would be that less drastic alternatives to ending an intolerable situation have been exhausted. To take Rhodesia as an example, they would note that, at the time of the UDI, Great Britain could have ended the rebellion with a minimum of armed force, but chose not to do so, primarily for domestic political reasons. Economic sanctions proved ineffective, in part because South Africa and Portugal openly refused to go along with them—despite a clear obligation under the UN Charter that they do so—and many other states violated the sanctions on a *sub rosa* basis. Even the United States violated the sanctions system by importing Rhodesian chrome for a period of time. The Security Council in theory could itself have employed force to bring the illegal rebellion to an end, but declined to do so. Hence the UDI was succeeding and would have continued indefinitely except for the use of force supported by third-party states.

Similar arguments could be advanced with respect to the two crucial trouble spots remaining in southern Africa—Namibia and South Africa. With respect to Namibia, South Africa has continued its control over the territory despite an advisory opinion by the International Court of Justice that it has no authority to do so.[27] At this writing the Security Council has declined to impose a Rhodesia-style embargo against South Africa, limiting its actions to an embargo on arms. South Africa's willingness to negotiate over Namibia is probably based on pressure from SWAPO's military activities in the territory, not on any respect for the authority of the United Nations or the International Court of Justice.

As to South Africa itself, the primary arguments would focus on the issue whether *apartheid* and its enforcement by South African authorities through the use of armed force can constitute a threat to international peace and security. Although Western powers resisted this conclusion for a substantial period of time, the Security Council has now determined that the situation does constitute such a threat in deciding to impose a mandatory embargo on arms sales to South Africa.[28]

Although it has not yet reached the level of intensity that exists in Namibia, guerrilla activity in South Africa is increasing and is being abetted by the supply of arms from the outside. This trend is likely to continue because *apartheid* domination by a white minority over a black majority in a nation on a continent composed of states with large black majorities is simply insupportable. If it is not ended by peaceful means, it will be destroyed by violence, with all of the hardship that will follow.

With respect to Namibia, the United Nations has played a constructive role toward peaceful settlement as well as taken steps arguably supportive of revolutionary violence. Most particularly, through the efforts of Secretary-General Waldheim acting in concert with five Western States, it helped to bring about an agreement in principle between South Africa and the South West Africa People's Organization (SWAPO) for a cease-fire, demilitarization of the territory with the assistance of a UN peace-keeping force, and free elections to establish Namibia as an independent state. On September 29, 1978, the Security Council approved a plan for a UN civilian and military operation in Namibia, designed to pave the way for elections leading to the country's independence.[29] At this writing, however, it is uncertain whether the agreement will be implemented, since recent successes by the South African army against SWAPO, including incursions against guerrilla bases in Namibia and Angola (engaging Angolan army units as well), may make South Africa more intransigent. Moreover, the Reagan Administration favors an alteration in the basic plan whereby the "Zimbabwe formula" would be adopted, i.e., the future laws of the country would be worked out in negotiations before an election took place.[30] The current United Nations sponsored plan for Namibia provides that elections would be held first to set up a constituent assembly that would in turn draft laws. In any event, United Nations participation would be indispensable to a peaceful settlement of the dispute over Namibia. Most particularly, the United Nations would be needed to serve as a mediator; to supervise elections to ensure their impartiality; to establish a peace-keeping force in connection with the demilitarization of the territory; to supervise elections to ensure their impartiality; and to assist the final transition to independence. Failure to implement a plan along these lines would result in a continuation and intensification of the guerrilla war in the territory.

Conversely, a peaceful settlement of the dispute over Namibia could be a major step toward the ultimate dismantling of *apartheid* in South Africa itself. Major steps toward the dismantling of *apartheid* in Namibia have reportedly already been taken, and these might serve as a model to induce South Africa to reconsider its own internal practices. More generally, both Zimbabwe and Namibia might be regarded as experiments in multiracial living in southern Africa. Should such experiments prove successful, the more enlightened and moderate elements in South Africa might be greatly strengthened and encouraged to push for similar reforms in South Africa itself.

The United Nations and the world community—particularly the superpowers—have an obligation to explore all possibilities of resolving the problems in southern Africa without violence. Any other course of action is incompatible with United Nations responsibilities for maintaining international peace and security and promoting respect for the principle of equal rights and self-determination of peoples.

Southern Africa has been a focal point for the United Nations before. Indeed, the largest UN peace-keeping operation and its most substantial effort to cope with revolutionary violence took place in the early 1960s with the outbreak of violence in the Congo (now Zaire). That effort warrants a relatively extensive examination.

THE UN OPERATION IN THE CONGO

By way of background, it should be noted that the violence in the Congo broke out on July 5, 1960, only five days after the end of Belgian colonial rule.[31] The Belgians had ill-prepared their former colony for independence, and the end of their colonial administration had come after only a six-month transition period. In part this was because Belgium expected to be able to maintain control over such important Congolese policy areas as defense, foreign affairs, currency, and telecommunications, and hence believed that the real transfer of power would take place sometime long after June 30, the nominal date of independence.

The Congolese, however, had different ideas. Most of the population expected that independence would usher in a wave of prosperity equal to that which the Belgians had enjoyed. The harsh reality of the situation was that the old problems remained and increased in severity. Particularly galling to the Congolese military was the fact that their officer corps continued to consist entirely of Belgians. Their mutiny against these officers spread quickly across the country and resulted in violence when the troops began attacking Belgian citizens.

The mutiny and the spread of violence throughout the country were followed shortly, on July 10, by the arrival of Belgian paratroopers in the Congo. Although the Congolese government needed assistance to control the violence and the Belgian government was prepared to render it, the Congolese were unwilling to invite their erstwhile colonial masters. They did call upon the United States for help, but obtained only a suggestion that they refer their problem to the UN. The Belgians defended their intervention as required to maintain order and to protect their citizens, but the Congolese characterized the action as an attempt by Belgium to reestablish a colonial regime.

The central government in Leopoldville faced other problems as well. On July 11, only one day after the Belgian government had sent paratroopers into the country, the Katanga government, headed by Moise Tshombe, proclaimed independence for its territory on the basis of self-determination, although prior to independence agreement had been reached on a strong national government. When the government in Leopoldville, headed by President Joseph Kasavubu and Prime Minister Patrice Lumumba, refused to call in Belgian troops, the Belgian government granted Tshombe's request for assistance in retraining his army.

In response to the Belgian intervention and Tshombe's proclamation, the government in Leopoldville requested military assistance from the United Nations "to protect the national territory of the

Congo against the present external aggression which is a threat to international peace."[32] Upon receipt of cables from President Kasavubu and Prime Minister Lumumba, Secretary-General Hammarskjöld, acting for the first time under Article 99 of the Charter, requested the president of the Security Council urgently to convene the council. Pursuant to the plan developed by the secretary-general, the Security Council adopted a resolution[33] that called upon Belgium to withdraw its troops from the Congo and authorized the secretary-general, "in consultation with the Government of the Republic of the Congo, to provide the Government with such military assistance as may be necessary until, through the efforts of the Congolese Government with the technical assistance of the United Nations, the national security forces may be able, in the opinion of the Government, to meet fully their tasks." It is noteworthy that the resolution speaks only in terms of "military assistance" and nowhere mentions the word "force." The effect of this was to leave the determination of the nature of the assistance to be given the Congolese government to the secretary-general.

To be sure, the secretary-general was not operating in a vacuum. In his initial statement to the Security Council, Hammarskjöld indicated that he intended to create a peace-keeping force on the basis of principles distilled from the UNEF experience. These principles included: the autonomy of the force and the operation; non-intervention in internal affairs; and avoidance of the use of force except in self-defense. As we shall see below, these principles proved to be much easier to state in the abstract than to apply in practice.

The secretary-general's initial legal rationale for the peace-keeping force was decidedly cautious. He characterized the crisis as a "situation" within the meaning of Article 34 of the Charter, which, by definition, did not require the presence of parties and could cover an internal situation as long as it affected international peace and security. By focusing on the aspect of the crisis involving a breakdown in law and order, the secretary-general avoided any implication that the UN force would be used in relation to the withdrawal of Belgian troops, although the presence of the UN operation would allow Belgium to withdraw without loss of face.

Unfortunately, it proved more difficult than expected to dislodge Belgium from the Congo, and the secretary-general had to return to the Security Council to obtain a new and more sweeping mandate. Hammarskjöld was especially concerned that Belgian troops withdraw from Katanga so that the central government of the Congo might be able to protect the territorial integrity of the country. On July 22, 1960, the council adopted a resolution[34] that expressly authorized the secretary-general "to take all necessary action" to secure the withdrawal of Belgian troops and requested "all States to refrain from any action which might tend to impede the restoration of law and order and the exercise by the Government of the Congo of its authority and also to refrain from any action which might undermine the territorial integrity and the political independence of the Republic of the Congo."

Even armed with this express authority, the secretary-general encountered substantial difficulty in carrying out his mandate because of the intransigence of Moise Tshombe. It soon became apparent that, even with the withdrawal of Belgian troops, the central government would have difficulty in assering its authority over the whole of the Congo. Again Hammarskjöld returned to the Security Council for additional authority and again the council obliged him. On August 9, it adopted a resolution[35] that reaffirmed the previous mandate to the secretary-general to secure the withdrawal of Belgian troops and declared that "the entry of the United Nations Force into the province of Katanga is necessary for the full implementation of this resolution." At the same time the resolution "*Reaffirms* that the United Nations Force in the Congo will not be a party to or in any way intervene in or be used to influence the outcome of any internal conflict, constitutional or otherwise."

This express qualification notwithstanding, the council's resolution of August 9 set the stage for what was to be the most heated legal and political argument over UN actions in the Congo: whether the use of force against Tshombe's government in Katanga constituted an impermissible intervention by the organization in the internal affairs of a member state.

Hammarskjöld himself was ambivalent and troubled over what the United Nations should do with respect to Katanga. On the one hand, he believed strongly that the organization should not take sides in a civil war by lending assistance to one side and not to the other; in particular, according to Georges Abi-Saab, he believed that "the U.N. should not act as a Holy Alliance between the existing governments of member states against all revolutionary movements in these States."[36]

On the other hand, the secretary-general did not believe that Katanga's attempt to secede was authentically indigenous, but rather a facade for outside intervention by Belgium. If this was the case, as was strenuously argued by several delegates in Security Council debates, UN action in Katanga would not constitute an intervention arguably precluded by Article 2(7) of the Charter, but rather a counterintervention in response to a Belgian intervention that had already turned the situation into one of an international character.

Whatever the scope of the force's authority, Hammarskjöld's goal was to deploy it peacefully in Katanga and to secure the peaceful withdrawal of Belgian troops. He hoped this would provide Tshombe with a diplomatic means out of secession and induce him to agree instead to some kind of federation with the central government.

Tshombe did agree to the deployment of UN troops in Katanga as well as to the withdrawal of Belgian troops, but only under certain conditions. These were, among others, that the withdrawal of Belgian troops would not include those officers who were detached to the provincial government of Katanga nor those who came to be directly employed by it, i.e., mercenaries. By the time the UN forces were deployed in Katanga, the Belgian troops had disarmed and neutralized those forces in Katanga loyal to the central government, and the need for them was slight. Tshombe did need the officers and the mercenaries, however, to help build up his own forces and consolidate his control over the territory. As long as the UN forces did not hinder this task, their presence would not interfere with Tshombe's aims and might even further them by making Katanga's secession look less dependent on Belgian aid.

Tshombe's aims were clear to Lumumba, who protested vehemently to Hammarskjöld over the UN's actions. In Lumumba's view the Security Council resolutions required that the United Nations not act as a neutral organization, but place all its resources at the disposal of the central government. He contended that the secretary-general's discussions with Tshombe without consulting with the central government, and particularly the assurances given Tshombe, constituted an intervention in the internal conflict in the Congo contrary to the terms of the Security Council resolutions.

The secretary-general resisted this view, and his relationship with Lumumba deteriorated rapidly. He also came into conflict with the Soviet Union over its providing military aid to the central government. Such aid, according to Hammarskjöld, was "contrary to the spirit of the Security Council resolutions" and was as unacceptable as Belgian assistance to Katanga.

The already complex situation in the Congo became considerably more complicated with the onset of the constitutional crisis caused by President Kasavubu's announcement that, using his constitutional powers, he had dismissed Lumumba and six other ministers and had asked Mr. Ileo, the president of the senate, to form a new cabinet. Lumumba challenged the president's constitutional authority to dismiss him, declared that Kasavubu would be relieved of his duties as president, and stated that this was an internal dispute in which neither the United Nations nor any outside power had any right to interfere.

Despite the injunction from Lumumba, on the night of September 5, Andrew Cordier, then commander of the UN force, ordered the closure of all major airports in the Congo to all but UN traffic. On the following morning he ordered the shutting down of the radio station at Leopoldville, which at the time was clearly in the hands of Lumumba supporters. Cordier defended these actions on the ground that they were necessary to maintain law and order, but friends of Lumumba, including most prominently the Soviet Union, sharply criticized them as gross interference in an internal dispute. They noted that the closing of the radio station and the airports clearly favored Kasavubu (who had asked for them) and undermined Lumumba's position.

Hammarskjöld's defense of Cordier's action pointed out that, in the context of the constitutional crisis, it was not clear with whom UN officials on the spot should consult—and indeed choosing one or the other faction would itself amount to an interference in the internal struggle. Further, he argued, a primary mission of the UN force was to maintain law and order, and faced with its breakdown in the Congo, the commander of the force either had to take steps to maintain it—even at the risk of affecting the internal political situation—or abandon the mission in the Congo and withdraw the force from the territory.

There is no doubt that the *effect* of the UN's actions was to deal a fatal blow to Lumumba's chances of winning out in his struggle with Kasavubu, and there was strong evidence that Hammarskjöld was aware that this would be the effect of the actions. Closing the airports prevented Lumumba from receiving any military or political support from other areas of the country favorable to him. Similarly, closure of the radio deprived Lumumba, a much more effective speaker and charismatic leader than Kasavubu, of a powerful means of gaining widespread support. Hammarskjöld even went so far as to express the opinion that the constitution of the Congo empowered the president (Kasavubu) to dismiss the prime minister (Lumumba), but contained no authority for the prime minister to dismiss the president. This provoked an especially harsh response from Lumumba, who suggested that it was the role of the Congolese Parliament to interpret the constitution, not that of the secretary-general.

The negative Soviet reaction to the UN's actions in closing the airports and shutting down the radio station in Leopoldville resulted in an inability, for the first time, of the super powers to reach agreement in the Security Council. The Soviet Union was unwilling to accept a draft resolution introduced by the United States that would have required that all aid to the Congo be channeled through the United Nations because this limitation was so obviously directed against Soviet aid to Lumumba.

For its part the United States rejected a draft resolution introduced by the Soviet Union that would have censured the secretary-general. When the Soviet Union vetoed a compromise draft resolution introduced by Tunisia and Ceylon that would have limited the channeling of aid through the United Nations to military aid, the United States submitted a draft resolution to convene an emergency session of the General Assembly under the procedure of the Uniting for

Peace resolution. This resolution was adopted despite a Soviet negative vote, the veto not being applicable to a procedural matter.[37]

In the General Assembly, the secretary-general saw his policies in the Congo vindicated. On September 20, 1960, the assembly adopted a resolution[38] that, among other things, requested the secretary-general to continue "to assist the Central Government of the Congo in the restoration and maintenance of law and order throughout the territory ... and to safeguard its unity, territorial integrity and political independence ..." and called upon all states "to refrain from the direct and indirect provision of arms or other materials of war and military personnel and other assistance for military purposes in the Congo ... except upon the request of the United Nations through the secretary-general. ..." The vote on the resolution was seventy in favor to none opposed, with eleven abstentions: the Eastern-bloc countries, France, and South Africa.

Meanwhile, back in the Congo, the impasse between Kasavubu and Lumumba over who could fire whom had led to an army takeover led by Colonel Mobutu. Lumumba remained at his official residence in Leopoldville under UN protection while his supporters set up a government in Stanleyville. The UN force thwarted several attempts by Kasavubu and his supporters to arrest Lumumba, much to their disgust and objection that the UN action constituted an interference in the internal affairs of the Congo.

The decision on November 24 to seat Kasavubu's delegation in the General Assembly was strongly disapproved by Hammarskjöld, who felt its timing interfered with efforts by the UN Conciliation Commission to bring about a reconciliation of the various factions in the Congo. He reportedly viewed it as a partisan decision brought about by pressure from the Western powers, especially the United States, because of their strong dislike of Lumumba.[39]

Lumumba soon became the focus of a much more intense dispute. On November 27, he left Leopoldville (and UN protection) to join his supporters, but was captured by central government troops on December 1 and later transfered to Katanga, where he was murdered.

The news of Lumumba's death came on February 13, when the Security Council was meeting in response to a request made by the Soviet Union at the time of Lumumba's arrest. Upon the announcement of his death, the Soviet Union issued a statement indicating it held the secretary-general directly responsible and that it would no longer recognize him as a UN official.

For a time it appeared that it would be impossible to reach agreement in the Security Council on any resolution. But a continuing deterioration of the situation in the Congo, including the murder of six prominent Lumumbists, finally led the council to adopt on February 21 a resolution[40] that, for the first time, expressly characterized the situation in the Congo as a "threat to international peace and security" and authorized the use of force beyond self-defense in the carrying out of one of the functions of the force under the mandate, namely, the prevention of civil war. The resolution also urged the convening of the Congolese Parliament and a reorganization of the Congolese armed forces with a view to neutralizing their interference in politics. Significantly, the resolution made no mention of the secretary-general, either to commend him for his past actions or to entrust him with a mandate to carry out the resolution. This omission was deliberate to avoid a Soviet veto.

Thus, for the first time, the council had invoked Chapter VII of the Charter in dealing with the crisis in the Congo. It was not clear, however, what articles of Chapter VII the council's resolution was based on. Hammarskjöld later characterized the operation undertaken pursuant to the resolution as "provisional measures" under Article 40. He apparently viewed Article 42 enforcement measures as inapplicable to an internal conflict—i.e., that they can only be taken against a "state." He may also have believed that it is difficult, if not impossible, to determine—under traditional definitions in international law—who is the aggressor against whom enforcement measures might be taken. The secretary-general's view was not shared by all states or by all commentators; a number believed that the proper Charter basis was Article 42. Georges Abi-Saab suggests that the resolution may be based on both Article 40 and Article 42:

> In fact, the general tenor of the resolution indicates the direction of a plausible legal explanation: paragraph 1 *urges* the U.N. to "take immediately all appropriate measures to prevent the occurrence of civil war in the Congo, including arrangements of cease-fires, the halting of all military operations, the prevention of clashes" before it adds "and the use of force, if necessary, in the last resort." The first category of measures are of the nature of provisional measures in the meaning of article 40. Article 40 provides in its last sentence: "The Security Council shall duly take account of failure to comply with such provisional measures." In other words, although provisional measures are "without prejudice to the rights, claims or position of the parties concerned," ordering by the Security Council of enforcement measures against the non-complying party, orders which in turn can be limited to the enforcement of the provisional measures. The "use of force, if necessary, in the last resort" in the resolution of 21 February accords perfectly with this hypothesis.[41]

The central government in Leopoldville reacted strongly to the resolution, interpreting it as allowing the United Nations to use force to disarm its army and to reconvene the parliament. This hostility led to attacks on UN units by some Congolese soldiers. Strenuous negotiations by the secretary-general and by his representatives, however, ultimately resulted in an agreement with Kasavubu by which he recognized the obligation of the Republic of the Congo "to carry out the resolution of the Security Council" and, for its part, the United Nations reaffirmed "its respect for the Sovereignty of the Republic of the Congo in the implementation of the resolution."[42] This agreement was followed by a settlement of the constitutional crisis when a *rapprochement* took place between Leopoldville and Stanleyville, and an agreement between their respective representatives was reached on June 19, 1961, on the reconvening of Parliament. No such settlement, however, was reached between the central government and Katanga; quite the contrary, the latter's attitude toward secession had hardened over the past year.

In the meantime, Russian attacks on Hammarskjöld had escalated and culminated in Khrushchev's speech on September 23, 1960, to the General Assembly in which he heatedly denounced the secretary-general and proposed he be replaced by a "troika," representing the Western, socialist, and neutralist countries (see Chapter 5 above for discussion of this proposal). After considerable struggle the Russian initiative failed, and, on April 15, 1961, the assembly adopted a resolution[43] generally regarded as a strong vote of confidence in the secretary-general.

Shortly after resolution of the constitutional crisis united the central government in the Congo, UN forces, in the first of what were to be three rounds of fighting, clashed with the Katanga gendarmerie in their efforts to remove foreign mercenaries from Katanga. The legal rationale for the use of force by the United Nations was self-defense; according to Conor Cruise O'Brien, Hammarskjöld's representative in the Congo, however, the purpose of the UN action was not to remove foreigners, but to end the Katanganese secession.[44] If so, the goal proved difficult to accomplish, and the first clash ended in a stalemate. It was while travelling to negotiate a cease-fire that Dag Hammarskjöld died in a plane crash on September 18, 1961, under suspicious circumstances.

A cease-fire between the United Nations and Katanga was arranged, but in October the central government decided to launch an attack of its own against Katanga. This attack was unsuccessful and was accompanied by a breakdown of discipline among Congolese troops and terrorization of the civilian population.

On November 3, the Security Council unanimously recommended U Thant as Acting Secretary-General until the end of Hammarskjöld's term in 1963, and the General Assembly approved the recommendation the same day. The Security Council then again turned its attention to the Congo, and the result was the adoption on November 24 of a resolution[45] that went significantly beyond its predecessors in several respects. Most particularly, the resolution explicitly authorized the secretary-general to use force to remove mercenaries as well as to prevent civil war, and to control the movement of persons and goods across the borders to prevent the entry of foreign military personnel and material into the Congo.

During debate on the resolution, the French, Belgian, and British delegates contended that the resolution put too much emphasis on force and not enough on conciliation, that it was contrary to the Charter because it went against the principles of non-use of force and nonintervention, and that it would set a dangerous precedent in putting the United Nations at the beck and call of any state with a dissident minority within its borders.

In December 1961 new fighting broke out in Katanga as UN forces attempted to insure freedom of movement and to restore law and order. This fighting ended with an agreement to reintegrate Katanga into the Republic of the Congo. However, this agreement was not implemented, despite prolonged further negotiations to this end throughout 1962. Fighting broke out again in December 1962 and, after UN forces occupied strategic points in Elizabethville, Jadotville, and Kolwezi, Tshombe announced on January 14, 1963, that the Katanganese secession was at an end.

Although Katanga had finally been reintegrated into the Congo, the central government now faced continuing conflict and a herculean task of modern nation building. The conflicts were not resolved, and, at the time UN forces withdrew on June 30, 1964, a third of the country was under the control of rebel forces. In a supremely ironic twist, Tshombe returned from exile on July 9, 1964, to accept the post of prime minister of the central government and promptly hired mercenaries to deal with the rebels. The situation continued to deteriorate, however, as demonstrated most vividly by the airborne assault on Stanleyville on November 24, 1964, by Belgian paratroopers transported in American aircraft to free rebel-held hostages. A year later, on November 25, 1965, Mobutu once again assumed power. He has remained in power up to the time of this writing. But the situation in the Congo continues to be extremely unstable, as demonstrated by the several (so far) unsuccessful attempts to overthrow Mobutu by force of arms.

The UN operation in the Congo raises a plethora of legal and political issues. For present purposes we will focus on four of them. The first three are basically legal in nature. The fourth is highly political.

Was the UN Operation in Violation of Article 2(7) of the Charter?

Although this argument has been made by some critics, it is difficult to sustain upon the evidence. The initial UN intervention came at the express invitation of the central government of the Congo and after Belgian troops had intervened without invitation from central government authorities. Moreover, the fact of Belgian intervention with its colonial overtones as well as the threat of intervention by other states belied claims that the situation was a matter essentially within the domestic jurisdiction of the Congo. Some have argued that, at least in the later stages of its operation, the United Nations was engaged in enforcement measures that Article 2(7) expressly exempts from its coverage. For reasons we shall examine, these arguments are not well founded.

It has also been contended that, at the least, the United Nations violated the spirit of Article 2(7) when it took actions—closing the airports in Leopoldville and shutting down the radio—which favored Kasavubu over Lumumba during the constitutional crisis over who had the authority to fire whom. But the UN actions should be evaluated in the context of a rapidly developing crisis. The primary mandate of the UN force, as set forth in Security Council resolutions, was to prevent civil war in the Congo. Had Andrew Cordier not ordered the airports closed and the radio shut down, the likelihood of civil war between the Kasavubu and Lumumba factions would have been great. Indeed, there was a strong possibility that assistance from outside states to Lumumba, especially from the Soviet Union, would have precipitated civil war.

Was the UN Operation Consonant with the Principle of Self-Determination?

Far from sustaining the contention that the UN operation in the Congo frustrated the exercise of the right to self-determination, the evidence indicates that the operation strongly protected and promoted it. The contention to the contrary is based on the view that Katanga's attempt to secede from the Congo was a legitimate exercise of the right to self-determination. However, as we have seen above, Katanga's secession was promoted by states outside the territory, especially Belgium, and Tshombe did not enjoy support from the majority of the people in the territory. Moreover, the recent independence of the Congo from Belgium was a valid exercise of the right of self-determination. Tshombe's attempt to secede, backed by the former colonial power, threatened the viability of the newly won Congolese independence. The United Nations helped to meet and defeat this threat.

Was the UN's Use of Force against Katanga Contrary to the Charter?

This was perhaps the most hotly debated issue concerning the UN operation in the Congo. Critics contend that, although Security Council resolutions authorized the UN operation in the Congo to prevent civil war, even to use force to this end "as a last resort," and to disarm and expel foreign mercenaries, they did not permit the UN force to use military means to reintegrate Katanga into the Congo. Nowhere in these resolutions, these critics continue, is there an authorization for an Article 42 enforcement type of action against Katanga. Far from preventing civil war, the critics conclude, the UN force participated in the civil war on the part of the central government and brought it to a close by defeating Katanganese forces.

These arguments are not easily dismissed. The primary argument made by UN officials at the time in support of the widespread military operations in Katanga leading to Tshombe's capitulation was that the UN forces were merely exercising their right of self-defense when they were attacked while attempting to carry out their mandate to disarm foreign mercenaries and expel them from Katanga. This borders on the disingenuous. Coupled with this justification was an argument that the United Nations was required to use force to ensure its freedom of movement throughout the Congo. In effect the United Nations interpreted the right of self-defense of its forces so broadly as to authorize the defeat of the Katanganese military to ensure that there would be no future attacks coming from that quarter.

If the UN operation, at least after the adoption of the February 24, 1961, resolution by the Security Council, could be characterized as an enforcement rather than a peace-keeping action, there would seem little doubt that it stayed within its mandate. But no UN official made such a claim, several states, including the United States, during debate on the February 24 resolution rejected Article 42 as a basis for it, and in the Certain Expenses Case[46] the International Court of Justice advised that the UN operation was a peace-keeping rather than an enforcement action. Hence it would appear that Article 40, with its provision for emergency measures, was indeed the Charter basis for the UN operation.

The fact of the matter is that the UN force, as a practical matter, simply could not carry out its mandate from the Security Council to maintain territorial integrity, prevent civil war, and remove foreign mercenaries without bringing the Katanganese secession to an end. Further, from a political perspective, by February 24, 1961, the situation had developed to the point where there were no longer strong objections from member states to bringing the Katanganese secession to an end by force, if necessary. There was still a disinclination to invoke Article 42, however, because that would have raised the legal question of the need for Article 43 agreements to govern the use of the force and would have set an undesirable precedent. The result was a UN operation in the Congo that was something less than a coercive international enforcement action under Article 42 and something more than a mere peace-keeping force operating solely with the consent of the parties to the dispute. Katanga's lack of status as a "state" under international law was a major and perhaps the determinate factor in the unwillingness of the majority of the International Court of Justice to classify the UN operation as an enforcement action.

Did the UN Operation in the Congo Contribute to the Control of Revolutionary Violence?

Assuming that the UN operation in the Congo can be upheld on a legal basis, the crucial question remains: Did it contribute to the control of revolutionary violence? The answer, in this commentator's opinion, is a qualified yes. And the yes is qualified only if one views the UN operation in the Congo from an ideal rather than a real perspective.

Ernest Lefever has compared the situation in the Congo with that which erupted four years later in Tanganyika, where local troops rebelled against their British officers, the Tanganyikan government asked for and received British military assistance, the mutiny was put down, and the British troops were then replaced by Ethiopian and Nigerian troops, which stayed for about a year.[47] Lefever suggests that prompt and decisive disciplinary action along the Tanganyikan model by the Belgian officers against the mutinous soldiers could have nipped the crisis in the Congo in the bud.[48] Perhaps. But the fact remains that no such action was taken. Moreover, one can understand the reluctance of the central government, with both Kasavubu and Lumumba in agreement on this point, to call in Belgian troops to restore order, in view of the bitterness attending Belgian colonial rule and Congolese suspicions regarding Belgian motives for intervening. These suspicions were confirmed, in the Congolese view, when Tshombe declared independence upon Belgian intervention and with Belgian assistance. Military clashes between Belgian and Congolese troops exacerbated the problem.

Lefever has also suggested that the United States might have accepted the Congolese invitation to intervene militarily and put down the rebellion and that the United States was oversensitive regarding possible charges of "neocolonialism."[49] But for the United States to intervene militarily in the Congo, even at the express invitation of the Congolese government, would have entailed substantial risk of counterintervention on the part of the Soviet Union or its proxies, in view of the great strategic and economic importance of the Congo. Lefever may also have underestimated the strength of third world reaction to such American action.

In any event, even assuming that early Belgian or American action would have been preferable to UN involvement, it was not forthcoming. And for the secretary-general not to respond positively to the request of the Congolese government that the United Nations render assistance to cope with a situation that clearly threatened international peace and security would have been irresponsible.

Lefever does acknowledge that the United Nations helped the central government to restore law and order and to avoid a great power conflict in the Congo as well as to preserve its territorial integrity.[50] These are no small accomplishments. It is true, as Lefever notes, that the UN operation failed to bring about a true peace in the Congo and that, when the UN force withdrew in 1964, revolutionary violence was widespread. But political and economic pressures on the United Nations to withdraw at that time were simply overwhelming. Moreover, the consensus in the Security Council that supported the forceful reintegration of Katanga had broken down. The central government had signed aid agreements with Belgium, Canada, Italy, Israel, Nigeria, Norway, and the United States; and communist and militant African states were aiding the rebels. The cold war was waging in the Congo, and, as Vietnam later demonstrated, the United Nations can do little to control revolutionary violence under such circumstances.

In the aftermath of the Congo crisis, some commentators suggested that the UN operation there might serve as a model for the future.[51] This has not proven to be the case. The closest analogies have been the UN peace-keeping forces in Cyprus and Lebanon, both situations characterized by high levels of revolutionary as well as traditional manifestations of international violence. As we saw in Chapter 4, UN forces have performed well in these two situations under the most difficult of conditions. In neither case, however, is there any question of UN forces moving to defeat one party to a conflict as they did with respect to Katanga. Nor has the United Nations been very successful in either case with respect to peace-making as compared to peace-keeping. One cannot fault the United Nations for this failure, however. In both cases powerful member states have deemed it in their interests to keep the conflict alive and have blocked efforts by the United Nations and others toward peaceful settlement. At the same time UN forces have played an indispensable role in circumscribing the scope of violence and lessening the chances of large-scale outside intervention.

Similar resistance to UN involvement, especially on the part of the great powers, has greatly minimized, or even excluded, a UN role in many recent instances of revolutionary violence. With respect to the civil war in Angola, for example, the United Nations has been able to do little more than express a pious hope through a statement by the secretary-general for unity. Largely because of American attitudes, the United Nations was unable to have anything more than a marginal impact on the revolutionary violence in

Vietnam. Similarly, reluctance on the part of various member states to have the United Nations involved has prevented the organization from exercising its primary responsibility for the maintenance of international peace and security in such diverse places as the Dominican Republic, Ethiopia, El Salvador, Guatemala, Western Somalia, Nicaragua, etc.

The United Nations has also been able to take constructive, although modest and not always totally successful, steps toward the control of revolutionary warfare in numerous other instances. We turn to these in the next chapter.

NOTES

1. Bard E. O'Neill, William R. Heaton, and Donald J. Alberts, *Insurgency in the Modern World* (Boulder: Westview Press, 1980), p. ix.

2. John Baylis, Ken Booth, John Garnett, and Phil Williams, *Contemporary Strategy, Theory and Policies* (New York: Holmes & Meier Publishers, Inc., 1975), p. 136.

3. Tad Szulc, "The Refugee Explosion," *New York Times Magazine,* Nov. 23, 1980, pp. 136, 138, quoting Lincoln P. Bloomfield, Professor of Political Science, Massachusetts Institute of Technology, who notes that during the last 10 years, 90 percent of small wars were fought in the third world. According to Bloomfield, a decade ago those parts of the world averaged a total of less than one new conflict a year, now the rate is 1.6 a year and "will be the same over the next decade."

4. Edwin Brown Firmage, "The 'War of National Liberation' and the Third World," John Norton Moore (ed), *Law and Civil War in the Modern World* (Baltimore: The Johns Hopkins University Press, 1974), pp. 304, 310–14.

5. Ibid., p. 313.

6. Edwin Brown Firmage, "Summary and Interpretation," Richard A. Falk (ed.), *The International Law of Civil War* (Baltimore: The Johns Hopkins University Press, 1971), p. 405.

7. Lassa P. Oppenheim, *International Law,* 7th ed., H. Lauterpacht (ed.), (London: Longmans Green, 1952), vol. 1, p. 249, quoted in Richard A. Falk, "Introduction," *International Law of Civil War,* pp. 1, 12.

8. See generally, Ann Van Wynen Thomas and A. J. Thomas Jr., "International Legal Aspects of the Civil War in Spain, 1936–39," Richard A. Falk (ed.), *International Law of Civil War,* pp. 111–78.

9. Leland M. Goodrich, Edvard Hambro, and Anne Patricia Simons, *Charter of the United Nations* (New York and London: Columbia University Press, 1969), p. 68.

10. This background is drawn largely from Abram Chayes, Thomas Ehrlich, and Andreas F. Lowenfeld, *International Legal Process* (Boston: Little, Brown & Co., 1969), vol. 2, pp. 1313–1402; and *New York Times,* March 29, 1979, p. 20.

11. See e.g., G. A. Res. 2012(XX) (1965); S.C. Res. 202 (1965).

12. S.C. Res. 217 (1965).

13. S.C. Res. 253 (1968).

14. See e.g., Dean Acheson, "The Arrogance of International Lawyers," *International Lawyer* 2 (1968):591–99.

15. See Myres S. McDougal and W. Michael Reisman, "Rhodesia and the United Nations: The Lawfulness of International Concern," *American Journal of International Law* 62 (1968):1–19.

16. John Polakas, "Economic Sanctions: An Effective Alternative to Military Coercion?"*Brooklyn Journal of International Law* VI no. 2 (1980):289, 301–20.

17. For the text of the agreement, see *International Legal Materials* 19 (1980):287–408.

18. Executive Order No. 12, 183, 44 Fed. Reg. 74,787 (1979). S.C. Res. 460 (1979).

19. G.A. Res. 31/34 (1976). For a statement of the U.S. position on the resolution, see Department of State, *Digest of International Law* (1976), pp. 12–13.

20. G.A. Res. 2625 (XXV) (1970).

21. G.A. Res. 3314 (XXXIX) (1974).

22. Stephen M. Schwebel, "Wars of Liberation—as Fought in U.N. Organs," John Norton Moore (ed.), *Law and Civil War*, pp. 446, 453.

23. Ibid., p. 453.

24. For analysis of some of these arguments, see especially, Rosalyn Higgins, "Internal War and International Law," Richard A. Falk and Cyril E. Black (eds.), *The Future of the International Legal Order* (Princeton: Princeton University Press, 1971), vol. 3, pp. 81–121. Compare Thomas M. Franck, "Who Killed Article 2(4)," *American Journal of International Law* 64 (1970):809–37, with Louis Henkin, "The Reports of the Death of Article 2(4) Are Greatly Exaggerated," *American Journal of International Law* 65 (1971):544–48.

25. See L. C. Green, "The Legalization of Terrorism," Yonah Alexander, David Carlton, and Paul Wilkinson (eds.), *Terrorism: Theory and Practice* (Boulder: Westview Press, Inc., 1979), pp. 175–97.

26. See Edwin Brown Firmage, "National Liberation and the Third World," John Norton Moore (ed.), *Law and Civil War*, pp. 304, 324–38; Jean-Pierre L. Fonteyne, "Forcible Self-Help by States to Protect Human Rights: Recent Views from the United Nations," Richard B. Lillich (ed.), *Humanitarian Intervention* (Charlottesville: University of Virginia Press, 1973), pp. 197–221.

27. Advisory Opinion on the Continued Presence of South Africa in Namibia (South West Africa) [1971] I.C.J. Rep. 16.

28. S.C. Res. 418 (1977).

29. S.C. Res. 435 (1978).

30. *New York Times*, April 1, 1981, p. 1.

31. The following background to the UN operation in the Congo is drawn largely from Georges Abi-Saab, *The United Nations Operation in the Congo 1960–1964* (Oxford: Oxford University Press, 1978), pp. vii–xvi, 1–206; Donald W. McNemar, "The Postindependence War in the Congo," Richard A. Falk (ed.), *International Law of Civil War*, pp. 244–302.

32. U.N. Doc. S/4382, July 13, 1960.

33. U.N. Doc. S/4387, July 14, 1960.

34. U.N. Doc. S/4405, July 22, 1960.

35. U.N. Doc. S/4426, August 9, 1960.
36. Georges Abi-Saab, *United Nations Operation,* p. 40.
37. Ibid., p. 72.
38. G.A. Res. 1474 (ES-IV) (1960).
39. Georges Abi-Saab, *United Nations Operation,* pp. 88–89.
40. U.N. Doc. S/4741, Feb. 21, 1961.
41. Georges Abi-Saab, *United Nations Operation,* p. 105.
42. Ibid., pp. 111–12.
43. G.A. Res. 1600(XV) (1961).
44. See Donald W. McNemar, "Postindependence War in the Congo," p. 255, fn. 40.
45. U.N. Doc. S/5002, November 24, 1961.
46. Advisory Opinion on Certain Expenses of the United Nations [1962] I.C.J. Rep. 151.
47. Ernest W. Lefever, *Uncertain Mandate* (Baltimore: The Johns Hopkins University Press, 1967), pp. 217–18.
48. Ibid., pp. 218–19.
49. Ibid., pp. 219–20.
50. Ibid., pp. 212–213.
51. Donald W. McNemar, "Postindependence War in the Congo," p. 302.

NINE

Revolutionary Violence

Oscar Schacter has usefully listed ten ways in which the United Nations may play a role in those internal conflicts which it has determined to be of international concern.[1] These include:

1. Public debate and the expression of international concern.
2. Quiet diplomacy, good offices, and conciliation.
3. Inquiry and reporting.
4. Assistance in ascertaining the "will of the people."
5. On-the-spot observation and surveillance.
6. Consensual peace-keeping and policing.
7. Economic assistance and technical cooperation.
8. Determination of governments entitled to representation in the United Nations.
9. Sanctions and enforcement measures.
10. The elaboration of norms and criteria of conduct.

Already in the previous chapter we have considered some examples of UN elaboration of norms and criteria of conduct; sanctions and enforcement measures; consensual peace-keeping and policy; public debate and the expression of international concern; and quiet diplomacy, good offices, and conciliation. The United Nations has employed these methods in a variety of other circumstances as well; it has also utilized the other measures noted by Schachter.

For example, a common response of the United Nations to revolutionary violence has been the conduct of an inquiry by a subsidiary body or by the secretary-general himself or his representative. This especially has been done in instances where there have been charges lodged of outside involvement, i.e., subversion or support of armed rebels. Examples would include Hungary (1956), Lebanon (1958), Laos (1959), Yemen (1963–64), Dominican Republic (1965), Bahrain (1970), Greece (1970), Senegal (1971), and the Western

Sahara (1975). Although, as Schacter has pointed out,[2] these fact-finding exercises have not been successful in bringing violent conflicts between contending factions for governmental authority or ones involving a threatened secession to an end, they may serve as a means of disclosing subversion and perhaps for discouraging further foreign intervention.

On several occasions the United Nations has utilized determination of the government entitled to representation in the organization as a means of influencing disputes involving revolutionary violence. However, the effect of these actions has not necessarily been beneficial. We have already seen Hammarskjöld's displeasure with the General Assembly's decision to seat the Kasavubu delegation during the constitutional crisis in the Congo. Similarly, the assembly's recognition in 1962 of the Republican delegation as the legitimate government of Yemen as against its rivals the Royalists was taken on the basis of political rather than legal criteria. By taking sides regarding the internal conflict, the United Nations undermined its effectiveness as an institution for controlling the revolutionary violence in that dispute and blocking intervention by outside states.[3] The United Nations compounded the problem when, having recognized the Republicans as the legitimate government of Yemen, it acted as if the Royalists didn't exist. Dr. Ralph Bunche, sent by the secretary-general on a mediation mission in connection with the Yemen internal war, was instructed not to talk with the Yemeni Royalists, but only with the Republicans, the Saudis, and the Egyptians. As a result, the Saudis, who backed the Royalists while the Egyptians were supporting the Republicans, refused to talk with Bunche, and he was unable to function effectively as a mediator. It wasn't until the end of 1963 that the United Nations changed its attitude and began talking to the Royalists along with the other parties to the dispute over Yemen. Most recently, the General Assembly has refused to accept the credentials of the delegation from South Africa.[4] Besides being of dubious desirability as a political matter, the assembly's action was of most questionable legality.[5]

TWO EXAMPLES

Western Sahara

The United Nations has managed to take, on the whole, more constructive actions concerning the Western Sahara and East Timor, two primary examples of revolutionary violence during the 1970s.[6] With respect to the Western Sahara, the International Court of Justice, in an advisory opinion requested by the General Assembly,[7] rejected Moroccan and Mauritanian claims that, because of historical ties to the territory, they had the right to exercise sovereignty over it. Rather, in the opinion of the court, the Sahrawi population had a right to self-determination. The exercise of this right could result in a decision for something other than independence, i.e., free association or even integration with another state. But the choice had to be based on "the freely expressed wishes of the territory's peoples acting with full knowledge of the change in their status, their wishes having been expressed through informed and democratic processes, impartially conducted and based on universal suffrage."[8]

During the time the court was deliberating, a UN visiting mission was traveling in the territory with a view to determining, among other things, what the wishes of the Sahrawis regarding their future might be. On the basis of extensive travel and interviews, the mission reported that there was an overwhelming consensus among the population in favor of independence and against integration with any neighboring country.[9]

Morocco's reaction to the court's opinion and the mission's report was to institute, on October 18, 1975, the so-called "Green March" of 350,000 "unarmed civilians" to enter the Western Sahara and pressure Spain to turn over the territory. The Security Council's reaction to this blatant violation of the right to self-determination was indecisive, as it was not until November 6 that the council could summon the political will to deplore the march and call for Morocco to withdraw.[10]

The Moroccan ploy worked in that, on November 14, a communique was issued in Madrid that announced an agreement among Spain, Morocco, and Mauritania to partition the country between Morocco and Mauritania, with Spain retaining a 35 percent interest in Fosbuccra, the 700 million dollar Saharan phosphate company. Algeria, left out of the Madrid negotiations, refused to recognize the validity of the agreement and announced that it would arm POLISARIO, the pro-independence movement in the Sahara.[11]

On December 10, 1975, the General Assembly passed two conflicting resolutions. The first [12] reaffirmed "the inalienable right of the people of the Spanish [Western] Sahara to self-determination ..." and called upon the secretary-general "to make the necessary arrangements for the supervision of the act of self-determination." But the second[13] took note of "the tripartite agreement concluded by Morocco, Mauritania and Spain," recognized the "interim administration" established by the three countries, and called on that administration to permit "free consultations" with the population. The second resolution thus seriously weakens the strong affirmation of basic principle expressed in the first.

Since the passage of these resolutions, Mauritania has relinquished its claims to the Western Sahara, but Morocco remains locked in a vicious battle with POLISARIO guerrillas supported by Algeria. The General Assembly recently called upon Morrocco to enter into negotiations with POLISARIO and to withdraw from the territory.[14] At this writing Morocco has declined to do so, and the United Nations has not followed up its call with more forceful action.

East Timor

Indonesia's seizure of Portuguese (East) Timor paralled in time and was similar in rationale to Morocco's occupation of the Western Sahara.[15] When, as a result of the Portuguese revolution of April 25, 1974, Portugal radically changed its policies towards its overseas territories and announced its intention that the population of Timor would be given the right to decide by referendum whether the territory should become independent, continue to be Portuguese, or become part of Indonesia, Indonesia at first expressed support for this approach, indicating that it would in no way seek to influence the choice of the people.

It proved difficult to determine the choice of the people, however. Three political parties developed, each favoring a different option: FRETILIN, a Marxist group, which favored independence; UDT, which favored continued union or federation with Portugal, gradually leading to independence; and APODETI, which favored union with Indonesia. Interparty violence developed, and Portugal was unable to arrange for an orderly act of self-determination.

On November 28, 1975, FRETILIN, now in effective control of most of the territory, issued a unilateral declaration of independence, establishing the Democratic Republic of Eastern Timor. In response, on November 30, UDT and APODETI issued a counterdeclaration proclaiming the unification of East Timor with Indonesia. On December 7, claiming close ethnic ties with the people of the territory, historic title, and the need to protect the population from terrorist acts by FRETILIN, Indonesia moved massive numbers of troops into East Timor.

After heated debate, the General Assembly passed a resolution[16] on December 12, 1975, by a vote of seventy-two to ten, with forty-three abstentions, strongly deploring "the military intervention of the armed forces of Indonesia in Portuguese Timor," and calling upon Indonesia "to withdraw without delay . . . in order to enable the people of the Territory freely to exercise their right to self-determination and independence," while recommending to the Security Council "that it take urgent action to protect the territorial integrity of Portuguese Timor and the inalienable right of its people to self-determination." Strong language indeed. But the abstentions of forty-three countries, including the United States, substantially lessened its impact.

For its part, the Security Council adopted a resolution[17] on December 22 unanimously reiterating the assembly's call on Indonesia to withdraw without delay from the territory and recognizing Portugal's continuing status "as administering power" with the obligation "to cooperate with the United Nations so as to enable the people of East Timor to exercise freely their right to self-determination." The resolution also requested the secretary-general "to send urgently a special representative to East Timor for the purpose of making an on-the-spot assessment of the existing situation and of establishing contact with all the parties in the Territory and all States concerned in order to insure the implementation of the present resolution. . . ." This was followed by a later resolution[18] again calling upon Indonesia to withdraw its forces without further delay, but failing to note Indonesia's disregard of the earlier resolution. The United States abstained on the second resolution, and Indonesia rejected it, claiming that "the majority of the people of Timor . . . have already demonstrated their strong desire to be reunited with the Indonesian people in the exercise of their right of self-determination."[19]

At this writing, both Portugal and the United Nations have continued to press for self-determination in East Timor.[20] But Indonesia has not been responsive to these initiatives, and in the absence of more substantial pressure than has been applied up to this point, appears unlikely to be so.

CONCLUSIONS AND RECOMMENDATIONS

Revolutionary violence represents the most serious challenge that the United Nations has had to face since its establishment in 1945. Unfortunately, with a few exceptions, it has not proved equal to the task.

The organization's failure to meet this challenge is not due to deficiencies in its Charter or operating procedures or to ambiguities in the law relating to intervention. Rather, the problem lies in the reluctance of member states to involve the United Nations in situations involving revolutionary violence.

The reasons for this reluctance are several. Increasingly, as in the case of traditional international violence, the parties to the conflict are not interested in its peaceful resolution; they are pressing hard for victory, i.e., the defeat of their opponents and their replacement in power with allies. This is especially true in situations of intervention in local conflicts.

In instances where there is little or no intervention by outside states, the parties to revolutionary violence may be even more reluctant to call upon the United Nations. Incumbent governments are unwilling to acknowledge that they are unable to handle a local rebellion, much less that it has gotten so out of control as to threaten international peace or security. Similarly, an incumbent government will not admit that the rebels have a right to self-determination or that its own barbaric record on human rights makes the conflict a matter of legitimate international concern rather than one essentially within its domestic jurisdiction.

Insofar as there are institutional attempts to control revolutionary violence, these have often been those of a regional organization such as the Organization of American States or the Organization of African Unity. These efforts have not been notably successful, and, in some instances, may have exacerbated the problem and been contrary to the UN Charter. Nonetheless, when a regional organization has assumed jurisdiction over a case of revolutionary violence, the United Nations has usually refrained from becoming involved.

Charges that the United Nations has supported revolutionary violence in South Africa and the Middle East have, as we have seen above, a measure of validity. At the same time, the United Nations has taken a number of constructive steps toward curbing revolutionary violence in these areas and may play an indispensable role in future arrangements designed to bring the unhappy conflicts to an end.

Moreover, the record indicates the United Nations has made positive contributions toward controlling revolutionary violence in a number of other instances. Some of these have been modest yet important steps such as fact finding, mediation, conciliation, or just providing a forum for debate or behind the scenes quiet diplomacy. Others have been more substantial, with the UN operation in the Congo representing the high water point and those in Cyprus and Lebanon also being of substantial scope and magnitude. The key question is, what of the future?

An improved record for the United Nations in dealing with revolutionary violence may well depend on the intelligence, courage, energy, and diplomatic sensitivities of the secretary-general. He should use his considerable authority under Article 99 of the Charter to bring to the attention of the Security Council more instances of revolutionary violence—even if the parties to the confict are unwilling to do so themselves. To minimize criticism and attempts to undermine his efforts, the secretary-general should emphasize his responsibilities under the Charter to help maintain international peace and security, and ensure that his actions are entirely supportable under international law and practice. A strong legal basis for his actions could help the secretary-general to meet criticisms based on political motivations more effectively. Hammarskjöld demonstrated this quite effectively in the Congo.

Suggestions for improvement in the UN's fact-finding capacity have been made so often that they have become commonplace. Nevertheless, they bear repeating, especially with respect to the control of revolutionary violence. Formal, permanent commissions of inquiry should be utilized for this purpose. In practice, this has not proved possible. But the secretary-general himself or, more likely, his representatives might be able to perform this function on a more systematic basis.

Suggestions have also been advanced by several commentators that the United Nations should draft guidelines on intervention for both states and the organization itself,[21] and eminent jurists have themselves drafted sophisticated provisions to serve as models.[22] Some commentators have even proposed that these guidelines be incorporated into an international code in binding treaty form.[23]

Desirable as such an exercise would appear to be at first blush, this writer believes that it would be ill-advised—at least at this time. Because of the current political climate, the risk would be that the guidelines would open more loopholes for revolutionary violence than they would close. It took a major effort to avoid this happening in the drafting of the Declaration on Friendly Relations, and, as we have seen, the effort was not entirely successful. Further efforts at this time of great tension between the superpowers and between developed and less developed states are likely to be less successful. There is, moreover, a danger in attempting to codify rules to cover an infinite variety of situations that vary from case to case in terms of the perceived interests of states in intervention or nonintervention.

The better approach would be to rely on the terms of the United Nations Charter and on those authoritative declarations drafted to date. These declarations, because of their wording and drafting history, favor an interpretation and application of the Charter that denies the legitimacy of revolutionary violence, except in situations where all other recourse to peaceful means of settlement have been exhausted. Most important, these declarations deny the legitimacy of intervention by outside states in support of revolutionary violence. Instead of drafting formal codes, the process of customary international law-making may afford some possibilities for overcoming problems created by lack of preexisting political consensus on issues such as the scope of the right to self-determination, aid to incumbent governments that violate fundamental human rights, wars of national liberation, etc.

Efforts to deny the legitimacy of support for revolutionary violence will have little chance of success, however, if the United Nations and the world community in general do not take more strenuous steps to provide realistic peaceful alternatives. Thus, unless more progress is made in resolving conflicts in southern Africa and in the Middle East, in particular, revolutionary violence will continue and increase in intensity. Similarly, unless there is greater success in promoting fundamental human rights and eliminating such barbaric practices as state torture, the revolutionary milieu will expand. At a minimum military and economic aid to a government that engages in such practices should be denied *before* revolutionary violence against it becomes widespread. It must be recognized that a government's forceful denial of fundamental human rights creates a situation fraught with the potential for revolutionary violence. Such denial also greatly increases the likelihood of involvement by outside states in support of revolutionary violence on the ground that this is justified by the doctrine of "humanitarian intervention."

To be sure, the subject of the proper approach to protect fundamental, internationally recognized human rights, and its relationship to violence, is currently being hotly debated. Jeane J. Kirkpatrick, American ambassador to the United Nations, has contended that the Carter Administration's human rights policies destablized friendly (to the United States) authoritarian regimes in third world countries such as Nicaragua, and led to their overthrow by hostile, totalitarian regimes that suppress all human rights and export revolutionary violence to their neighbors.[24] A discussion of the validity of this thesis is beyond the scope of this chapter. Suffice it to say for present purposes that one can accept the validity of Ambassador Kirpatrick's thesis that aid should not be withdrawn from a friendly government at a time when it is the target of widespread revolutionary violence and still argue in favor of strong support for human rights before the outbreak of violence. Strong support for the protection of internationally recognized human rights through unilateral, regional, and UN efforts—including, as a last resort, economic sanctions—should be regarded as an alternative to revolutionary violence.

One conclusion can be stated categorically. The United Nations will be more successful in controlling revolutionary violence only if the major powers wish it to be so. The United States and the Soviet Union, in particular, are currently on a dangerous collision course in promoting their respective candidates in internal struggles and risking eventual direct confrontation between themselves. Unless there is a shift away from confrontation and toward cooperation between the great powers the successes of the United Nations in controlling revolutionary violence will necessarily be few.

NOTES

1. Oscar Schacter, "The United Nations and Internal Conflict," John Norton Moore (ed.), *Law and Civil War in the Modern World* (Princeton: Princeton University Press, 1974), pp. 401, 409–10.

2. Ibid., p. 429.

3. Kathryn Boals, "The Relevance of International Law to the Internal War in Yemen," Richard A. Falk (ed.), *The International Law of Civil War* (Baltimore and London: The Johns Hopkins University Press, 1971), pp. 303, 308–09.

4. *Kansas City Times,* Sept. 5, 1981, p. A18.

5. The general criterion followed by the United Nations in deciding whether to accept a delegation's credentials is whether it represents a government exercising effective authority and control. In the case of South

Africa, the argument is made that this cannot be the only criterion applied because its application in this instance would run counter to such Charter principles as those directed to the promotion of human rights and even the maintenance of international peace and security. However, such a decision constitutes a type of sanction or enforcement not taken in accordance with the constitutional procedures set forth in the Charter for such action. See Oscar Schacter, "The United Nations and International Conflict," pp. 438–39.

6. For general background to the situations in the Western Sahara and East Timor, see Thomas M. Franck, "The Right of Self-Determination in Very Small Places," *New York University Journal of International Law & Politics* 8 (1976):331–86.

7. Advisory Opinion on Western Sahara [1975] I.C.J. Rep. 12.

8. Ibid., pp. 32–33.

9. Thomas M. Franck, "The Right of Self-Determination," p. 340.

10. S.C. Res. 380 (1975).

11. Thomas M. Franck, "The Right of Self-Determination," p. 341.

12. G.A. Res. 3458A (XXX) (1975).

13. G.A. Res. 3458B (1975).

14. See *UN Chronicle* January 1981, p. 19.

15. See Thomas M. Franck, "The Right of Self-Determination," pp. 342–50.

16. G.A. Res. 3485 (1975).

17. S.C. Res. 384 (1975).

18. S.C. Res. 389 (1976).

19. Letter from the Deputy Permanent Representative of Indonesia to the United Nations to the Secretary-General, Feb. 17, U.N. Doc. S/1196, Annex. pp. 1–2 (1976).

20. See *UN Chronicle,* January 1981, p. 18.

21. See e.g., Louis B. Sohn, "Civil Wars: Guidelines for States and the United Nations," John Norton Moore (ed.), *Law and Civil War in the Modern World* (Baltimore and London: The Johns Hopkins University Press, 1974), pp. 582–87.

22. John Norton Moore, "The Control of Foreign Intervention in Internal Conflict," *The Virginia Journal of International Law* 9 (1969):209–342.

23. Evan Luard, *The United Nations* (London and Basingstoke: The Macmillan Press Ltd., 1979), pp. 161–62; P.E. Corbett, "The Vietnam Struggle and International Law," Richard A. Falk (ed.), *The International Law of Civil War* (Baltimore and London: The Johns Hopkins University Press, 1971), pp. 348, 401–04.

24. Jeane Kirpatrick, "Dictatorships and Double Standards," *Commentary* 68 (1979):34–45.

TEN

Unconventional Violence: Wars of Assassination and International Terrorism

SOME WORKING DEFINITIONS

If revolutionary warfare is "the principal form of conflict on our planet today," the kind of violence addressed in this chapter is increasingly characteristic of the current milieu. As used in this chapter, "unconventional violence" covers first, so-called "wars of assassination" and second, international terrorism.

The war of assassination has become an increasingly popular method of dealing with one's enemies. Instead of marching armies into the territory of an adversary state in the traditional manner or fomenting revolutionary violence against its government, an alternative approach is to utilize an agent—either a government employee, perhaps a "diplomat," or a private hired gun—to assassinate the leading government official or officials of that state. Another manifestation of this form of violence is to arrange for the assassination of domestic enemies who have fled abroad to seek sanctuary. In both cases, the potential for precipitating inter-state conflict is considerable.

Reports of "international terrorism" are constantly in the news, yet neither member states of the United Nations nor scholars have agreed on a definition of the term. Indeed, as we shall see later, this failure to reach agreement on its definition has greatly hampered efforts in the United Nations toward the prevention and suppression of international terrorism.

There are some who believe that the term is indefinable and ought to be dropped, at least for purposes of analysis and efforts to combat those acts loosely described as international terrorism.[1] The problem with many definitions of international terrorism is that they attempt to include too much within their scope. Depending upon the particular perception, three basic categories have been utilized to describe the kinds of acts characterized as international terrorism.

State Terrorism

This category comprises the use of terror by governments in order to intimidate the population—the archetypical case is the "reign of terror" during the French Revolution of 1789–94. Techniques include the use of torture and other cruel and inhumane treatment of individuals. The international dimension is supplied by the fact that these activities violate internationally recognized norms of human rights. Most commentators, including this one, believe that it is preferable to approach this problem as a matter covered by international human rights law.

Terrorism in Armed Conflict

Included in this category are acts inflicting terror in the context of "armed conflict" covered by the laws of war. Examples would include the killing of defenseless prisoners of war and the wanton slaughter of civilian noncombatants.

Terrorism by Private Individuals

This is the category of violence most often denominated "international terrorism;" it will be the focus of this chapter. A working (although by no means uniformly agreed upon) definition of this category would be "the threat or use of violence by private persons for political ends, where the conduct itself or its political objectives, or both, are international in scope."[2]

Another working definition might be Professor Paust's description of terrorism as "the purposive use of violence or the threat of violence by the perpetrator(s) against an instrumental target in order to communicate to a primary target a threat of future violence so as to coerce the primary target into behavior or attitudes through intense fear or anxiety in connection with a demanded (political) outcome."[3] As an example where the instrumental and primary targets might be the same person or groups of persons, Paust cites an attack on a military headquarters in order to instill terror or intense anxiety in the military elite of that headquarters. He notes further that "the instrumental target need not be a person since attacks on power stations can produce a terror outcome in the civilian population of the community dependent upon the station for electricity."[4] So defined, international terrorism might include—assuming the presence of a terror outcome, a political goal, and an international dimension—

the explosion of bombs in the market place, the taking of hostages, attacks on international business persons and diplomats, the hijacking of airplanes, the possible use of nuclear materials or chemical and biological weapons, and attacks on energy resources such as pipelines, off-shore oil rigs, and tankers carrying oil or natural gas.

With these working definitions in mind, we turn to an examination of the historical and political context in which unconventional violence has taken place.

HISTORICAL AND POLITICAL CONTEXT

Wars of Assassination

Assassinations, of course, are nothing new. The assassination of Julius Caesar on the Ides of March, 44 B.C., was an early example.[5] The word "assassin," derived from Arabic and literally translated as "hashish-eater," was applied to a sectarian group of Moslem fanatics who, acting under the influence of intoxicating drugs, murdered prominent Christians and other religious enemies.

Assassinations gained ideological support in the sixteenth and seventeenth centuries with the development of the theory of tyrannicide. The leading exponent of the doctrine of tyrannicide as the remedy to despotism was Juan de Mariana, the Spanish Jesuit scholar. In Mariana's words: "If in no other way it is possible to save the fatherland, then the prince should be killed by the sword as a public enemy. . . ."[6] Ten years later the French King Henry IV was assassinated by the mad monk François Ravaillac. The regicide's credo was perhaps most vividly stated by John Wilkes Booth as he leaped onto the stage of the Ford Theater after having shot President Abraham Lincoln: "*Sic semper tyrannis*" (Thus always to tyrants).

State support of assassins is also not unknown to history, although it was relatively late developing since government officials have generally regarded the assassin as their common enemy. On June 28, 1914, the heir to the imperial throne, Archduke Franz Ferdinand, was murdered by a nineteen-year-old assassin trained by the Black Hand, a secret Serbian organization acting at the direction of the Serbian government. Within one month's time, events set in motion by the assassination of the Archduke culminated in the outbreak of World War I.

The last few years have seen a virtual explosion in state support of assassinations as a form of surrogate warfare. Most of these assassinations have involved the murder of political enemies in exile. The governments of Syria, Iran, Iraq, and, most particularly, Libya have openly sought the assassination of enemies in the United Kingdom, Italy, France, Greece, the Federal Republic of Germany, and the United States.[7] Reportedly, ten Libyan exiles were liquidated in Rome, Athens, Bonn, and London between March and mid-June 1980. Libya's leader, Colonel Muammar el-Qaddafi, has even officially admitted his responsibility and warned that: "The only chance our exiles have to save their lives is to contact our embassies immediately and prepare to return to Libya. Otherwise they will be liquidated wherever they may be."[8] The shooting of a Libyan student in Colorado and evidence that Libyan diplomats were supporting such activities and planning more of them led the Reagan Administration to declare these diplomats *persona non grata* and to require the closure of the Libyan "People's Bureaus" in Washington.[9]

Other states have apparently gotten into the act. There is strong evidence that the government of Chile was behind the 1976 murder of former Chilean ambassador Orlando Letelier by an explosion in his car on Embassy Row in Washington. Similarly, there was strong evidence that a Bulgarian defector, Georgi Markov, was the victim of a Bulgarian sponsored "umbrella murder" in London in September 1978. A London court ruled, on January 2, 1979, that Mr. Markov had been murdered by being stabbed on a busy London street with an umbrella that injected a poisonous pellet into his thigh. The pellet was the same as that taken from the body of another Bulgarian defector, Vladimar Kostov, in Paris.[10]

Except for the American action in expelling the Libyan diplomats, there has been little response by states whose territory has been the site of such assassinations. Neither Britain nor Italy, for example, protested Qaddafi's threat. The West Berlin government, under pressure from the government of the Federal Republic of Germany, set free and deported two Iraqi diplomats who had been held on charges of having planned and prepared a bomb attack against a group of Kurdish students. Since the men were accredited to East Germany, they had no diplomatic immunity in West Berlin. The reason for the West German government's pressure on the West Berlin government was reportedly that Iraq had promised to prohibit training in its country for West German urban guerrillas if the Iraqi diplomats were set free.[11]

International Terrorism

The origins of the word "terrorism" can be traced back to the era of the French Revolution and the Jacobin Reign of Terror. In this form terrorism was identified with state action that had as its purpose political repression and social control.

The first concerted efforts at international control of private acts of terrorism came in response to increased terrorist activity following World War I.[12] In the late twenties and early thirties, a series of meetings were held under the auspices of the International Conference for the Unification of Penal Law. As in earlier years, some extradition treaties were revised to exclude certain terrorist acts from the category of "political offenses," thereby making them extraditable. In particular, the exclusion was effected in three traditional ways:

1. By incorporating the so-called "Belgian" or "attentat" clause according to which certain acts against Heads of State are not to be considered political offenses.
2. By providing that certain specified activities or crimes beyond those covered under the "attentat" clause shall also not constitute political offenses. Examples of this kind usually stress a distinction between social terrorism and political terrorism. "Social terrorism" is directed at governments, states, or political systems in general, rather than against one regime.
3. By including in extradition treaties a clause to the effect that an offense in which the common crime element predominates is not a political offense.[13]

The event that stimulated intense worldwide focus on the problem of international terrorism was the assassination at Marseilles on October 9, 1934, of King Alexander of Yugoslavia and Mr. Louis Barthou, foreign minister of the French Republic. This in turn led to the Convention for the Prevention and Punishment of Terrorism, concluded at Geneva under the auspices of the League of Nations on November 16, 1937.[14] Under the convention terrorism was defined broadly to include criminal acts directed against a state and intended to create a state of terror in the minds of particular persons, or a group of persons, or the general public. Possibly because of the breadth of this definition, only one member state of the League ratified the convention, and it never came into force.[15] World War II interrupted any further consideration of the convention. Since it was not listed among the treaties and conventions for which the League was a depository and with respect to which the United Nations had taken any responsibility, the convention may be considered a dead letter.

UNITED NATIONS LAW AND PRACTICE:
DESCRIPTION AND ASSESSMENT

Wars of Assassination

United Nations law relevant to the subject of wars of assassination is substantial and clearly prohibitive of the practice. Assassination of a state's leaders undertaken at the direction of another state clearly violates such UN Charter provisions as Article 2(1), which provides that the organization is "based on the principles of sovereign equality of all its members" and Article 2(4), which prohibits "the threat or use of force against the territorial integrity or political independence of any state," as well as Charter principles on nonintervention and self-determination. Similarly, assassination of domestic enemies who have sought asylum abroad violates, among other things, Charter principles on human rights, sovereign equality of states, and territorial integrity. Numerous UN resolutions affirm these Charter principles. The case under the UN Charter against the legality of wars of assassination is so clear as to obviate any further discussion of the subject.

In practice, however, the United Nations has not come to grips with the issue. To this writer's knowledge, despite strong evidence of Libyan, Iraqi, Bulgarian, and other state sponsorship of assassination, there has been no discussion, much less debate or other action, in the United Nations of the problem. The reason for this is that no state has been willing to put the subject on the agenda.

One may speculate that this unwillingness is motivated by the same considerations that seem to explain states' reluctance to face the problem squarely outside of the UN context. For many Western European states, Libya is an important trading partner, which delivers oil and buys a substantial amount of goods and machinery. France has close ties with Iraq and Syria, which makes it reluctant to attempt to bring either of these countries to account. This is so even though these assassinations are often arranged under diplomatic cover—a clear abuse of diplomatic immunity that threatens the security of legitimate diplomats everywhere.

This lack of will on the part of UN member states is shortsighted. Wars of assassination have the potential to set off a spiral of violence and counterviolence that could lead to major inter-state conflict. Surrogate warfare may evolve to the point of traditional armed conflict involving a large number of states. The problem of assassinations should be dealt with at this stage while it is still manageable.

International Terrorism

As noted above, the United Nations made no attempt to revive the League convention. Nor did it make an effort to replace it with one of its own. However, a similarly broad approach to the problem was taken by the International Law Commission in its 1954 Draft Code of Offenses against the Peace and Security of Mankind.[16] The Draft Code provided as to terrorism that "the undertaking or encouragement by the authorities of a State, or the toleration by the authorities of a State of organized activities calculated to carry out terrorist acts in another State" is declared to be an offense against the peace and security of mankind and a crime under international law.[17] But the General Assembly decided to defer consideration of the Draft Code until greater progress had been made in arriving at a generally agreed definition of aggression. Now that the assembly has adopted a general definition of aggression, work on the Draft Code has resumed. But its fate is uncertain at this writing.[18]

A dramatic increase in hijacking of and acts of violence against airplanes led to the conclusion of three conventions in the International Civil Aviation Organization (ICAO), a United Nations specialized agency. These conventions include: the 1963 Tokyo convention,[19] which in effect requires states parties to return a plane and passengers if they have been hijacked; the 1970 Hague convention,[20] which provides that states parties must either extradite or prosecute the hijackers; and the 1971 Montreal convention,[21] which contains the same requirement with respect to those who engage in any kind of sabotage of aviation, such as blowing up planes on the ground. None of these conventions makes any reference to terrorism, but rather describes the acts covered as crimes or "offenses." The objectives of these conventions are basically twofold. First, they seek to protect the safety and property of persons involved in civil aviation as passengers or crew; and second, they attempt to ensure the freedom of movement and travel so essential to international intercourse.

However, the Tokyo, Hague, and Montreal conventions, especially the latter two, were not ratified by the states that were providing sanctuary for hijackers. The refusal of these states to ratify precipitated efforts within ICAO toward the adoption of measures that might be brought to bear against states acting contrary to the principles of these conventions. The United States at one point supported the concept of an independent convention which would have authorized states parties to suspend all air service to states that had not ratified the Hague and Montreal conventions and that allowed hijackers to use their territories as sanctuaries. But this proposal never reached the stage of consideration in plenary discussion in the Extraordinary Assembly of ICAO, which met at Rome from August 28 to September 21, 1973. Nor was the conference able to agree on any other proposals to enhance the security of civil aviation.[22] As we shall see below, however, later resolutions of the General Assembly have called upon member states to ratify the ICAO conventions, and there has been a dramatic increase in the number of states parties to these conventions in recent years.

The kidnapping and killing at Munich on September 6, 1972, of eleven Israeli Olympic competitors by Arab terrorists, as well as a number of other spectacular acts of terrorism, resulted in the introduction by the United States on September 25 of a Draft Convention for the Prevention and Punishment of Certain Acts of International Terrorism.[23] In introducing the convention and in subsequent debates on it, United States representatives attempted to obviate the concern of some member states that the convention was directed against wars of national liberation. To this end, they pointed out that the convention was limited in its coverage to "any person who unlawfully kills, causes serious bodily harm or kidnaps another person. . . ." They noted further that, even as to these acts, four separate conditions had to be met before the terms of the convention applied. First, the act had to be committed or take effect outside the territory of a state of which an alleged offender was a national. Second, the act had to be committed or take effect outside of the state against which the act was directed, unless such acts were knowingly directed against a nonnational of that state. Under this provision an armed attack in the passenger lounge of an international airport would be covered. Third, the act must not be committed either by or against a member of the armed forces of a state in the course of military hostilities. And, fourth, the act had to be intended to damage the interests of or obtain concessions from a state or an international organization. Accordingly, United States representatives pointed out, exceedingly controversial activities arguably terrorist in nature, such as fedayeen attacks in Israel against Israeli citizens and a wide range of activities by armed forces in Indochina and in southern Africa were deliberately excluded from the convention's coverage.[24] A particularly broad loophole was the requirement that the act be committed or take effect outside of the state of which the alleged offender was a national. This provision would have excluded from the scope of the convention most terrorist attacks in Latin America and elsewhere against transnational business personnel and facilities.

The United States purpose in drafting a convention of such limited scope was to meet the concern of third world countries that the American initiative was directed against wars of national liberation and thereby to gain as wide an acceptance of the convention as possible. As to persons allegedly committing offenses covered by the convention and apprehended in their territories, states parties would have been required to establish severe penalties for covered acts and either to prosecute such persons or to extradite them to another state party for prosecution. The decision whether to prosecute or extradite the alleged offender would have been left to the sole discretion of the state where he was apprehended.

The United States draft resolution[25] accompanying the draft convention would, among other things, have had the assembly decide to convene a plenipotentiary conference in early 1973 with a view to adoption of such a convention, call upon all states as a matter of urgency to become parties to and implement the ICAO conventions on hijacking of and other offenses against aircraft, and request ICAO to draft as an urgent matter a convention on arrangements to enforce the principles of the conventions. From the outset, however, it was apparent that the United States initiative faced substantial opposition from the Arab states, China, and a block of African states. In the general debate this opposition was expressed in perhaps its most extreme form by the Libyan representative, who described the United States initiative as a "ploy ... against the legitimate struggle of the people under the yoke of colonialism and alien domination" and warned against the United Nations becoming an "instrument in local election campaigns and a pawn of international propaganda based on falsehood and deceit."[26]

In response the United States representative admitted the necessity of studying the underlying causes of terrorism, but contended that progress in eliminating such causes would by necessity come slowly and that in the meantime there was an urgent need to agree on measures to prevent and prosecute acts of international terrorism against innocent individuals. He noted that "[w]e do not hesitate in our domestic laws to prohibit murder even though we have not eliminated all sources of injustice or identified all the causes which lead men to commit violent acts."[27] As to the questions of wars of national liberation and self-determination, the United States representative quoted from Secretary of State William Roger's speech to the General Assembly:

> The issue is not war—war between states, civil war, or revolutionary war. The issue is not the strivings of people to achieve self-determination and independence.
>
> Rather, it is whether millions of air travelers can continue to fly in safety each year. It is whether a person who receives a letter can open it without the fear of being blown up. It is whether diplomats can safely carry out their duties. It is whether international meetings—like the Olympic games, like this Assembly—can proceed without the everpresent threat of violence.[28]

Finally, the United States representative warned that, should the United Nations fail to take meaningful action on international terrorism, like-minded states would agree among themselves on controls and sanctions with respect to transport and other facilities under their control, or private groups such as airline pilot associations and labor organizations would take action in their own defense. Such actions by groups of states or by private organizations, he said, would be less than fully effective and might "do more harm than good to the delicately interwoven and interdependent structure of modern communication and transportation."[29]

In an effort to reach a compromise, Italy and a number of cosponsors introduced a draft resolution which would have provided for a full study and analysis of the underlying causes of international terrorism and stressed the right of every government and all people to sovereign equality, to equal rights, and to self-determination. At the same time, it requested the International Law Commission to prepare a convention on international terrorism for submission to the 28th session of the General Assembly.[30]

This compromise approach was not accepted by the great majority of the committee members, and on December 11, 1971, the Sixth Committee (Legal) of the General Assembly adopted a draft resolution submitted by Algeria and other cosponsors by a vote of seventy-six to thirty-four (U.S.), with sixteen abstentions.[31] On December 18, the assembly approved the committee's decision by adopting Resolution 3034 (XXVII) by a roll call vote of seventy-six to thirty-five (including the United States) with seventeen abstentions.[32] Resolution 3034 (XXVII)—while expressing *"deep concern* over increasing acts of violence which endanger or take innocent human lives or jeopardize fundamental freedoms," and inviting states to become parties to existing conventions on international terrorism and to take appropriate measures at the national level to. eliminate terrorism—focuses its primary attention on "finding just and peaceful solutions to the underlying causes which give rise to such acts of violence." The resolution also *"Reaffirms* the inalienable right to self-determination and independence of all peoples under the colonial and racist regimes and other forms of alien domination and upholds the legitimacy of their struggle. . . ." By way of implementation the resolution invites states to study the problem on an urgent basis and submit their observations to the secretary-general by April 10, 1973, and decides to establish an *ad hoc* committee, to be appointed by the President of the General Assembly, to study these observations and to submit a report with recommendations for elimination of the problem to the 28th session of the Assembly. The committee was appointed. However, after meeting from July 16 through August 10, 1973, the committee reported to the 28th session of the General Assembly that it was unable to agree on any recommendations for dealing with the problem.

With the benefit of hindsight, one should not be surprised by the strikingly large majority of states that rejected the United States draft resolution and accompanying draft convention. The timing of the United States initiative was most unfortunate and ensured its defeat. On September 6, the killing of Israeli Olympic competitors by Arab terrorists took place at Munich; on September 8, the secretary-general, due in large part to the strong urging of the United States, requested that an international terrorism item be placed on the assembly's agenda; and on September 25, Secretary of State Rogers introduced the United States draft resolution and convention to the assembly. The Arab states regarded this scenario as a hostile United States-Israeli plot endangering their vital interests and succeeded in convincing a number of states that the United States initiative was directed against all liberation movements. Even many of those states which saw no such intent in the terms of the United States draft resolution and convention were unwilling to support proposals which many Arab states believed were directed specifically at them.

To be sure, the United States made valiant efforts to quiet these fears and objections. As we have seen, the terms of its draft convention were narrowly drawn so as to exclude from its coverage such controversial actions as fedayeen raids into Israel or Israeli responses thereto. In their public statements American representatives sought to assure member states that their draft resolution and convention were not directed against national liberation movements or intended to affect the right to self-determination. But such reasoned responses were of no avail in the heated atmosphere engendered by the Munich killings and by the charges and countercharges passing between Israel and the Arab states.

Also, again with the benefit of hindsight, one may perhaps view more kindly the action of the General Assembly in adopting Resolution 3034 (XXVII). Although by this resolution the assembly did not take or even propose any immediately effective measures to combat international terrorism, it did require the world community to focus its attention on this problem and on possible measures toward its control. In accordance with the resolution, possible measures toward the control of international terrorism were considered and debated by member states and by the *ad hoc* committee established by the resolution, and, as we shall see below, these efforts eventually resulted in the United Nations taking more constructive actions.

One constructive action took place on December 14, 1974, when the General Assembly adopted by consensus the Convention on Prevention and Punishment of Crimes Against Internationally Protected Persons, Including Diplomatic Agents.[33] The convention is patterned after a similar convention concluded by the Organization of American States in 1971, which, although prepared by a regional organization, is open to participation by states outside the region.[34] United Nations work on the protection of diplomats preceded Secretary-General Waldheim's initiative on international terrorism and then proceeded simultaneously with the assembly's consideration of the American draft convention. In 1971, in response to a large number of terrorist attacks on diplomats, the UN International Law Commission (ILC) proposed to prepare a set of draft articles on the protection of diplomats. During the initial deliberations of the ILC, some participants expressed a preference for a wide-ranging convention that would attempt to protect mankind generally from terrorist attacks. However, the majority of member states was of the opinion that, in view of the traditionally protected status of diplomats under international law, a convention focusing on the diplomatic victim was urgently needed and that the "elaboration of a legal instrument with the limited coverage of the present draft is an essential step in the process of formulation of legal rules to effectuate international cooperation in the prevention, suppression, and punishment of terrorism."[35]

The convention provides for international cooperation in preventing and punishing attacks against diplomats and other persons enjoying a special status under international law. As of January 1, 1981, fifty-two states were parties to the convention.[36] Some critics, however, do not regard the United Nation's adoption of the convention as a positive development.[37] These critics point out that the General Assembly resolution[38] accompanying the convention *"[r]ecognizes also* that the Convention could not in any way prejudice the exercise of the legitimate right to self-determination and independence . . . by peoples struggling against colonialism, alien domination, foreign occupation, racial discrimination, and *apartheid."* They then claim that this language permits attacks on diplomats if they are committed in the name of self-determination. But this contention is not well founded. The resolution is not part of the convention, even if it is by its terms related to it and is to be published with it. Moreover, the language of the resolution appears merely to state the self-evident fact that the convention cannot in any way prejudice the right to self-determination and is not able to affect the legal obligations set out in the convention itself.

If most commentators would hail the United Nation's adoption of the convention as a positive contribution toward combatting terrorism, opinion is much more divided on the organization's response to the international hostage-taking incidents at Entebbe, Uganda and Teheran, Iran. We turn to these in the next two subsections of this chapter.

THE SECURITY COUNCIL AND ENTEBBE

The salient facts of the incident at the Entebbe airport in Uganda may be briefly summarized as follows.[39] On June 27, 1976, four terrorists, members of the Popular Front for the Liberation of Palestine, a radical branch of the Palestine Liberation Organization (PLO), hijacked an Air France jet with over 250 passengers including 96 Israelis on board shortly after it had taken off from the Athens airport. The hijackers first flew their hostages to Benghazi, Libya, for refueling, and then to Entebbe airport in Uganda, where they were held for six days in an unused passenger terminal. Israeli discussions with President Idi Amin of Uganda, as well as intelligence reports and other sources of information, indicated quite conclusively that not only was President Amin not making efforts to free the hostages and apprehend the hijackers; he was actively involved in support of the hijacking operation.

There was substantial objective evidence that the Uganda government was actively supporting the hijacking operation. To cite only a few examples, when the aircraft landed in Entebbe, six Palestinians, members of one or more divisions of the PLO, joined the hijackers. Ugandan soldiers assisted the hijackers in their surveillance of the hostages. Shortly after landing at Entebbe, the hijackers demanded that fifty-three prisoners be released (forty incarcerated in Israel, the other thirteen elsewhere). President Amin informed the hostages that the hijackers had no grudge against them, but "only against the fascist Israeli government—and if the latter does not agree to the guerrillas' demands, it does not care about the fate of its citizens."[40] The day after the plane arrived in Uganda, all Israelis were segregated in another part of the airport. On June 30, forty-seven non-Israeli women and children were released and allowed to go to Paris. On July 1, one hundred French hostages were released and allowed to leave the country. The ninety-six Israelis remained at Entebbe under the guard of the hijackers, who were relieved from time to time by Ugandan armed forces.

As all available evidence began to point ineluctably to the futility of attempts to resolve the problem diplomatically, the Israeli government decided to go ahead with a military raid on Entebbe in an effort to rescue the Israeli hostages. Accordingly, on July 3, under cover of darkness, three planeloads of Israeli commandos made a surprise landing at the Entebbe airfield and within less than an hour were airborne with the remaining Israeli hostages. In the course of the raid, one Israeli soldier, three hostages, twenty Ugandan soldiers, and apparently all of the hijackers were killed. An uncertain number of other persons were wounded. Ten Ugandan aircraft were destroyed, and considerable damage was done to various parts of the airfield. One Israeli woman, who had been taken to a Ugandan hospital earlier in the week, had to be left behind. Never heard from again, she apparently was murdered by Ugandan soldiers in retaliation for the raid. After stopping in Nairobi to refuel and to carry out emergency surgery on the wounded—at least the tacit consent of the Kenyan Government to do so had been secured in advance—the hostages arrived back in Israel Sunday morning, exactly a week after their takeoff from Lod Airport aboard Air France Flight 139.

Five days after the raid on Entebbe, the Organization of African Unity (OAU) submitted a complaint to the Security Council regarding "an act of aggression" by Israel against Uganda.[41] Not surprisingly, their version of the facts regarding the raid at Entebbe differed sharply from those just set forth. The foreign minister of Uganda, Juma Oris Abdalla, and the representative of Mauritania, Moulaye El Hassen, speaking on behalf of the African group, argued that the Israeli raid constituted aggression under Article 2(4) of the UN Charter in that it had violated the territorial sovereignty and political independence of a member of the United Nations. According to their version of the facts, not only was the government of Uganda innocent of any collusion with the hijackers, it was making every effort, in cooperation with other governments and the secretary-general, to obtain the freedom of the hostages. Further, they contended that these efforts were leading to a peaceful resolution of the problem when Israel "decided to take the law into its own hands." Accordingly, they argued, the council should adopt a draft resolution, introduced by Benin, Libya, and Tanzania, that would have had the council condemn Israel's flagrant violation of Uganda's sovereignty and territorial integrity and demand that Israel meet the just claims of Uganda for full compensation for the damage and destruction inflicted during the raid.

In response, the Israeli ambassador to the United Nations, Chaim Herzog, sharply disputed Uganda's version of the facts, repeatedly stressing evidence of Uganda's collaboration with the hijackers and of the imminent danger to the Israeli hostages. On the basis of this version of the events, Herzog turned to a defense of the raid at Entebbe under principles of international law.

Ambassador Herzog first contended that Uganda had violated a basic tenet of customary international law in that it had failed to protect foreign nationals on its territory. He further argued that Uganda's actions constituted a "gross violation" of the 1970 Hague Convention for the Suppression of Unlawful Seizure of Aircraft, which both Israel and Uganda have signed and ratified.

Herzog did not claim that these violations of customary and conventional international law by themselves justified Israel's use of armed force on Ugandan territory. Rather, in this regard he stressed two primary lines of argument. First, he contended that Israel's raid did not violate Article 2(4) of the Charter because that provision does not "prohibit a use of force which is limited in intention and effect to the protection of a State's own integrity and its national's vital interests, when the machinery envisaged by the United Nations Charter is ineffective in the situation."[42] Second, he invoked the right of a state under the doctrine of self-defense to take military action to protect its nationals in mortal danger as long as such action is limited to cases where no other means of protection are available and to securing the safe removal of the threatened nationals. In Herzog's view, the situation at Entebbe was in complete accord with the classic formulation set forth in the *Caroline* case, in that there was a "necessity of self-defense, instant, overwhelming, leaving no choice of means and no moment for deliberation."[43]

By way of precedent, Herzog referred, among other things, to France's use of force just a few months before the raid at Entebbe in order to rescue a busload of children held hostage on the Somalia border. The representatives of the terrorists in Somalia had made demands on the French government and had announced that, if their demands were not met, they would cut the children's throats. In response, French soldiers attacked the terrorists on the Somalia border, killing them and rescuing the children, except for one child who was killed by the terrorists and one child who was taken to Somalia but later returned alive. During the attack by the French soldiers, fire was directed at them from a Somalia frontier post, seriously wounding a French lieutenant. The French forces returned the fire into Somali territory, causing casualties and damage to the Somalis. Although Somalia complained of the incident to the Security Council, it received little support, and the council took no formal action.

The United States strongly supported the legality of the Israeli raid at Entebbe, but it did so cautiously. In the Security Council debate, Ambassador William Scranton "reaffirmed" the principle of territorial sovereignty in Africa. He also stated that Israel's breach of the territorial integrity of Uganda, although short in duration and only temporary, would normally be impermissible under the UN Charter. However, according to Scranton, the situation at Entebbe involved "unique circumstances," which it was hoped would not arise again in the future. In his words:

There is a well-established right to use limited force for the protection of one's own nationals from an imminent threat of injury or death in a situation where the state in whose territory they are located either is unwilling or unable to protect them. The right, flowing from the right of self-defense, is limited to such use of force as is necessary and appropriate to protect threatened nationals from injury.[44]

After four days of debate, the Security Council failed to take any formal action. On July 14 the United States and the United Kingdom introduced a resolution that would have had the Security Council condemn hijacking and all other acts that threatened the lives of passengers and crews and the safety of international civil aviation, and call on all states to take every necessary measure to prevent and punish all such terrorist acts. Under the resolution, the council would also have deplored the tragic loss of human life that had resulted from the hijacking of the French aircraft; reaffirmed the need to respect the sovereignty and territorial integrity of all states in accordance with the United Nations Charter and international law; and enjoined the international community to give the highest priority to the consideration of further means of assuring the safety and reliability of international civil aviation. The resolution failed to obtain the necessary majority. The vote was six in favor, none against, with two abstentions.[45]

The draft resolution sponsored by Benin, Libya, and Tanzania was not pressed to a vote.

In a statement made after the vote on the U.S.-U.K. resolution, the American representative, Ambassador W. Tapley Bennett, expressed his delegation's regret that the council had declined to take positive action against the hijacking of the Air France airliner, but he expressed satisfaction that "not a single delegation could bring itself to vote against such a balanced resolution."[46] He again stressed that the "sovereignty and territorial integrity of states must be sustained and protected." Specifically, he emphasized that the United States did not view the raid "as a precedent which would justify any future unauthorized entry into another state's territory that is not similarly justified by exceptional circumstances."[47]

In the end, then, the "defendant" (Israel) won, as the OAU sponsored resolution was never pressed to a vote. The situation in the Security Council, however, was topsy-turvy. The defendant should have been Uganda, not Israel. Must one conclude, therefore, as some critics have suggested, that the council totally abdicated its responsibility for the maintenance of international peace and security in this instance?[48]

Certainly the council's inaction on Entebbe was not one of its finest moments. Nonetheless, viewed in context, the debate on Entebbe served a useful function and may have been a first step toward later, more constructive council action against terrorist hostage-taking. One can understand the initial strong reaction of the OAU to a report that Israel had mounted a military expedition to the territory of a member state—a military expedition that resulted in a prima facie violation of Article 2(4) and in the death of Ugandans and the destruction of Ugandan property. As the debate unfolded in the Security Council, however, the extent of Uganda's support of the hijackers became clear even to the more radical OAU member states. This resulted in the unwillingness of the sponsors of the OAU resolution to press it to a vote. It did not, unfortunately, convince them that they should support the U.S.-U.K. resolution, which, it should be noted, did not condemn Uganda but only the hijacking itself. Apparently support for even this mildly worded resolution would have been too much of a reversal of the original OAU position to be acceptable. Still, at a minimum, the council's debates surely served an educational function in increasing the awareness of member states of the United Nations of the dangers state support of international terrorism can create for the maintenance of international peace and security. The next lesson on this subject was presented by Iran's seizure of American diplomats in Teheran.

THE IRAN HOSTAGE CRISIS

By way of brief background, it will be remembered that, on January 16, 1979, the Shah of Iran was deposed and left the country.[49] His place as ruler of the country was taken by the Ayatollah Khomeini, who arrived on February 4 from Paris. On October 22 the Shah was admitted to the United States for medical treatment. In protest, on November 4 militants, with the acquiescence of the Iranian government, seized the American Embassy in Teheran taking sixty-six American hostages and demanding that the United States return the Shah and his wealth to Iran.

Shortly after the seizure of its embassy, the United States took its case to the Security Council and, on November 9, the council responded by unanimously calling for the immediate release of the hostages.[50] The United States also brought an action against Iran before the International Court of Justice. Iran refused to recognize the jurisdiction of the court, contending by letter to the president of the court that the seizure of the hostages was merely a "secondary" or "marginal" matter, and declined to appoint an agent to argue its case. On December 15, 1979, the court unanimously issued an interim order[51] indicating, as "provisional measures" pending final judgment in the case, that the government of Iran should immediately ensure the restoration of the premises of the United States Embassy to the exclusive control of American authorities and the release of the hostages. Iran, however, failed to comply with the court's order. It similarly failed to comply with resolutions of the Security Council calling for the immediate release of the hostages. A mediation effort by the secretary-general in Teheran was equally unavailing. Consequently, on January 13, 1980, the United States sought to have the Security Council adopt mandatory economic sanctions against Iran under Articles 39 and 41 of the United Nations Charter. The council was prevented from doing so by a Soviet veto.[52]

From February 22 to March 10, 1980, a five-member UN commission of inquiry visited Iran. But this failed to lead to the release of the hostages when Iran insisted that the commission interview only those hostages selected by the militants as being implicated in anti-Iranian activities. Unwilling to accede to these conditions, the commission left Iran on March 10 and never returned.[53]

Iran continued to defy the court's interim order, and the situation in Iran continued to deteriorate, increasing the danger to the safety of the hostages. To meet this danger the United States launched a rescue mission on April 24, 1980. The rescue mission never got beyond the Iranian desert, however, because of equipment failure in the rescue helicopters. While in the process of withdrawing, two of the American aircraft collided on the ground following a refueling operation. Upon learning of the abortive mission, Iran dispersed the hostages to various locations in order to prevent any future rescue attempts.

On May 24 the International Court of Justice rendered its judgment,[54] holding unanimously that Iran must immediately terminate its unlawful detention of the hostages, release them from its custody, and ensure their departure from Iran. By a vote of thirteen to two (the Soviet and Syrian judges), the court also decided that Iran was obliged to pay the United States compensation for its unlawful detention of the hostages. The dissenting judges based their dissent, in part, on their view that the rescue mission violated an admonition in the court's interim order that both parties should refrain from any action that might exacerbate tensions, and on alleged American violations of international law in returning the Shah to power in 1953 and in interfering in Iran's internal affairs.

Iran, as expected, rejected the court's judgment. The United States made no effort to have the Security Council enforce the judgment through the application of mandatory economic sanctions or other pressures. The wisdom of this decision will be examined below.

Eventually, Iran released the hostages, but not to discharge its legal obligation to carry out the court's decision. Rather, it was conforming with a complex series of agreements concluded by the representatives of Iran and the United States on January 19, 1981.[55] Apparently the last significant involvement of the United Nations in the Iran hostage crisis was the May 24, 1980, judgment of the International Court of Justice.

On the basis of this survey it could be concluded that the United Nations proved largely irrelevant to resolution of the Iran hostage crisis. Such a conclusion would be too facile. To the contrary, the United Nations can be viewed as having "won back a measure of the standing that it has lost in recent years."[56] If the standing of the United Nations has indeed been enhanced because of its actions with respect to the Iran hostage crisis, this is not because these actions induced Iran to release the hostages—although it is at least arguable that the resolutions of the Security Council, the interim decision, the final judgment of the International Court of Justice, and the mediation efforts of the secretary-general may have had some cumulative effect in inducing Iran to reach a settlement with the United States. Rather, the primary value of the actions of the United Nations was that they served to reaffirm, in categorical terms, the principle of diplomatic immunity and the inviolability of diplomatic premises as well as to focus the world's attention on the problem of international terrorism and state support of it. As we shall see below, this helped to create an atmosphere in the United Nations that permitted the adoption of the International Convention Against Hostage Taking and other constructive measures.

Moreover, although on the whole UN institutions were used effectively during the Iran hostage crisis, there was one major exception. This was the failure of the United States to return to the Security Council after the final judgment of the International Court of Justice in order to seek mandatory economic sanctions from the council for Iran's failure to carry out the judgment and release the hostages. To be sure, the skeptic might note that the Soviet Union had already vetoed an earlier attempt to get the Security Council to impose economic sanctions and suggest that it would surely do so again. But the Soviet Union had been able to present a colorable case against the earlier effort to impose sanctions. It is debatable whether an interim order of the court—as compared with a final judgment—is binding on the parties.[57] The Soviets could also argue that imposition of sanctions would be premature, that further conciliatory efforts should be made to convince Iran that it should release the hostages.

These arguments would not have been available the second time around. There was no question but that Iran was bound by the court's judgment—a judgment supported by the Soviet judge as well as all the other members of the court. The Soviet Union could hardly argue that economic sanctions would be premature or that other more conciliatory means had not yet been exhausted. Probably the Soviet Union would nonetheless have cast its veto, but it would have done so with some embarassment in light of the patent weakness of its supporting arguments.

Moreover, by failing to return to the Security Council, the United States undermined a larger interest—support for the United Nations system of adjudication. The International Court of Justice has no enforcement powers of its own it can utilize if a state party fails to carry out a judgment. Rather, the Security Council is the UN organ with authority to enforce the court's judgments.[58] But it cannot operate on its own to do so; in the absence of a referral of the issue to it by the United States, the council was without authority to act.

Even if a Soviet veto had blocked the council from imposing economic sanctions against Iran, the effort would have been worthwhile. The United States would have expressed its strong support for the integrity of the court's jurisdiction and demonstrated the hyprocrisy of the Soviet position. A draft resolution reaffirming the court's judgment and prevented from being adopted only by a Soviet veto would have constituted a strong vote of confidence in the court and for the peaceful settlement of disputes. It was unfortunate that the council never had an opportunity to act.

THE HOSTAGES CONVENTION AND OTHER RECENT
DEVELOPMENTS

Perhaps stimulated by the murder of the Israeli Olympic competitors
at Munich, and subsequent kidnappings of German businessmen,
the Federal Republic of Germany first proposed the preparation of
an international convention on measures against the taking of hostages
during the Security Council debates on Entebbe.[59] Following up on
this proposal, on September 28, 1976, the Federal Republic submitted
a request to include on the agenda of the General Assembly the
topic of drafting such a convention. The assembly in turn inscribed
the item on the agenda and then created an *ad hoc* committee
composed of government representatives to draft a convention. This
amounted to a circumvention of the *ad hoc* committee on international
terrorism (Terrorism Committee) established in the wake of the
Munich murders, but whose work had been suspended since 1973
because of the inability of its members to reach any agreement.
Indeed, earlier suggestions in the Terrorism Committee for the drafting
of a convention against the taking of hostages had not been accepted.

The fascinating history of the drafting of a hostages convention
has been documented elsewhere.[60] For present purposes it suffices
to note that Israel's raid at Entebbe, West Germany's raid at Mo-
gadishu, Somalia, the hostage taking at Larnaca airport in Cyprus
and the abortive Egyptian rescue attempt there, and the seizure of
American hostages in Iran all served to dramatically illustrate the
need for the adoption of a hostages convention and to develop a
consensus in the United Nations to that end. Not the least of the
factors serving to induce third world states to join in the consensus
was a perception that most of these states were exceedingly vulnerable
to self-help measures by militarily advanced countries along the lines
of the Israeli raid at Entebbe.[61]

On December 17, 1979, the General Assembly adopted the International Convention Against the Taking of Hostages (hostages
convention) without objection.[62] The hostages convention is a significant step toward the control of international terrorism. Detailed
consideration of the convention appears in other forums.[63] Only a
few highlights will be noted here.

Patterned on the approach embodied in the Hague and Montreal
conventions against aircraft hijacking and sabotage and in the UN
Convention on the Protection and Punishment of Crimes Against
Internationally Protected Persons, including Diplomatic Agents, the
primary purpose of the hostages convention is to ensure that those
who take hostages will be subject to prosecution or extradition if
they are apprehended within the jurisdiction of a state party to the
convention—thus denying safe haven to those who engage in the
crime of hostage taking as defined by the convention. Equally im-

portant is the obligation that states parties to the convention have to cooperate in the prevention of acts of hostage taking by internal preventive measures and by exchanging information and coordinating measures to prevent such acts.

The hostages convention also contains several noteworthy innovations not found in other UN antiterrorist conventions. The most important of these is the clear rejection of the thesis, advanced by some radical third world states, that the pursuit of equal rights and self-determination by liberation groups can justify acts of terrorism such as hostage taking. To the contrary, Article 12 of the convention[64] achieves the goal of ensuring that a state party will be obligated to prosecute or extradite hostage takers under the hostages convention, unless it is equally bound to do so under the 1949 Geneva conventions on the law of armed conflict and the 1977 Additional Protocols. The legal effect of this complex article is that for states parties to the hostage convention, the obligation to prosecute or extradite extends to *all* cases of international hostage taking.

The General Assembly has also taken several recent steps that, although modest, could eventually result in a major tightening of legal controls of international terrorism. For example, the General Assembly has passed several resolutions urging member states to become parties to the Hague and Montreal conventions. These seem to have had some effect. As of January 1, 1981, the number of states parties to the Hague convention was 109; to the Montreal convention 107.[65]

Also, on December 17, 1979, the assembly adopted a resolution[66], which, among other things:

(i) urges states to incorporate special clauses in bilateral treaties to ensure that the state where the alleged terrorist is found will either itself prosecute him or extradite him to a country requesting his extradition pursuant to the treaty. Such clauses are now the exception rather than the rule in bilateral extradition treaties.

(ii) invites governments to submit observations regarding the need for additional international conventions on international terrorism.

(iii) requests the secretary-general to prepare a compilation of national legislation regarding international terrorism. Such data, when collected, should prove extremely useful to states wishing to structure their law and policy so as to combat terrorism effectively while safeguarding fundamental human rights and should facilitate international cooperation between law enforcement officials.

This resolution was followed by resolutions in 1980 and 1981[67] that set up a system of data exchange regarding terrorist attacks against diplomats and call upon member states to report to the Secretary General on measures taken to bring the offender to justice and the final outcome of the proceedings against the offender, as well as measures aimed at preventing a repetition of such violations.

CONCLUSIONS AND RECOMMENDATIONS

Wars of Assassination

As indicated above, the United Nations has simply not come to grips with the problem of wars of assassination. The question is what, if anything, should or could the organization do?

One possible approach would be the drafting of a convention within the United Nations that would classify assassinations with an international dimension as international crimes. The problem with this approach, especially if it were the basis of an initiative by the United States, is that it might suffer the same fate that befell the American draft convention on terrorism in 1972. That is, it might be perceived, indeed correctly, as an initiative directed against certain radical Arab states and the communist countries, with a resultant highly charged political atmosphere. Drafting an international convention in the context of the Arab-Israeli or East-West conflict is not likely to be a productive enterprise.

Accordingly, a more modest approach might be in order. This might include placing the topic of assassinations on the agenda of the General Assembly; general debate on the subject; and, at an opportune time, the introduction of a resolution. The resolution might "reaffirm" the principle that the assassin is the enemy of mankind; deplore reports that some states are utilizing assassins as a form of surrogate warfare; and call upon all states to adhere to their obligations under the UN Charter and general principles of law recognized by civilized nations to cooperate toward the eradication of such practices.

At a minimum, debate on such a resolution would serve to focus the attention of the world community on the problem of assassinations and, one would hope, might cause states that engage in the practice to have second thoughts about the wisdom of their actions. As noted above in the section on international terrorism, for purposes of defining the political offense exception to extradition requirements, states have long regarded the assassin as the enemy of mankind and hence without the scope of the exception. For states to employ assassins for their own political purposes is to ignore the profound dangers assassinations pose for their own interests. In today's world no one is safe from the assassin. The common interest lies in combatting him, not in supporting him. Extensive debate in the

General Assembly might help states to recognize their own enlightened self-interest.

International Terrorism

As the above survey of UN practice with respect to international terrorism demonstrates, the organization's record in this regard has improved steadily since the days of the debacle over the murders at Munich of the Israeli Olympic competitors. The United Nations has now adopted five international antiterrorist conventions and has taken a number of other constructive steps as well. There may even have developed a consensus among UN members that terrorism is indeed a serious problem and that further cooperative efforts towards its control are needed. Some commentators have pointed out that moments of agreement regarding the threat of international terrorism are rare, and have suggested that there is now a unique opportunity to conclude more antiterrorist agreements.[68] Others have suggested that the need is for an omnibus antiterrorist convention of wide-ranging scope and the establishment of new methods of enforcement such as an international criminal court.[69]

Perhaps. But this commentator would sound a note of caution. We have probably not quite yet reached the stage of ambitious schemes to combat international terrorism. At this stage it would seem preferable to take vigorous steps to induce more states to ratify existing antiterrorist agreements and, most important, to ensure that they are utilized more effectively. The unhappy fact is that these conventions remain largely mere paper documents rather than the basis for a working system of international cooperation for combatting international terrorism.

The basic purpose of these conventions is to establish a framework of international cooperation between states toward preventing and suppressing international terrorism. With respect to prevention—to use the UN convention on internationally protected persons, (e.g., diplomats) as an example—states parties are required to cooperate in order to prevent preparations in their territories for attacks on diplomats within or outside their territories and to exchange information and to coordinate the taking of administrative measures against such attacks. Unfortunately, there is little evidence that states parties to this or to the other UN antiterrorist conventions are engaging in such cooperative measures on any regular or systematic basis. Most of the decline in aircraft hijacking since the conclusion of the ICAO conventions has been due to the preventive techniques of airport and aircraft security and not to cooperative arrangements worked out under the terms of the conventions.

Similarly, although there is ample evidence that hijackers have been submitted to prosecution either in the states in which they have been found or in the states to which they have been extradited or expelled, it is unclear the extent to which this has been based on the terms of the ICAO Conventions. Expulsion or deportation has been a more frequently utilized method of return of hijackers than has extradition,[70] and the extradition of hijackers that has taken place appears to have been effected pursuant to bilateral treaties rather than the multilateral conventions.[71] Some prosecutions of terrorist attacks on diplomats have also taken place, at times under legislation enacted to implement a state's obligations under the UN convention. But, to this writer's knowledge, the UN convention has not been utilized as a basis for extradition. What the practice will be under the hostages convention remains to be seen.

In short, if these conventions are to be an effective means for combatting international terrorism, they will have to be used. Conclusion of antiterrorist conventions is only the first step in the process; unfortunately, most states parties seem to regard it as the last.

The United Nations would seem an ideal forum for facilitating the kind of cooperative efforts envisaged by the conventions. The Secretariat, in particular, could be an extremely helpful source of basic data relevant to antiterrorist efforts. However, the Secretariat's services can be helpful only if they are used; otherwise they will remain a largely untapped resource.

None of this should be taken as a suggestion that there should be no initiatives that might involve the drafting of new antiterrorist conventions. Quite the contrary. For example, one promising possibility has been proposed by Professor Rubin as a corollary to Article 12 of the hostage convention.[72] That is, Professor Rubin has suggested extension of the law of armed conflict to terrorist operations—at least to the extent that it would cover terrorist actions that would constitute "grave breaches" were they committed within the context of armed conflict as that term is currently defined under international law. Grave breaches are those "war crimes" so heinous that states parties to the 1949 Geneva conventions have undertaken special obligations to "search for persons alleged to have committed, or to have ordered to be committed, such grave breaches" and to "bring such persons, regardless of their nationality, before [their] own courts" or hand them over "for trial to another High Contracting Party concerned." Grave breaches under the Geneva conventions of 1949 and the 1977 Additional Protocols include such terrorist activity as "willful killing," the taking of hostages, making the civilian populations or individual civilians the object of attack, and making a person the object of attack in the knowledge that he is *hors de combat*. Accordingly, if the regime of the law of armed conflict were extended to cover terrorist activities of this nature, the terrorist would have no ability to claim asylum based on his political motivation. Rather, states concerned would have an obligation to search him out and bring him to trial or hand him over to another high contracting party concerned.

To be sure, states might object, for a variety of reasons, to an extension of the law of armed conflict to private acts of individual terrorism.[73] But, at a minimum, they might be willing to agree, in principle, upon an exclusion from the political offense exception for those terrorist activities that, if they were committed in an armed conflict as defined under the Geneva conventions and the Additional Protocols, would be categorized as war crimes and grave breaches. At the least, Professor Rubin's proposal is the kind of imaginative suggestion that deserves serious consideration.

The current wording of the terrorism item on the General Assembly's agenda dates from the days of the Munich murders and illustrates some of the reasons the United Nations has had difficulty in making progress in combatting international terrorism:

> Measures to prevent international terrorism which endangers or takes innocent human lives or jeopardizes fundamental freedoms, and study of the underlying causes of those forms of terrorism and acts of violence which lie in misery, frustration, grievance and despair and which cause some people to sacrifice human lives, including their own, in an attempt to effect radical changes.

In light of all the emotional and political baggage that this item carries, it should be dropped and new initiatives for combatting terrorism introduced under more precisely focused agenda items. The piecemeal approach to combatting international terrorism would still seem to be the most realistic, because more ambitious initiatives unfortunately tend to lead UN debates into the quagmires of "state terrorism" and the causes of terrorism, which, while important subjects in themselves, so overload the agenda that the United Nations proves incapable of constructive action.

At the same time skepticism about the current feasibility of omnibus approaches to combat international terrorism should not preclude the exploration of more modest initiatives. Moreover, if such initiatives are found feasible, they should be vigorously pursued in the United Nations. It would be unfortunate to lose the momentum toward progress that developed in the wake of the Iran hostage crisis. The moment should be seized.

NOTES

1. See, e.g., Baxter, Richard, "A Skeptical Look at the Concept of Terrorism," *Akron Law Review* 7 (1974):380–85.

2. Alona E. Evans and John F. Murphy (eds.), *Legal Aspects of International Terrorism* (Lexington and Toronto: Lexington Books, 1978), p. xv.

3. Jordan J. Paust, "Terrorism and the International Law of War," *Military Law Review* 64 (1974):1, 3–4.

4. Ibid.

5. See Robert A. Friedlander, *Terrorism* (Dobbs Ferry: Oceana, 1979), vol. 1, p. 7.

6. Quoted in ibid, p. 9.

7. Jacques de Vernisy, "The New International Terrorism," *World Press Review,* Nov. 1980, pp. 23–25.

8. Ibid, pp. 23–24.

9. See *American Journal of International Law* 75 (1980):937–39.

10. *New York Times,* January 3, 1979, p. 5.

11. Ibid., Sept. 16, 1980, p. 3.

12. See Thomas M. Franck and Bert B. Lockwood, Jr., "Preliminary Thoughts Towards An International Convention on Terrorism," *American Journal of International Law* 68 (1974):69–90.

13. Study Prepared by the Secretariat for the Sixth Committee (Legal), November 2, 1972, UN Doc. A/C 6/418, at 16 (1972).

14. The text of the convention can be found in Friedlander, *Terrorism,* p. 253.

15. See Thomas M. Franck and Bert B. Lockwood, Jr., "Preliminary Thoughts," p. 70.

16. 9 UN GAOR, supp. 9, at 11–12, UN Doc. A/2693 (1954).

17. Article 2(5) of the Draft Code.

18. See Benjamin B. Ferencz, "The Draft Code of Offences Against the Peace and Security of Mankind," *American Journal of International Law* 75 (1981):674–79.

19. Convention on Offenses and Certain Other Acts Committed on Board Aircraft, Sept. 14, 1963 [1969] 3 UST 2941, TIAS No. 6768.

20. Convention for the Suppression of Unlawful Seizure of Aircraft, Dec. 16, 1970 [1971] 22 UST 1641, TIAS No. 7192.

21. Convention for the Suppression of Unlawful Acts Against the Safety of Civil Aviation, Sept. 23, 1971, TIAS No. 7570.

22. See *Department of State Bulletin,* Vol. 69 (October 29, 1973), pp. 550–51.

23. Draft Convention for the Prevention and Punishment of Certain Acts of International Terrorism (Draft Convention to Prevent the Spread of Terrorist Violence), UN Doc. A/ C. 6/ L. 850 (1972). The text of the convention may also be found in Friedlander, *Terrorism,* p. 48.

24. Statement of Ambassador W. Tapley Bennett Jr., to the Sixth Committee (Legal) of the UN General Assembly, *Department of State Bulletin,* Vol. 68 (January 22, 1973), pp. 81, 94.

25. See John F. Murphy, "United Nations Proposals on the Control and Repression of Terrorism," M. Cherif Bassiouni (ed.), *International Terrorism and Political Crimes* (Springfield: Charles C. Thomas Pub., 1975), pp. 493, 499.

26. Ibid.

27. Ibid., p. 500.

28. Ibid.

29. Ibid.

30. Ibid.

31. Ibid., p. 501.

32. Ibid.

33. G.A. Res. 3166, 28 U.N. GAOR Supp. (No. 30), U.N. Doc. A/9030 (1973).

34. For the text of this convention, see *American Journal of International Law* 65 (1971):898–901.

35. Report of the International Law Commission, 2 U.N. GAOR Supp. (No. 10) 90, U.N. Doc. A/ 8 10/Rev. 1 (1972).

36. See Department of State, *Treaties in Force,* January 1, 1981, p. 356.

37. See L.C. Green, "The Legalization of Terrorism," Yonah Alexander, David Carlton, and Paul Wilkinson (eds), *Terrorism: Theory and Practice* (Boulder: Westview, 1979), pp. 175, 186.

38. U.N. Doc. A/940, at 63, 64 (1973).

39. This summary of the facts is largely based on the account given in William Stevenson, *90 Minutes at Entebbe* (New York: Bantam Books, 1976).

40. Ibid., at 27.

41. The following summary of the debate in the Security Council on the raid at Entebbe is based primarily on excerpts from *UN Chronicle,* August–September, 1976, pp. 15–21, 67–76; and William Stevenson, *90 Minutes at Entebbe,* pp. 148–208.

42. William Stevenson, *90 Minutes at Entebbe,* p. 172.

43. Ibid., at 174.

44. See Statement by Ambassador William Scranton, *Department of State Bulletin,* Vol. 74 (August 2, 1976), p. 181.

45. *UN Chronicle,* Aug. 1976, p. 15.

46. Statement by Ambassador W. Tapley Bennett Jr., *Department of State Bulletin* 74 (August 2, 1976):185.

47. Ibid.

48. See especially the letter to the editor of the *New York Times,* from Myres S. McDougal and William M. Reisman, *New York Times,* July 16, 1976, p. 20.

49. For general background to the crisis, see Joseph Jude Collins and Michael H. Collins, "Reflections on the Iranian Hostage Settlement," *American Bar Association Journal* 67 (1981):428–33.

50. S.C. Res. 457 (1979), *UN Chronicle,* January 1980, at 13.

51. The Order of the Court, December 15, 1979 [1979] ICJ Rep. 7, reprinted in *American Journal of International Law,* Vol. 74, pp. 266–77 (1980).

52. See Joseph Jude Collins and Michael H. Collins, "Reflections on the Iranian Hostage Settlement," p. 430.

53. See *UN Chronicle,* March 1981, pp. 12–13.

54. "United States Diplomatic and Consular Staff in Tehran," *International Legal Materials* 19 (1980):553–84.

55. The text of these agreements may be found in *International Legal Materials* 20 (1981):223–40.

56. Remarks by Stephen M. Schwebel, on "Legal Responses to the Afghan/Iranian Crises," *Proceedings of the 74th Annual Meeting of the American Society of International Law,* April 17–19, 1980, pp. 265–266.

57. See Leo Cross, "The Case of United States Diplomatic and Consular Staff in Tehran: Phase of Provisional Measures," *American Journal of International Law* 74 (1980):395–410.

58. Article 94 of the UN Charter provides:

1. Each Member of the United Nations undertakes to comply with the decision of the International Court of Justice in any case to which it is a party.

2. If any party to a case fails to perform the obligations incumbent upon it under a judgment rendered by the Court the other party may have recourse to the Security Council, which may, if it deems necessary, make recommendations or decide upon measures to be taken to give effect to the judgment.

59. This general background is taken from Robert Rosenstock, "International Convention Against the Taking of Hostages: Another International Community Step Against Terrorism," *Denver Journal of International Law and Policy* 9 (1980):169–95.

60. Francis A. Boyle, "International Law in Time of Crisis: From the Entebbe Raid to the Hostages Convention," *Northwestern University Law Review* 75 (1980):769–856.

61. Ibid., p. 828.

62. International Convention Against the Taking of Hostages, G.A. Res. 34/146, 34 U.N. GAOR, Supp. (No. 46) 245, U.N. Doc. A/34/46 (1979).

63. Robert Rosenstock, "Against the Taking of Hostages," Francis A. Boyle, "International Law in Time of Crisis."

64. Article 12 of the Convention provides:

In so far as the Geneva Conventions of 1949 for the protection of war victims or the Additional Protocols to those Conventions are applicable to a particular set of hostage-taking, and in so far as States Parties to this Convention are bound under those conventions to prosecute or hand over the hostage-taker, the present Convention shall not apply to an act of hostage-taking committed in the course of armed conflicts as defined in the Geneva Conventions of 1949 and the Protocols thereto, including armed conflicts mentioned in article 1, paragraph 4, of Additional Protocol I of 1977, in which peoples are fighting against colonial domination and alien occupation and against racist regimes in the exercise of their right of self-determination, as enshrined in the Charter of the United Nations and the Declaration of Principles of International Law concerning Friendly Relations and Cooperation among States in accordance with the Charter of the United Nations.

65. Department of State, *Treaties in Force,* January 1, 1981, pp. 264–65.

66. G.A. Res. 34/145 (1979), *UN Chronicle,* January 1980, p. 86.

67. G.A. Res. 35/168, December 11, 1980; U.N. Doc. A/361 667, November 11, 1981, G.A. Res. 36/33.

68. See Gail Bass, Brian M. Jenkins, Konrad Kellen, David Ronfeldt, *Options for U.S. Policy on Terrorism* (Santa Monica: Rand Corp., 1981), p. 12.

69. See e.g., Leo Cross, "International Terrorism and International Criminal Jurisdiction," *American Journal of International Law* 67 (1973):508–11.

70. See Alona E. Evans, "The Apprehension and Prosecution of Offenders: Some Current Problems," Alona E. Evans and John F. Murphy (eds.), *Legal Aspects of International Terrorism* (Lexington and Toronto: Lexington Books, 1978), pp. 493–521.

71. Remarks by M. Cherif Bassouni on "International Procedures for the Apprehension and Rendition of Fugitive Offenders," *Proceedings of the 74th Annual Meeting of the American Society of International Law* (1980), p. 277

72. See Alfred P. Rubin, "Terrorism, Grave Breaches, and the 1977 Geneva Protocols," ibid., pp. 192–96.

73. See ibid., p. 195.

ELEVEN

Nontraditional Violence: Overview, Conclusions and Recommendations

OVERVIEW AND CONCLUSIONS

By any standard, be it idealistic or realistic, the United Nations' performance with respect to the control of nontraditional international violence is disappointing. This is especially the case with respect to revolutionary warfare. Although by no means the primary reason for the UN's failure, the provisions of the Charter itself are vague and elliptical on the subject. Article 2(4), for example, was drafted with traditional violence in mind, and an expansive reading of terms is required for it to apply to revolutionary warfare. Moreover, Article 2(7) reflects a strong bias by member states against UN intervention in domestic affairs, and there are no criteria in the Charter—and no agreement among member states regarding such criteria—to determine when an internal or civil war has become an international matter, rather than one essentially within the domestic jurisdiction of a state.

The highwater mark of UN involvement with revolutionary warfare was the Congo experience. Since that time, with certain exceptions such as southern Africa, the practice of the United Nations has been to err on the side of caution in assuming jurisdiction over revolutionary warfare. Arguably, this constitutes an abdication of responsibility since revolutionary warfare is the primary threat today to international peace and security. Increasingly, revolutionary warfare is not a matter essentially within the domestic jurisdiction of a single state, but threatens involvement or often actually causes involvement by states outside of the conflict. At a minimum this participation consists of supplying arms and materials; recently, it has involved the intro-duction into the conflict of troops from third-party states. States seem more and more inclined to participate in such armed intervention, as demonstrated by the presence of Cuban troops in Angola and Ethiopia and of Libyan troops in Chad. Other states seem to view such armed intervention with equanimity. Indeed, in some circles, there appears to be a revival of romantic notions of armed conflict.[1] The ghastly horrors of Vietnam and Biafra appear to have been forgotten.

Coupled with the ambiguity of Charter provisions and a revival of romantic notions of armed conflict as stimulants of revolutionary warfare is the recrudescence of the just war concept. This is the gravest challenge to the United Nations' capacity to control international violence because the most fundamental principle underlying the UN Charter categorically rejects the use of force as a means of settling international disputes. Under the Charter no use of force by states is "just." It may be permitted, but only to the extent necessary for a country's self-defense or as authorized by the United Nations. Any use of force that goes beyond the requirements of self-defense and constitutes a punishment or reprisal against an adversary is a violation of the Charter.

The response to this line of argument is that a categorical prohibition against outside intervention in a revolutionary warfare context would have the effect of denying a people's right to rebel against an oppressive government. Arms from the outside are needed, the argument continues, to counteract the oppressive government's virtual monopoly over the means to wage war, especially in a situation where the United Nations is unable or unwilling to employ even economic sanctions against the oppressive government.

There is a measure of cogency in this argument, but it implies that the peaceful settlement mechanisms of the United Nations simply cannot function in the revolutionary warfare milieu. We should hesitate to accept such a pessimistic conclusion, for its adverse implications for world peace would be profound.

Admittedly, it is easy to become pessimistic regarding the prospect for peaceful settlement when one considers the phenomenon of wars of assassination. At this writing, the Reagan Administration is alleging that Libyan President Qaddafi has hired "hit teams" to assassinate the president and other high ranking American officials. Rumors abound that the administration has threatened to employ armed force against Libya in response—perhaps not excluding the use of counterassassination. Nonetheless, the United Nations has still not been asked to address the issue.

With respect to international terrorism, on the other hand, as the preceeding chapter indicates, the recent record of the United Nations is a substantial improvement upon the debacle over the Munich murders in 1972. Whether this progress will continue remains to be seen.

RECOMMENDATIONS

Chapters 8, 9, and 10 contain a number of suggestions for possible improvement in the United Nations performance with respect to the control of nontraditional violence. These will not be repeated here. It may be useful, however, to identify and emphasize a few general themes. For example, elaborate efforts to draft new conventions or wide-ranging guidelines concerning nontraditional violence are likely, on the whole, to be more harmful than helpful.[2] Instead, existing law and institutions should be utilized more creatively and energetically. At the least such problems of nontraditional violence as wars of assassination must be raised in UN organs, and the organization should be used as a forum for quiet diplomancy toward their resolution.

Also, while discussions of the causes of revolutionary warfare or international terrorism have often diverted the United Nations into heated debate and prevented it from taking constructive steps to cope with these problems, there is no doubt that the causes of nontraditional violence cannot be ignored if progress is to be made. Most particularly, the United Nations can and should play a major role in resolving the conflicts in southern Africa and the Middle East—sources of so much nontraditional violence. Similar UN attention should be directed toward the situation in Central America and the Carribean. Again, however, as has been pointed out several times in earlier chapters, the United Nations has little capacity to act on its own. It must be utilized by member states as a forum for peaceful settlement.

Further, with respect to the causes of nontraditional violence, organs of the United Nations designed to protect and promote human rights should be employed more forcefully to deal with egregious violations of fundamental human rights. It must be recognized that a government's forceful denial of the right to life, liberty, and the pursuit of happiness creates a situation fraught with the potential for nontraditional international violence. Contrary to the arguments of some, these are not just "Western" values; they are universal. Nor are they, as is sometimes contended, incompatible with the promotion of economic, cultural, and social goals. Economic, cultural, and social goals can hardly be promoted in an atmosphere conducive to revolutionary warfare, wars of assassinations, and international terrorism. Unless outrageous violations of human rights can be brought under control through peaceful means—including use of the United Nations—they will be combatted by the gun. The tragedy is that history demonstrates this method seldom leads to replacement of repressive regimes by far-sighted governments supportive of fundamental freedoms. Rather, the French Reign of Terror is the archtypical model.

Index

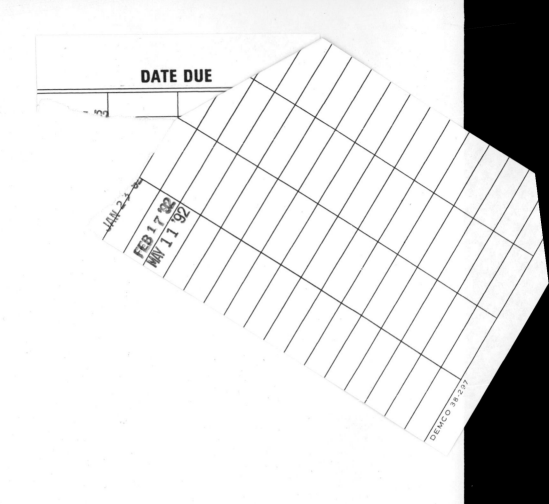